D1359777

THE COSMIC DEITY

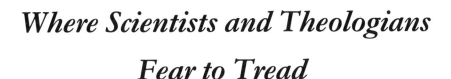

Where Scientists and Theologians

Fear to Tread

Robert G. Neuhauser

Mill Creek Publishers
www.millcreekpublishers.com
mcp@paonline.com
Lancaster PA 17602

2-14-05
Lan
Gift

THE COSMIC DEITY
Where Scientists and Theologians Fear to Tread

first printing

Copyright © 2005 by Robert G. Neuhauser
Lancaster, PA 17602

All rights reserved.
No part of this book may be used or reproduced in any manner
whatsoever without the written permission of Robert G. Neuhauser

The cover design was created in cooperation with
Kerry Burkhart of Albert Bogner Design Communications

Logo for Mill Creek Publishers by Lois "Kelsey" Kelso

Library of Congress Number:- 2004113544
ISBN: 0-9759043-0-2

Library of Congress Cataloging-in Publication data forthcoming
Neuhauser, Robert G.
The Cosmic Deity: Where Scientists and Theologians Fear to Tread
Includes bibliographical references and index.

1. Creation. 2. Creationism. 3. Religion and science.
I. Title.
BL227.N48 2004   213   QBI04-200442

Printed on Recycled Paper

Printed in the United States of America
Mill Creek Publishers
Web Site: www.millcreekpublishers.com
email: mcp@paonline.com
PO Box 10892
Lancaster PA 17602

Table of Contents

Appendices

PREFACE

Imagine a creation, created in an instant, that has imbedded within its very nature an intelligence or a genius. This creation contains within itself the ability to make this ongoing creation happen. Vision with me the way this "intelligently designed" universe creates our world and the expansive cosmos we inhabit *in which we live and move and have our being.* For the most part I will avoid the use of the word, God, since this word has many emotionally charged meanings. Instead I will use the word, Creator, since this implies the source of everything. "The Creator" is a basic concept implicit in many religions and cultures. In these traditions "The Creator is" the starting point, the origin of everything.

The prevailing image of a "God" is of a being that became active in the affairs of a small tribe several thousand years ago. It is a being who controls the affairs of the world and desires petitions to have oversights corrected. This image does not have much resonance with a person who has absorbed the essence of knowledge of the creation that has been attained over the past century and a half.

In an attempt to maintain the continuity and the authority of these religious traditions, the average attender at religious services and activities is exposed to words, concepts and images that seem to be mired in the 17th century. The world of the 16th and 17th century was of a world about 10,000 years old. It was a world in which diseases were caused by evil spirits or were punishments for transgressions. It was a world where some sort of spirit animated plants, animals and humans. Mental illness was an invasion of evil spirits. A heaven was just up there beyond the clouds. Humans were being watched over from above as well as being judged. Earthquakes, floods, fires, volcanoes and plagues were "acts of God." The God/spirit deliberately animated every event and could be petitioned to act favorably for those who pleased this higher power. It was a world created intact and complete with an amazing interdependence of all creatures with everything having a purpose. In a word, the common knowledge up through the 16th century prompted people believed in magic. Magic was the only rational explanation of the cause of events that were taking place in the world wherein humans had little or no solid concept of what was taking place and little or no control over events.

Preface

The world was a large place, largely unknown, inhabited by strange or lesser people. The stars of the night sky seemed limited and inconsequential, except for the wandering planets. Many people ascribed magical powers to these planets and decided that they could influence human personalities and their actions.

Suddenly, in only the last 150 years, there has been an astounding explosion of knowledge about the creation. Diseases are now attributed to microbes, viruses, gene malfunction or stress. Life began evolving billions of years ago and each living creature contains a code specifying its unique nature. The world is not a large isolated planet, but only a small but seemingly unique planet circling an ordinary star among the 100 billion or so stars in our galaxy. Our observable universe seems to be populated by hundreds of billions of similar galaxies with a total number of stars that are equivalent in number to the grains of sand on every beach in the world.

The creation is not only populated by this unimaginable number of stars and their associated and diverse planets, but these are spread over a breadth of space that light can traverse in no less than about 13 billion years. The creation has existed for at least these 13 or so billion years and has continually evolved throughout this time. All parts of the creation have been evolving and continually changing throughout this expanse of time. Living creatures are not the only evolving entities!

Perhaps even more profound it was discovered that four and only four forces control and/or manipulate all creation, and that events involving those smallest parts of the creation are indeterminate or unpredictable. Time and space are interrelated and matter and energy are interchangeable.

For many observers, there is this persistent evidence that there seems to be a genius evident in the creation. This genius configured the creation in such a way that the creations continual evolution was enabled. If there is intelligent design in the creation, it is present within the very nature of the creation.

A comprehensive vision seems nowhere to be found. Inquiring minds within the world's religions are divesting themselves of the image of a Creator/God that micro-manages the creation and the affairs of humans, yet they voice no credible or understandable alternative to the ancient views.

From the other part of our culture, the scientists confine their studies to what and how and but not why. They studiously avoiding attributing any purpose or intent to the Creation. They seem to scrupulously avoid attributing any uniqueness to the creation processes that they are studying. They do however, marvel at the very unique characteristics of the creation that allow it to evolve and produce the stupendously diverse universe that we inhabit.

From the scientific side, the creation's emergences from the primordial energy or power and the course of the creation's on-going saga are becoming firmly established in the realm of common knowledge. Coming from the honest searching inquiring minds of the Religious traditions, the concept of a Creator present and imminent in every portion of the creation is gaining acceptance. Both the scientist's perspectives and the religious concepts are vague and parochial as they are currently articulated.

When the scientist sees this uniquely tuned creation she resorts to a lottery. This creation is seen as only one of an infinitude of universes, each one occurring by chance. From the religious perspective theologians find it difficult to identify a Creator too closely with the apparently aimless course of creation and the apparent chaos operating at its numerous levels.

The Creator/creation is an effort to make sense of these dichotomies and present a new insight into the Creation/Creator inquiry. Some 40 years ago when the revolution in genetics was unfolding with the discovery of the mechanism of the double helix of DNA and its determination of the course of all life, when the echoes of the Big Bang were confirming the speculation of the origin of the universe, and the interchangeability of matter and energy was being burned into our consciousness, the author began to write and speak of the relation of these discoveries to our understanding of the creation. Tentative models of the Creation/Creator were lofted for criticism and stimulation of thought.

In recent times, thoughtful free thinkers have been approaching this problem from many directions. Sallie McFague published her *Body of God* as a tentative model of God, but veered off when she tried to tie it closely to her personal faith. Recently Bishop John Spong has been wrestling with the image of a Theistic God occupying a two or three level universe and intervening in the course of events and finds that concept unrealistic. In *Why Christianity Must Change or Die* he postulates a God/Creator intimate in every bit of the entire creation with only a vague description or insight into the nature of such a God/Creator. Ian Barbour in his award winning book *When Science Meets Religion,* investigates and compares many aspects of contemporary religious thought and scientifically based philosophy, and concludes that the only avenue for a God/Creator to intervene in the cosmos is at the uncertainty level of action of the fundamental particles of the universe. He too envisions a God/Creator present and imminent in all of the creation.

The scheme of things as proposed in this book arises out of the Quaker tradition. George Fox, the founder of Quakerism (Religious Society of Friends) threw out the current dogma of his time and asserted that there is a bit of God/Creator in each person. This book takes the next step in this tradition by exploring the assertion that each of us (and all of creation) are a bit of the Creator.

From the Science corner, scientists such as Brandon Carter, J.D. Barrow and F. Tipler point out that the creation is superbly fine-tuned to produce the evolution of a universe that could evolve humans or other observant creatures. Minute differences in the basic properties of the universe would preclude biological evolution as we understand it. Physicists of many viewpoints generally are unwilling to attribute any intelligence/mind behind or within the creation that would determine its unique composition. Instead, they describe our universe as only one of an infinitude of universe, ours being the only one of these many universes that could evolve as our universe has done.

Here we embark on an effort to meld these disparate approaches into a "workable" image. We will do this by describing the Creator's adventure throughout the breadth of the creation which extends over nearly 13 billion light years of observable space and the depth of 13 billion years of time. Then we will submerge our observations within the bits and pieces of the creation and examine how they operate and to what forces they respond, explore the source of these forces and try to understand how these forces participate in the nearly unbelievable continuity and diversity of the evolutionary process.

Preface

Herein are the observations of a working scientist, engineer, and technical designer, experienced in putting things together that work. I draw from both the science disciplines and a deep personal immersion in two western religious traditions in an attempt to bring these divergent perspectives together into a rational view of the creation that concludes a Creator. This vision of the Creator encompasses a "God" that permeates and determines the very nature of our seemingly unique creation and is present throughout the breadth of space and the depth of time.

Robert G. Neuhauser
Lancaster PA.
May 2004

Chapter 1

Is the Creator the Creation?

"Whatever one may call the "Creator,"
his only authentic revelation is the Universe.
Science is the study of the work of the Creator,
a kind of divine service, a search for truth,
searched with uncompromising honesty."

Dr. Albert Szent-Gyorgi, Nobel Laureate

"With all of your learning, gain knowledge; with all of your knowledge, gain wisdom; with all of your wisdom, gain understanding." These words echo down through the heritage of humanity's western culture, illuminating the dim era of oral history. The need to understand things seems to be an internal necessity for humans. We need to understand things for our own internal satisfaction. We also need to have an understanding of the world about us because of nothing less than for sheer survival. Why do things happen? Why the storms, why the migration of animals, why the waxing and waning of the warmth of the sun, why plants grow and why new humans are born are age old concerns. These things matter! They bear on both survival and peace of mind. This drive to understand seems to have been, and still is, a basic and universal human preoccupation.

Our ancestors discussed these ideas as their language abilities progressed. Attempting to understand the unseen "hand" that made things happen was a common theme. This unseen motivating presence was given a name or a description that defined their concepts of its nature and how it operated. The tendency was to form an image of this unseen force in human terms and then name it accordingly. This force became their God. With their human horizons limited, these variously named Gods became the custodians of their immediate territory or of a particular group of people.

All was fine and good until cultures collided. Then there was the inevitable feeling of; my God is better than your God. Of course there was also the conclusion that the different gods reigned over and controlled different geographical regions. When things went badly for one tribe, they probably investigated the nature of a neighboring god to see if that god might be a better bet by being more powerful and more obliging. Gods competing for territorial control became part of their thoughts.

Around a nighttime campfire several thousand years ago, some thoughtful people probably began to ask one another the question as to why there was something rather than nothing. Where did this world and its sun, stars, planets, rains and clouds come from? What was the force or being that created it. Where did all of the creatures come from? If the different gods created their own territory, why was it that all of the different territories were of the same cut, the same design, made of the same stuff?

These profound and ponderous thoughts produced the idea of a Creator. The Creator was the source of all things. It was an all-powerful force. Thus arose the One-God concept. God was no longer just the ruler and controlling force in a local geographic area but the Creator of everything. This concept of the Creator continues to dominate most western religious thought. The nature of the Creator seems to be an enigma, the greatest unknown.

How can we come to grips with an "infinity", with the all-powerful Creator of the vastness of space inhabited by its unimaginable diversity? Religions for the most part are an attempt to put it all together, to describe the Creator, to define the Creator's realm, to contemplate the possible goals of the Creator and to explore humankind's relationship to the Creator and the creation. The inquiring minds of our ancestors had precious little to go on. They only had the traditions, dreams, astute observations and oral legends passed down through the centuries. These concepts were variously interpreted by the different generations. This intense effort to gain an understanding occupied the minds of the curious and the intellectually gifted members of society. The surviving literature attests to their logic and to the careful preservation of the best of their thoughts and conclusions.

Our world is not the world of our ancestors. In the words of the author who described the efforts of the early geologists who discovered that this earth was not thousands but untold millions of years old:

"We are at the "beginning of an era, not yet over, that has been marked ever since by the excitement and astonishment of scientific discoveries that allowed human beings to start at last to stagger out from the fogs of religious dogmas and to come to understand something certain about their own origins and those of the planet they inhabit."   Simon Winchester, *The Man That Changed The World*

Truly the past 150 years have produced an absolute revolution in our knowledge. Our concepts of the nature of the creation are now laced with certainties. Our view of the creation has been expanded from a tiny planet circulating about the sun to include a universe populated by innumerable suns, black holes, quasars and galaxies of stars, not to mention the millions of species of living creatures on this planet. This creation extends over distances so vast they can hardly be encompassed by the human mind. Beyond this mind-stretching realization is the understanding that the creation has existed and evolved over a period of tens of billions of years. How then can we hope to understand or comprehend the nature of the Creator?

Just as the concept of a single creator was a clarifying insight, the basic knowledge gained by the process of scientific inquiry during the past century and a half has simplified and clarified our understanding of the creation. Just consider how present day anthropologists study the clues that exist in the artifacts of our human and animal ancestors to understand their nature. We can use our new knowledge of the creation as clues to assist us to confidently examine the course of and the nature of creation. We can do this because we can now see more clearly and understand more thoroughly, thanks to that wealth of knowledge of the creation that we now possess.

Our knowledge of the creation has grown explosively in magnitude and quality in the past hundred or two hundred years. Doesn't this put us into a much better position to contemplate the mechanisms and the past course of the creation? Our knowledge equips us to more effectively contemplate the course of the creation throughout the breadth of space and the depth of time. Perhaps this will also lead us to a better understanding of the nature of the Creator.

Where shall we start? In the beginning, there was only a vast power, an incomprehensibly large concentration of energy. This power manifested itself as devoid of any other feature until the moment it transformed itself into what we call the creation; that vast explosion of creativity that exhibits, in human terms, genius, wisdom and, if I may say so, love. This power, this energy, became the creation. In and at that event, the energy transformed itself into the creation.

This is the transforming intuition of our era. It is blossoming into a new and universal creation myth, interwoven into our consciousness and remaking our story of ourselves. It is emerging as thinkers try to put together and harmonize the hitherto disconnected discoveries in physics, earth science, biology, and cosmology revealed during the century just ended. They are being woven into a fresh creation narrative that attempts to put these newly understood fundamentals into an understandable story, the story that also explains our own origins and experience within the breadth of unimaginable stretches of space and the depth billions of years of time. It is becoming a universally accepted creation myth.

And what an exciting challenge! As children we readily learned the old creation myths together with all the ways our ancestors had analyzed the universe. No matter where we grew up, we learned of the way they viewed the principles of the natural world, its fundamental moving parts, its internal processes. In this sense, we are returning to an old wellspring, even if the water may seem new.

What does this new story mean, in words both ancient and modern? Is it just possible that this immense power that transformed itself into the creation was the Creator itself? At first this implication that the primal power transformed itself into the creation may seem so improbable that you shake your head in puzzlement. Perhaps you have accepted the concept of the Creator as being the biosphere, that intimately interlinked web of living, moving, creative creatures which are the doers, the changers, the thinkers, the builders. Surely, you may think, the Creator does not encompass such inert "dead" things such as rocks, dirt, dust, chemicals, comets, asteroids, and planets.

But look again. These apparently unchanging things are anything but inert. Each is seething and vibrating, stable yet changing. All of creation is composed of the now familiar bits and pieces which are at once both matter and the bearers of forces and fields. The forces and fields transfer energy and power, providing the stability that permits the matter to exist as well as the compulsion that transmutes it into something new and different.

All things living and dead are composed of these same bits and pieces, or as we could say, building blocks. Within each different entity the uniquely organized pattern of those tiny common bits produces a different and changing "creature" with its own essential properties and its own internal dynamism. All these building blocks together with all their forces and fields exploded into existence at the same instant, at the moment when unimaginable energy became the creation. This initial "power" has infused every part of the creation, indeed has *been* the creation, ever since its beginning.

We are a part of that creation. Doesn't this revolutionary intuition yields a new foundation for human thought and action? Just as our new world view is propelled by the discoveries of modern science, our revolutionary *self-view* defines us as an intimate part of the this creation, sharing in its immortality and in its grand adventure, but at the same time stripping away from us any cherished uniqueness.

Will our rich cultural heritage survive under such a new understanding of our existence? Can we make the emotional leap to a new paradigm? I believe we can, *if* the new understanding is a satisfactory replacement for the previous comforting and nurturing patterns of thought that defined our culture, our religion, and the myths that produced our all-important inner security. I believe that this new understanding, as it permeates our conscious and subconscious thoughts, can be more satisfying and integrating than the old. As we shall see, our inward journey reflects the creation's own adventure in the direction of complexity, affinity, consciousness, love, and ultimately, mutual responsibility.

Join with me, then, on a thoughtful exploration, reflecting on this grand adventure of the creation. Look around with me and see who and where we are. We know, if we stop to think about it, that you and I have accompanied the creation on this wonderful venture ever since each and every part of us materialized in the womb of creation. We can now see that we have existed for a mind-numbing length of time as a part of the creation and yet we have traveled through only the tiniest fraction of the unimaginable reaches of the creation. We have come from and participated in the explosive moment when creation began. Now we have come to the point where we see more clearly its grandeur and majesty and feel that we are an everlasting part of the creation. In a way we have existed forever.

Surely, you may think, all this cannot mean that every part of the creation is a part of the Creator? Are the atoms, quarks, suns, black holes, butterflies and microbes, rays of light, human minds, whales, mice, clouds, and rocks all parts of the Creator in a creation spanning distances measured in billions of light years of voids and galaxies, suns, quasars, and gas clouds? A creation enduring for tens of billions of years? Is the Creator everything, everyone, and everywhere?

Let us explore that premise of a simple oneness. Is the Creator the indeed the creation, a unity of matter and energy in which all substances and forces, all value systems and esthetics qualities, inhere?

Creation Traditions

This concept of the Creator *as* the creation initially flies in the face of all conventional wisdom. It clashes with our gut reactions as well as our wishes and desires. When we reason, we deal in analogies. We assume that the Creator is the builder, the shaper, the genius of creation, the father, the rule-giver. All of these are human terms, being analogous to the human characteristics we deal with every day. Many of us tend to heap on additional desired characteristics, such as being a just, forgiving, compassionate, all-knowing, all-powerful judge and friend.

At rock bottom, most systems of philosophy or religion contain the concept of a Creator, one who is or manifests the power that brought the creation into being at its beginning. As we view the immensity and complexity of the creation, and as we understand its diversity and ever-changing nature, then we stand in awe of the power that caused it to be. We revere the genius evident in the creation and in the Creator to whom we attribute its existence.

Every human imagination feels this sense of awe and wonder. Every human society tells and retells its children rich and insightful stories of a creation time, often invoking a ritualized image of the Creator, passing on its collective wisdom from one generation to the next.

Power and wisdom are the common denominators of our creation traditions. An awesome power created a rich and unfathomable universe. In these traditions, the creation exhibits the creative "mind" of genius, the wisdom of the Creator.

Implicit in most of these traditional views is a two-level universe, a Creator apart from the creation and yet exerting some form of control over it. Theologians concentrate on the Creator, and scientists wrestle with the creation.

In the distant past the theologian was also the scientist and the educator. Religious institutions and traditions were the repositories of all knowledge. These institutions attempted to make sense of everything seen and experienced. Gradually and sometimes painfully, those applying the methods of scientific inquiry, and those upholding the traditions of theology and its reasoned and "revealed" knowledge diverged to the point that religion often excommunicated science and science denounced religion as both myth and addicting drug.

In recent times, fresh insights have forced science and religion to begin to converge again. Strangely, the scientists are leading this convergence, because their recent discoveries require a rethinking of the dichotomy of Creator and creation.

What Can We Learn from Knowledge Generated by Science?

The scientist-philosopher Kenneth Boulding has written of science: *"It is concerned with developing testable statements about the world, which in turn create images of the world which correspond to what the world is really like."* Science is based on measurements and relating these measurements to the sensations that reach the human mind via our eyes and ears. Science tries to discover basic cause-and-effect relationships that can be demonstrated again and again. Science does not produce science, it produces knowledge!

In pursuing the unity of the Creator and creation, we make use of these fundamental testable and tested statements produced by scientific inquiry. Given authority by repeated observation, they appear to us as stubborn facts that will not go away. Because they have stood up under critical testing and thinking, more and more they form the bedrock of our understanding of the world and the universe.

Despite the millions of years of human existence, most scientifically established knowledge has been elaborated only during the last 500 years. This knowledge is the result of the advance in human thought going beyond the conclusions of intuitive and philosophical thought. New disciplines of thought employed testable and mathematically provable techniques for figuring out how the universe operates.

What is the knowledge revealed by science that changed our understanding of the universe? What new facts propel us to rewrite our creation story? The most important of these discoveries are the following:

1. Matter (material) is convertible into energy. Energy is convertible into matter. Albert Einstein first proposed this as a formal and exact relationship testable by science. His renowned equation linking energy and matter is the elegantly simple: $E = MC^2$. (Energy equals Mass times the velocity of light squared)

2. All of the forces that control and organize matter, and then endlessly reorganize it, originate within the matter itself.

3. The material of our universe possesses both stability and instability at each of its organizational levels. These qualities give rise to both continuity and change.

4. There is continuity in the evolution of the universe. The universe has not always been as it is today. On the contrary, on every level it shows signs of having matured from previous and younger states. Its evolution begins with an initiating energy and the simplest forms of matter, extending through to the most diverse and complicated manifestations of the creation seen today. Scientists now believe that the universe started abruptly and without antecedents in a cataclysmic "Big Bang" many billions of years ago.

There are many ways to incorporate these facts into a creation story that is both scientifically and emotionally satisfying. The basic outline that emerges from these discoveries is also the premise of the first part of this book. The thesis may be summarized in a few simple postulates:

a. **The only substance is energy.**

b. **The only reality**[1] **is organization.**

c. **The creation organizes and reorganizes itself using the forces originating from within its own substance.**

d. **The creation is the Creator.**

e. **The Creator/creation is on an adventure.**

What I would like to do now is to explore the thought processes that lead to these postulates, a sort of working backwards. We need to understand the knowledge revealed by science and how our reasoning has brought us to the creation story outlined here.

We need to see how the physical and chemical organization of living cells leads to purposefulness, consciousness, self-consciousness, spirituality, and ethics. We will call these qualities "emergent realities", i.e. properties that emerge in complex organizations which are not shown by their individual components. We shall see how these non-material manifestations of reality are also generated by the continual organization and reorganization of matter and energy in the great adventure called creation.

Then there is the exciting challenge of examining the *implications* of our new belief, a kind of working forwards. We will look at the difficult problems that this view of the Creator-as-creation poses to previous human thought, especially the disruption of our collective consciousness. We will explore problems of good and evil, the values and impediments of religious traditions, and the kind of genius evident in the creation. Ultimately we will examine the questions of whether the creation exhibits a "mind" and where the genius of the creation resides.

---

[1] I use the word reality in the sense that reality is what defines things and makes them what they are. In its broadest sense things include both the tangible material world and intangible things.

First, however, let us probe the basis of the knowledge upon which our understanding rests and recapitulate those discoveries.

Matter Is Energy

Albert Einstein forced a revolution in thinking about the physical world. It began with his speculations on how the world would appear to a person who was traveling past it at a speed close to the velocity of light. He put these thoughts and conclusions into a rigorous mathematical framework which he called the theory of relativity, a theory which decisively upset the applecarts of both science and religion.

Among Einstein's many conclusions drawn from the relativity theory and the many mathematical descriptions of the world that this theory generates, there is one mathematical equation that looks innocuous enough:

$$E = MC^2.$$

This equation relates matter to energy. The amount of energy E which is represented in any particle of matter is related directly to its mass and to the velocity of light. The mass of any particle of matter (M) (what we sometimes loosely call weight), multiplied by a very large number C^2 (C is the velocity of light), represents the equivalent energy of that particle.

This is an interesting mathematical relationship, but what does it really mean? In its most profound meaning, it means that a tremendous amount of energy is the equivalent of a minute amount of matter, and that a minute amount of matter is equivalent to a tremendous amount of energy. As we will later see, it also specifies the mass/energy relationship at the moment when an immense amount of energy transformed itself into all the matter of the universe.

The possibility of the transformation of matter into energy was not obvious at the start of the 20th century when Einstein first proposed it. Images of the destructive power of the nuclear bomb, however, have now burned it indelibly into our minds.

Before the bomb, Einstein's energy equation diffused only slowly through the consciousness of the scientific community. Scientists first began to understand the source of the immense amount of power that is radiated from the sun, a vast amount of energy sent out continuously every day for the past five billion years. This feat would be impossible if conventional chemical burning processes produced the sun's energy. We now know that both the nuclear bomb and the sun release energy when matter is converted into energy, occurring when the nuclei at the center of certain atoms either split or fuse together with other nuclei. In these processes a bit of their nuclear <u>mass</u> (or weight) converts into energy, releasing far more energy than could be generated by the "burning" of atoms in a chemical reaction.

Einstein's equation is a two-way street. Energy can also be converted into matter - converted into the protons, neutrons, and electrons that make up the stable parts of all creation. This has been unambiguously demonstrated by elegant experimentation, so accept it for now. Later we will look at the exciting scientific evidence and wonderful experiments that proved this convertibility beyond any doubt. A companion to the understanding of the conversion of matter into energy and the reverse side of the process, the conversion of matter into energy is that nothing is lost in the process and nothing is added. Any time a bit of matter gives off energy, it loses a bit of its mass also, however minuscule that loss may be.

Scientists were now ready to acknowledge an electrifying step in their theory, the Big Bang. This conception holds that the creation of the universe took place within a burst of explosive power. It began with the appearance of an unimaginable amount of energy fluxing at temperatures so high that the present material of the universe could not exist within it. Suddenly this power inflated. Next it "condensed" into every bit of the matter that comprises the universe, "exploding" in the Big Bang, initiating space-time and propelling the stuff of the universe through untold billions of light-years of expanding space.

We are examining the possibility that the Creator was and is this power which appeared inflated and then transformed most of its energy into the fundamental particles that make up our universe. These are the particles that organize themselves and reorganize themselves into the fantastic diversity of suns, moons, and creatures that comprise the creation.

If you would like to try to comprehend the incalculable power of the Big Bang, consider this. If we converted all of the matter in a small coin, say a dime, into energy, that amount of energy would be about equal to the energy or power of the two bombs that vaporized Hiroshima and Nagasaki. Conversely, that is the amount of energy that would have to be converted into matter to make enough metal to form a dime. Now multiply that amount of power released by those two bombs by the number of dimes it would take to make up our earth. Multiply again by the number of earths that it would take to make up the sun. Next, multiply that by the number of suns in the observable universe. (The number of suns in the universe is a hard number to comprehend. A close approximation proposed by Carl Sagan is the total number of grains of sand on every beach in the world). Multiply all of that by one billion. Then add the amount of power it would take to propel all of those suns and galaxies billions of light years through space at speeds approaching the speed of light. With that, finally, we come to an appreciation of the power or energy that represents the creation; the power of the Creator.

The Forces that Organize and Reorganize Matter

An early Greek experimental scientist, the renowned Archimedes, used to say that if you gave him a lever long enough and a sturdy enough fulcrum to rest it upon, he could move the world. He understood that forces were not abstract; they have to have a source and a means (instrument) in order to act upon a body. To move the world, he would need a lever and a firm place on which the lever could rest. Then he could use his own weight to produce the force.

In our time we ask: What are the forces that control the universe? What forces shape it and change it and produce the activity that we observe? What is the nature of these forces and where do they originate? What does each of the forces act upon?

During the 20th century scientists identified four forces, and only four forces, that apparently account for all of the activity of our universe. These four forces give direction to all matter. They are:

- **the electromagnetic force**

- **the strong nuclear force**

- **the weak nuclear force**

- **the force of gravitational attraction**

A huge body of scientific evidence shows that all parts of the universe feel these forces. Observations suggest that they act in a uniform way at all times, at all places, on all particles. Each force is exerted through a distinct and characteristic field of action wherever it occurs. Each type of particle, no matter where it may be located, feels a given force in a manner identical to that of a similar particle in another location. Each particle responds to certain forces and no others. Because of these simple relationships, scientists refer to these forces as "fundamental" forces obeying universal "physical laws."

The crucial question for us, in proposing a theory of creation/Creator is: Where do these forces originate? Where do they come from? The answer from observation and reflection is ... they inhere within. They are inherent aspects of the very particles that make up the universe! Let us see how this works.

The electromagnetic force operates between electrons, between protons, and between electrons and protons. Electrons repel one another and protons repel one another. Between electrons and protons, however, there is a mutual attraction. The *innate* electrical charges of the electrons and protons produce this attraction and repulsion; no outside agency is involved. Materials gain their strength and durability by the electric forces that bind atoms together.

This simple force of attraction and repulsion gives rise to huge effects. When electrons move in response to the electromagnetic force, they produce both magnetic fields and waves of electromagnetic radiation. This radiation includes the light and heat that warm us, the radio waves that inform us, and the ultraviolet and gamma rays that sometimes endanger us. The motion of electrons transmits energy on both the most minute scale - between atoms - and across the reaches of space.

The strong nuclear force holds protons and the neutrons together in the atomic nucleus and overcomes the strong electromagnetic repulsion that protons have for each other. The strong nuclear force gives long-term stability to the nucleus. It originates within the nucleus, operates only over the very short distance of a nuclear diameter, and is felt only by protons and neutrons[2]. Electrons and neutrinos do not generate or respond to this force.

The weak nuclear force imbues the nucleus with a certain degree of instability and is the agent of change at the nuclear level. It makes some nuclei more unstable than others and pushes unstable nuclei to transform themselves into more stable forms. Sometimes it transforms

---

[2] More about neutrons later

a neutron into a proton, an electron, and a neutrino. At other times it transforms a proton into a neutron by combining it with an electron. Such events are the sources of energy released in radioactive materials, atomic power plants, nuclear bombs, and the sun. As the process of nuclear rearrangement occurs, small amounts of matter are converted into large amounts of energy appearing as heat (electrons moving faster), radioactivity (the expulsion of high-energy particles), and gamma rays (high-energy electromagnetic waves). The above three forces are manifestations of the electrons, protons, and neutrons themselves. They act only on particles having corresponding inherent characteristics. They are not forces that reside elsewhere and act from outside.

In this regard they are different from **gravity**. Gravity is an attractive force that is felt between every particle of matter, between every iota of substance that has ever been condensed from the primal energy of the creation. Although gravity is by far the weakest force acting on and emanating from a given particle, there is no limit to the distance that its gravitational attraction can be felt.

The force of gravity holds together the sun, and binds the planets, comets, and their assemblage into a solar system. It molds the black holes, neutron stars, and the galaxies. When an accumulated mass of gas or particles becomes great enough, the crushing power of its gravity propitiates the nuclear reactions that "ignite" the mass into a great sun or supernova. Here on earth gravity sculpts the planet by slowly pulling down the mountains and driving the ocean tides. It is gravity that keeps both the earth tethered to the sun and the earth's inhabitants tethered to their terrestrial home.

Summary

The four fundamental forces, inherent in matter itself, account for all activity, events, and processes in the universe as well as for the transmission of matter and energy within it. Both the driving forces of change and the sustaining forces of stability result from these four fundamental forces.

The key idea which has advanced in this century from intuitive insight to established physical principles, is that the creation comes complete with its own internal workings and forces. No pushes and pulls other than those inherent in the simple nature of fundamental particles are required to explain the complex behavior of the universe.

Subsequent chapters examine these forces in more depth and show how they may all be interpreted as manifestations of a general underlying principle, namely affinity.

Stability and Instability, the Agents of Change and Growth

The Greek philosopher Heracleitus complained, "Most men fail to comprehend the universal principle through which all things are interrelated and all natural events occur, and thus live like dreamers with a false view of the world." He observed that all things continually change. His thoughts were concerned with determining the source of these changes.

Human thought tries to anchor its values to factual certainties, to unchanging principles, and to dependable structures. We use expressions such as "solid as a rock" to express basic realities or enduring principles. However, it is also true that nothing lasts forever. The entire universe itself has existed only since the power and energy transformed itself into matter at the Big Bang. In some far-distant future it may all transform back into energy again.

One mark of the genius inherent in creation is the tendency toward both stability and instability which is everywhere evident. For instance, even a rock that we may view as enduring and solid is probably a fourth or fifth-generation rock. Every crystal, every molecule has been eroded, melted, worn off, or vaporized three or four times before being reassembled into the rock that we see today. Like Heracleitus, we too shall seek the origins of change and growth as well as marvel at the kaleidoscope of creation's inventions thus far.

Instability and change manifest themselves at every level. In the minute sphere of the atomic nucleus, the protons and neutrons of certain nuclei are likely to undergo spontaneous change, converting a bit of mass to heat, radioactivity, and radiation. They may re-form into a more stable isotope of the same atom or they may split into two new atoms. This instability is *inherent,* that is to say, it is a property of the nuclei themselves and is not introduced from outside.

Similar events occur at the level of atoms and molecules, reflecting the spontaneous rearrangement of electrons. From the changes in electron motion and energy come everything from the simple evaporation of water to the most complex synthesis of a modern drug.

Going up higher on the ladder of organization, into the realm of living things where molecules and organisms replicate themselves, we know that each generation is slightly different from its parents. Even here there is no new force at work, only the playing out of the fundamental forces already described. The slight instability in the motion of electrons means that making a truly perfect copy of anything becomes unlikely when trillions upon trillions of electrons are involved.

Although our intuition might tell us to look for a guiding hand from above to explain why living things vary and subtly change, one of the achievements of modern science has been to show that such explanations are not necessary. Although people may continue to enjoy the concept of a benevolent external guiding hand for cultural reasons, the guiding hand itself will be found to dwell within the matter of the creation.

The **stability** inherent in the fundamental particles of creation allows complex entities to form and exist -- things like the suns, planets, solid continents, as well as the living creatures that inhabit them. Without stability the universe would consist of a seething mass of subatomic particles with no particular form or identifiable structures. Indeed, those regions of the universe characterized by crushing heat and pressure, e.g. the centers of hot stars, show something very like this elemental anarchy.

On the other hand, if matter was eternally stable, if a given arrangement of fundamental particles endured forever, there would be no change, no evolution, and no novelty. Since this is evidently not the case, modern scientists, as well as Heraclitus, have treated instability as *inherent,* as an essential aspect of all matter.

Fortunately our earth has enjoyed a balance between the forces of stability and instability such that new entities can come into being, exist for a while, and prove themselves to be enduring or not. Then the built-in forces of instability bring changes that either destroy the old forms or force them into a new and possibly more enduring forms. As we shall see, these complementary tendencies drive all the brilliant creativity we experience around us.

The Continuity of Evolution

No part of the universe appeared fully formed as it exists today. Each part of the creation has been built up step by step from the simplest particles that condensed out of the unimaginable energy of the Big Bang. In recent years physicists have hypothesized and named the most simple constituent particle the "quark." Quarks do not persist as quarks after their condensation from energy but almost instantly combine with other quarks. It is believed that in the first instants of the Big Bang the newly condensed quarks assembled themselves into protons and neutrons and set off the chain of events that also led to electrons and neutrinos.

The protons appeared with their inherent positive charge and the electrons with their opposing negative charge. The electromagnetic force appeared, and at the same instant the electrons began their motion towards the protons. When the temperature cooled sufficiently to allow orderly motion, the electrons settled into a pattern of spinning around and encircling the protons. In doing so they carried out the single most important change in the arrangement of matter that the Creation has ever experienced. They created the *atom*, the foundation of all subsequent matter.

When an electron goes into an orbit or envelope around a single proton, these two particles form the simplest (and earliest) atom, hydrogen. Amazingly, that hydrogen atom is a million billion times larger in volume than the single proton comprising its nucleus. Huge swarms of newly created hydrogen (and helium atoms) formed the first stars. The gravitational attraction of their combined weight produced immense heat and pressure. The heat and pressure in the interior of these solar furnaces in turn forged the nuclei of these lighter atoms into heavier and larger nuclei. The larger stars that exploded into supernovas fused these new nuclei into even heavier atoms. The matter thrown out by these exploding supernovas was later drawn back together by gravity into second-generation stars, comments and planets. In the cooling of the planets and comets, the dozens of new kinds of atoms began to liquify, solidify, and link to each other in fantastic variety. On our planet, mineral compounds appeared that formed the rigid plates of the continents of planets. Water formed and covered the low areas, and more mobile assemblies of atoms became the myriad of chemical compounds dissolved in the water. Some atoms and molecules tended to remain gases even at the lower temperatures, and these floated above the land and sea to form the atmosphere of our planet.

In the warm seas, more complex assemblies of atoms began to assemble and reassemble themselves into amino acids and other primitive "organic molecules." These few different building blocks of organic molecules eventually assembled themselves into the proteins and other structures that constitute every living cell and creature today.

Thus the same atoms and molecules compose both the living and non-living parts of our world. They are just linked in different patterns and have different levels of organization of their fundamental particles.

All living creatures are either single cells or are composed of a myriad of similar and diverse cells. Every cell has a membrane of interlinked molecules which encloses it, giving it form and protection. This membrane allows nutrient molecules to enter the cell and compounds produced by the cell to leave.

Inside every cell are chains of DNA, the information molecules that bear the code specifying the nature of the cell and of the organism. DNA is a chain of four different kinds of nucleic acid units, and sequences of these units ("genes") are the <u>code</u> of the recipes that the cell needs to function and reproduce. DNA recipes instruct the cell not only how to change its activities but also how to reproduce itself and eventually how to reproduce the organism. DNA is the agent of genetic heritage.

Summary

There is an unbroken continuity of evolution from quarks to protons to atoms to the human body. From the smallest proton to the largest and furthest celestial bodies, from unfeeling rock to the neurons of the brain that permit consciousness and self-awareness, there is an unbroken continuity of matter and energy that together make up the creation/Creator.

POSTULATES

From the above survey we may distill a brief list of postulates about the world which we inhabit -- and thus about ourselves. Together these postulates make a bracing and thrilling creation story; together they give us a foundation of self-awareness with which we can begin new spiritual and ethical reflection.

1. The Only Substance Is Energy

All of material creation is composed of particles that have condensed out of energy or power. Other energy in the form of heat, light, and electromagnetic radiation emanates from this material. There is no other matter or energy except that deriving from the power present at the moment of creation. This power transformed itself into the versatile and unique fundamental particles that subsequently assembled themselves into the whole of the great variety and diversity of the universe. Search where we will, such matter/energy is the only substance we can find.

2. The Only Reality Is Organization

The reality of anything is its organization. Its uniqueness, its properties, its characteristics, depend upon nothing intrinsic except the organization of its components. Consider the Taj Mahal. It is composed of marble, mortar, and metal -- just like the men's room in our city hall! The uniqueness of each is in its organization, in the design and the arrangement of its common components. One has become a monument to beauty and love. The other is a waste disposal facility.

To say that things have no essence except their complex organization is a major claim that could not be supported before modern science. To get a scientific feel for the scope of this postulate, let us look first at the atoms that constitute all of the material of our world and of the universe. Each kind of atom has distinctive properties, but *every* atom of *every* kind is composed of the same constituents -- the protons and neutrons in its nucleus and the shells of electrons surrounding it.

One species of atom differs from another only in the number of protons and neutrons in its nucleus. The number of protons in turn specifies the number of electrons in the outer shells. This number alone specifies the uniqueness and distinctness of that type of atom. The electron shells create an atom that is nearly a million times larger in diameter than the nucleus alone. Organized in this fashion, the atom interacts with other atoms in a predictable and relatively stable way. The electrons in the shells of one atom interact with those of another atom to form a new entity, a molecule, that has entirely different properties from the original atoms. The one hundred or so different kinds of atoms may be organized into a near-infinity of molecular species. *All* the characteristics of these molecules are accounted for by their organization and *only* by their organization.

There are no differences between the basic components of air and rocks, or those of a raindrop and a tree, or between the constituents of humans and insects. There is also a common chemistry of life. The same organic molecules compose every living thing. It is in the different organization of familiar molecules that the uniqueness of each creature takes shape. The uniqueness lies in the organization and not in the constituents, just as we have already seen for molecules and atoms.

In the realm of the intangible - especially in thoughts, ideas, words, language, literature - we find the same principle. In languages employing alphabets, every written passage uses the same letters of the alphabet. Each word is unique because of the organization of its letters. The uniqueness of a written thought lies in the organization or sequence of the words used to express it.

Energy is transferred between different parts of the universe by electromagnetic radiation. Whether this consists of radio waves, infrared heat waves, light, x-rays, or gamma rays, the essential difference lies only in the frequency of their oscillations. In fact the "pitch" of a moving wave is itself a type of dynamic organization. The magic colors of a sunset begin as a characteristic mix of light frequencies and intensities, whose pattern triggers a feeling of peace and joy in the human mind.

The realities of our existence are not always obvious. Things happen, creations abound, plants spring from the ground, the sun rises and sets. These phenomena mystified our ancestors. The unseen hand that set the "uncaused" features of the universe into motion was attributed to a spirit: some motivating force behind or within. Spirits gave impetus to animals, induced plants to grow, caused rain to fall, and brought on the calamities of thunder, lightning, and disease. Good and bad spirits also generated human motivation.

Today the reality behind objects, materials, and things can be seen to lie in the organization that determines their nature. The unseen creative hand is the self-organization and reorganization of matter that has been taking place without interruption since the creation. This is the "spirit" that impels the emerging characteristics of the evolving universe. As we shall see, this process also encompasses the development and function of the human brain.

The creation is everywhere full of materials and objects with "emergent properties," properties which are characteristic of the whole but not of its simpler components. Atoms frequently stack themselves into crystals but protons, electrons, and neutrons do not. Water vapor molecules freeze into a solid at about 0 degrees Celsius, whereas hydrogen and oxygen, its components, do not. Similarly, consciousness and motivation are among the emergent properties of the nervous systems of mobile creatures.

Even seemingly unorganized systems show their own characteristic form of "organization" when they are considered as a whole. Gases are a collection of atoms and molecules that do not adhere to one another. They randomly collide with one another and anything else that gets in their path. The reality of a gas is that its atoms act individually at random, yet this random action produces the pressure, density, and other characteristics of the gas as a whole.

Clearly the reality of everything we encounter lies in its organization, from the static relationship of atoms in a crystal of rock to the dynamic interrelationship of different people in a culture or a civilization. Organization defines the reality.

3. The Creation Organizes Itself

We have shown that all the forces acting upon the Creation originate within the creation and that the reality of all creation is organization. Therefore the organization is self-organization and the Creation truly organizes itself. The only "as yet unknown" forces are those that decree the condensation of new stable particles from energy in a creation event.

Within the very nature of these particles are the forces or affinities that compel them to organize themselves into larger entities that are both stable and unstable. The coexistence of stability and instability allows the persistence of a myriad of existing forms of creation as well as compels their continual evolution into new ones. All of these process of creation takes place from within.

4. The Creator Is the creation. The creation Is the Creator.

From all of this, can we conclude that the Creator is the unimaginably great power that transformed itself into matter at the beginning of space and time? By imbuing this matter with inherent forces of stability and change, it launched the universe in such way that the creation process must continue indefinitely. The common characteristic of the four fundamental forces inherent in matter is that of *affinity*. Affinity means the tendency to draw together, to match up, to seek like entities, or to attract an "opposite."

The creation everywhere exhibits creative affinities that bring about new objects or creatures in the broadest sense, including living things with their special powers of self-replication and awareness. These affinities are the creative forces of the Creator, and they are not limited to relationships between tiny particles. At the human level we may choose to call them love.

What after all is love but an affinity? It can variously be a propensity to closeness, a will to create new life and new associations, a feeling of identity with family members, or a drive to submerge oneself in a relationship that alters one's own reality. This powerful manifestation of the Creator/creation may be seen everywhere around us.

If the Creator *is* creation, the Creator must be immanent in all of its creation. Every one of us, and each part of us, is an integral part of the Creator.

Now we can perceive a Creator that has transformed itself into a ever-changing and ever-growing universe. This creation designed itself at the very start to include an eternal dynamic such that it is allowed and compelled to evolve and change forever, exhibiting its genius in this evolutionary method.

The Creator Is On an Adventure

Because we are human, we try to divine a purpose in natural events. We also project this view onto the Creator. So we ask: What is the purpose of the Creator? What is the purpose and the destiny of the creation? What is our purpose as a part of this creation?

Henry David Thoreau once observed, "*Sometimes when I drift idly on Walden Pond, I cease to live and begin to be.*" Living implies a journey or a purpose. Being implies an appreciation of existence for its own sake.

The creation is always creating, endlessly and differently across the vastness of the universe. It is creating time and space; it is also creating an endless variety of material "creatures." Each persists for a time as a new manifestation of the creation; each has a finite life; and each is eventually re-submerged within the Creator/creation.

We humans like to look backwards and trace the course of our lives and their antecedents. We see the historical continuity in evolution and like to think that we perceive a purpose, that purpose being ourselves as the crowning point of the creation. Now it is true that the human species seems to be the most complex single organism so far observed, certainly as far as the reasoning powers of the human brain are concerned. Further, the civilizations that humans evolve and in which they in turn evolve as individuals are far greater than the sum of the persons who participate in them. For these reasons it is tempting to conclude that the complexity of humans is the ultimate intent or purpose of the Creator.

The new understanding of creation offers an opposing view, however. We see the creation as exploring every possibility, producing an explosion of diversity. If the creation exhibits any one defining characteristic, it is this insistence on diversity. Every possible <u>combination</u> of material particle, every possible combination with every possible stability and instability <u>is being</u> created.

This exploration of diversity is not a journey from a starting point to a destination. It follows no plan or timetable towards a goal or ultimate form of creation. Rather it has the characteristics of an adventure, an exploration of the possible, an open-ended excursion. What *can* be *will* be. The Creator/creation is off on a grand adventure with no apparent ultimate purpose except the adventure itself. Awesomely, each and every speck, each and every object and creature, and each and every one of us is a part of that adventure.

Chapter 1 Bibliography

Brush, Stephen G., *How Cosmology Became A Science*, <u>Scientific American</u>, 267:62-70, August, 1992. The author describes the start of the revolution in knowledge resulting from scientific inquiry.

Ferris, Timothy, *Coming Of Age In The Milky Way*, New York, William Morrow and Company, Inc., 1988. Gives the reader a perspective on the scope of the known universe.

Fritzsch, Harald, *The Equation That Changed The World* , The University of Chicago Press, 1994. An imagined dialogue between Einstein, Newton and Haller, a cosmologist, that illustrates the thinking that Einstein used to discover the historic equation that related energy and matter.

Hawking, Stephen W., *A Brief History Of Time: From The Big Bang To Black Holes,* New York, Bantam Books, 1988. A classic popular description of our understanding of the creation of and evolution of the universe.

Osterbrock, Donald E., Joel A Gwinn and Ronald S. Brashear, *Edwin Hubble And The Expanding Universe*, <u>Scientific American</u>, 269:84-89, July, 1993. How Hubble discovered that the universe was more than our galaxy and was also expanding.

Weinberg, Steven, *Life In The Universe*, <u>Scientific American</u>, 271:44-49, October, 1994. An overview of the knowledge of our observable universe.

_____ *The First Three Minutes: A Modern View Of The Origin Of The Universe*, New York, Basic Books, Inc., Publishers, 1977. One of the first attempts to come to grips with what was happening in the Big Bang.

Chapter 2

Energy, the Origins of Matter

"Everything has changed but our thinking."
-Albert Einstein

It is just before sunrise, June 16, 1945. The clock is counting down toward zero. Men huddle in trenches or behind trucks, super-dark glasses over their eyes, waiting to see if their calculations and experimental knowledge will be vindicated. They are about to test an improbable new weapon.

Zero - above the sands of the remote valley of Alamogordo, New Mexico, flashes the most brilliant light and the most powerful explosion ever ignited by humankind. A few of the observers present note that the course of future world history has just changed. It occurs to no one that our retrospective story of the universe, our creation myth, is about to change as well.

In the following weeks this flash burns an indelible imprint in human consciousness. Later it will reverberate through science, politics, theology, and philosophy to an extent greater than any other event in history.

This crucial event at Alamogordo was of course the first human made atomic explosion, The Bomb. It confirmed without a doubt that matter is convertible into energy -- unimaginable amounts of energy. This has become a central and profound part of the scientific understanding of the world. The new view of the nature of our universe, borne out in part by this explosion, is at least as profound as the momentous event itself.

Unfortunately, for the past 60 years following that historic sunrise we have been preoccupied with atomic weapons and atomic power. But the more profound and enduring truth is that matter was converted to energy in that explosion as predicted in Einstein's famous equation $E = MC^2$. This is the revelation that concerns us here.

What about the other implications of $E = MC^2$? Is energy also convertible into matter? Was the matter of the universe created from energy? Could an unimaginable amount of energy have transformed itself into the universe? If so, could this energy that transformed itself into the universe actually *be* the Creator?

For many this leap of thought may be just too big a jump. As Einstein himself observed, well into the atomic age, "Everything has changed but our thinking." Now that the basic energy equation describing the universe is widely accepted, our thinking must indeed change. The remainder of this chapter shows the paths taken in the search for knowledge that leads to the same revolutionary conclusion: An awesome primal energy transformed itself into the universe at the instant of the Big Bang.

Einstein's World

Before the 20th century, the science of physics believed that matter could neither be created nor destroyed. However, there in that remote valley of New Mexico, matter, the "stuff" of which our universe is made, transformed itself into energy. The bomb makers illustrated beyond any doubt that matter/material is a form of energy or power.

Early in the 20th century this unknown and unconventional thinker, Albert Einstein developed his now-famous theory of relativity. Out of his many calculations and mathematical proofs came that one simple-looking equation:

$$E = MC^2$$

This equation said that the amount of energy E is equivalent to the amount of matter or mass M in a proportion involving the velocity of light squared, which is a constant term C^2. This relationship looked very clean and elegant on paper, but what were its implications? Was it just a numerical relationship or was there a larger meaning?

Einstein interpreted his equivalence statement in the same manner as a reversible chemical equation: matter could be converted into energy and energy could be converted into matter. For him the most interesting part of the equation was C^2. C is the speed of light, a very big number.

Light travels fast, fast enough to zip around the equator of the earth seven times in a second. Squared, it becomes an incredibly large number. Thus the equation predicts that a small amount of matter can turn itself into an awesome amount of energy. In the reverse process, a vast amount of energy or power is transformable into a small amount of matter.

Initially this equation was only treated as a mathematical abstraction. However, some physicists soon looked into it more deeply, repeating Einstein's calculations and testing them experimentally. Their conclusions were jolting. If the convertibility of matter into energy was possible and the convertibility of energy into matter was equally true, then it seemed that our well-worn old world might be unstable, prone to disappear in a flare of energy. At the very least physicists should be able to detect some energy-to-mass or mass-to-energy conversions taking place somewhere in the universe.

The first hint that matter can be converted into energy came when Henri Becquerel noticed x-ray-like radiation coming out of uranium salts. Marie and Pierre Curie investigated the phenomenon and found that radium too produced the penetrating rays. In addition, measurable amounts of heat emanated from their samples of radium. Both heat and x-rays are energy. It was not clear if they were the products of a chemical reaction, or, just possibly, of a different process that was somehow converting matter into energy. Of course, we now know that is exactly what was taking place! Some of the radium atoms were spontaneously splitting into two daughter atoms and giving off energy in the process. We will return to this splitting process a little later.

Within a few years numerous aspects of Einstein's theories, including the numerical equations describing his comprehensive relativity theory, were proved by sophisticated experiments and observations. The formula $E = MC^2$ was firmly imbedded in the mathematical models and in the experimental observations confirming those models. It appeared that either Einstein's simple formula was valid or his entire mathematical model and the experimental data that confirmed it were in error.

Searching for the Proof

The early part of the 20th century was an exciting time for the few physicists equipped to study the basics of nature. Although Newton's theories of gravitational attraction and planetary motion were sufficient to explain most of the commonly observed phenomena in the universe, they could not account for many things going on in the smaller world of the atom. Unexplained questions also remained in cosmology. Einstein's relativity theory set physicists to thinking along new lines regarding the interrelatedness of space and time, and matter and energy. Others explored more deeply the nature of the atom. Some developed new mathematical tools and experimental equipment. These either confirmed previous speculations or laid incorrect ones to rest.

One of the biggest mysteries rose every day in the east. The sun, which powers life on earth, produces energy in prodigious amounts. The source of its radiated power remained a mystery. There was no way, using conventional thermodynamics and chemical reactions, that anyone then could explain how the sun generated this awesome amount of energy for any length of time. Despite the sun's large size, none of the conventional energy reactions known on earth could come close to being the source of such a vast constant outpouring of energy. Even a sun composed of pure coal, swimming in a sea of pure oxygen, could not produce this total amount of heat energy.

By this time geologists had convincingly shown that the earth was far older than previously assumed. The record of fossils found in rocks suggested that the sun had been emitting a nearly constant stream of energy for hundreds of millions, if not billions, of years. The constant output of heat and light kept the earth's surface at a reasonably constant temperature allowing living creatures to exist and evolve through most of our planet's long history. Scientists had to conclude that the warmth we experience from the sun has not been the result of a burning process or any other familiar chemical reaction.

As an alternative, energy might be continually pumped into the sun by material falling into it, pulled in by the sun's gravitational attraction. When matter smashes into the sun, the force of the collision would heat it up. Rough calculations readily showed, however, that this could never account for its steady energy output over billions of years.

Einstein's equation pointed the way to the only viable explanation. Although physicists did not have the tools or the information to imagine the processes that might be taking place in the sun, they became convinced that the answer lay in $E = MC^2$.

The development and utilization of the *spectrograph* helped solve some of these mysteries. The spectrograph is an instrument that analyzes light and determines how much energy is in each wavelength. When it was used for solar and other astronomical observations beginning in the 1850s, it yielded information that started to break through the "cloud of unknowing" surrounding the outer universe. The spectrograph allowed scientists to analyze the light from the sun and stars and to determine which atoms were present in them.

Physicists had already used this tool as a rapid way of identifying many of the elements of the earth. Directed at the sun, the spectrograph immediately uncovered a strong unfamiliar pattern, the signature of the helium atom. Only later was helium gas actually discovered here on earth. Hydrogen was the predominant atom detected in the sun's spectrum, along with large quantities of helium and much smaller amounts of other of the lighter atoms.

By this time the mass, "weight," of most of the atomic elements was known with great precision. Similarly, the masses of the constituents of atoms (protons, electrons, and neutrons) had been precisely measured.

Making Sense of the Data and Theories

By the early 1930s enough of this information was available to physicist Hans Bethe to allow him to hypothesize and calculate the process that produced these prodigious amounts of energy. The process was the fusing together of the single protons of four separate hydrogen nuclei to form the nucleus of a helium atom.

It is a complicated process with several steps. The single protons of two hydrogen nuclei fuse together. Two other protons convert into neutrons. These neutrons and the paired protons then fuse together to form the new helium nucleus. Several tiny new particles (neutrinos) are expelled during this conversion. When Hans Bethe added up the mass of the four original hydrogen protons and electrons and compared it to the mass of the helium atom, a significant loss was noted. Even when the approximate mass and energy of the tiny expelled neutrinos were accounted for, there was still a significant loss of mass. The amount of lost mass represents the matter converted to energy in the proportion of $E = MC^2$.

This hydrogen-to-helium fusion process is now affirmed as the source of energy in the sun. A clearly visible demonstration of the proof of this knowledge is taking place every day right in front of everyone. If the amount of energy released when four hydrogen nuclei fuse into a helium nucleus is compared to the amount of energy obtained when four hydrogen atoms are burned in oxygen, it equivalent to comparing an atom bomb explosion to a campfire.

The sun has been shining and radiating this energy for billions of years, continually transforming some of its mass into energy. Four million tons of it per second! But do not worry, the sun has enough material to keep going for many more billions of years before it finally flickers out.

But back to our story: Once the fusion process in the sun was well established in scientists' thinking, nuclear physicists did not automatically run to their laboratories to try to fuse hydrogen into helium. Physicists realized that in order to make hydrogen atoms fuse together, they would first have to strip the electron shell away from the two nuclei. Then they would have to overcome the powerful, mutually repulsive positive charges of the two protons. Only in the center of the sun are temperatures and pressures great enough to strip the electrons from hydrogen atoms and force the protons close enough together to initiate a fusion process.

Great amounts of time and money are now being spent trying to fuse hydrogen nuclei together here on earth. Primarily, the physicists are seeking a controllable process for producing useful energy. Un-controlled fusion energy has already been released from man-made hydrogen bombs, in fearsome explosions that dwarf the explosions of the original atomic bomb.

The Consequences Are Unsettling

Compared to other-worldly fusion, the mass-to-energy conversion in nuclear *fission,* the splitting of atoms which powers both atomic power plants and the atomic bomb, seems almost familiar. In 1938, following the observations of Becquerel and the Curie's, Otto Hahn and Fritz Strassman detected the appearance of two lighter atoms in a bit of uranium that they had bombarded with neutrons. They realized that the bombardment had split the uranium atoms into two lighter atoms and had released both unexplained energy and a number of free neutrons. They established that it was now possible to split certain atoms deliberately in order to release large amounts of power.

With this discovery, the use of an atom-splitting process to produce useful energy was raised from a possibility to a good probability. Now the race was on to develop this potential new energy source. Let us slow down in order to explain certain terms in more detail. The *neutron* is a component of the nucleus of all atoms except the most simple hydrogen atom. It is slightly heavier than a proton, but unlike a proton, it has no electrical charge. A neutron can be thought of as a forced combination of a proton and an electron in which the negative charge of the electron neutralizes the positive charge of the proton. Although neutrons appear to be necessary to stabilize the more complex nuclei of heavier atoms, an inappropriate number of neutrons in a nucleus may also make it unstable.

Each atomic element, such as oxygen or carbon, may have different numbers of neutrons in its nucleus. For example, all carbon atoms have six protons in their nucleus but they can be found with different numbers of neutrons. Atoms with these different numbers of neutrons all behave chemically as carbon but have slightly differing weights. These are called the different *isotopes* of carbon. Some isotopes are stable, others are unstable. In unstable isotopes, such as the well-known carbon-14 used in calculating archeological time, the nuclear assembly of protons and neutrons sooner or later breaks down. If a neutron is expelled from the nucleus, the atom becomes a different isotope of carbon.

But sometimes a proton loses out and is expelled from the nucleus. When a proton is ejected the atom becomes a different species, i.e. it becomes a different element. When certain isotopes of uranium are bombarded with neutrons, the neutrons cause the fission or splitting of the uranium nuclei. Fission of these isotopes causes the creation of two different atoms as well as the expulsion of two or more neutrons from each of the splitting atoms. This leads to the possibility of a chain reaction. (Neutrons can go on to enter other uranium isotopes and split them.) From the time of this important discovery, it was a cinch that, with the proper engineering, atomic explosions or atomic power could be produced by nuclear fission. In just a few years the atomic age dawned with the momentous bomb blast over Alamogordo.

Getting to the Core: Matter Converted to Energy
In both the fusion and fission processes, the nuclear particles of atoms are reconfigured or rearranged into slightly less massive structures. The lost mass becomes energy. This raises some key questions: Can atoms be converted directly and entirely into energy? Is it possible to feed protons and neutrons into a nuclear furnace where they can be "burned" and converted entirely to energy? The answer is probably not, but protons, neutrons, and electrons can be annihilated

under certain conditions and in the process yield tremendous amounts of energy. We will return to this subject later.

Energy Transformed Into Matter

The other direction of Einstein's equation $E = MC^2$ implies that energy can be converted into matter, i.e. into the neutrons, protons, and electrons that make up our tangible universe. Can this really happen; can stable and enduring atomic building blocks be produced from energy alone?

We now know that the answer to that question is "yes." The conclusive demonstration is nothing less than the creation of the universe at the moment of the Big Bang. Unraveling the story of the conversion of energy to matter, like the story of matter to energy, is long and complicated. We must journey painstakingly through it because it leads to the Creator.

We are going to the very beginning of space-time, back to the core, to look at the creation of the universe. We are not going to look at it through the myths and legends that different peoples have devised to satisfy their curiosity about existence, although these may make delightful reading. We will look at the creation from the standpoint of the understandings that have been slowly and patiently accumulated from scientific experiments and observations. We will use only those facts that have been rigorously screened of any hopeful assumptions and unwarranted conclusions.

Let's first look at the sources of the different historical and scientific views of the universe. Early astronomical observers noted that the stars seemed to rotate about the earth appearing at different times and in different locations in a regular seasonal pattern except for "the Wanderers," that is, the planets. When Copernicus and Galileo later showed that the earth and the wandering planets rotated about the sun it seemed that the stars must be constant and immovable heavenly bodies. This became and remained the conventional wisdom for several centuries.

In Galileo's time it was not possible to detect any relative motion of the stars with the available instruments of his day. The distances to them were too great. It even took a long time to realize that the stars were suns similar to our own sun. The "heretic" Giordano Bruno was burned at the stake for that notion. The conventional view was that stars inhabited space, were fixed in their positions, and had probably been there since creation. Newton himself could not answer why the stars were neither drawing together nor orbiting around one another. One possibility was that if they had been created only recently, they would not have had enough time to move very far from their created positions. That argument was demolished, however, by the re-evaluations of the antiquity of the earth by geologists. The earth itself turned out to be billions of years old.

Einstein, when he was formulating his theories of relativity early in the 20th century, assumed that the stars were fixed in space. Even if the universe were infinite in size and there were equal pulls in each direction, close stars would be pulled together by the gravitational force that increases rapidly as bodies approach one another. Therefore Einstein went so far as to put an arbitrary "anti-gravity" constant into his formulas dealing with space and time. He assumed that there had to be a force acting at long distances that kept distant bodies from responding to the force of gravity and plunging toward each other. (He admitted later that this was one of his biggest mistakes although a similar phenomena is being considered today which is termed "a Dark Energy" that seems to have an effect on the expansion of the universe.)

By the 1920s it was clear that more than Newtonian gravity was at work. In 1929 the astronomer Hubble, using the newest and finest telescope of the day, studied the spectral pattern of light coming from near and distant stars and galaxies. Strangely, his results indicated that almost all the stars, instead of drawing together, were rushing away from one another! The new telescope took in so much light that Hubble could determine the distances of not only the nearby stars but also of galaxies far remote from our own. The further out the galaxies were, the faster they seemed to be moving away from one another.

Hubble detected the motion with a spectrograph, the same instrument that had previously found helium on the sun. When Hubble looked at the light from distant stars and galaxies with his spectroscope, he recognized the characteristic patterns of light from the different elements composing the stars. More important he noted that in the light from more distant stars the distinctive patterns were shifted toward the red end of the visible spectrum, the region of lower frequencies. The "music" of the distant stars was coming in at a lower pitch. Similarly, when a phonograph record spins at slower than normal speed the same music is heard but at a lower pitch. The spectrograph recognized the signature or tune of the different atoms in the stars emitting the starlight but noted that their pitch had changed.

This shift in pitch suggests that the object is moving away from the observer. This is akin to the tone of a train horn being lower in pitch when it is traveling away from an observer than when it is standing still or moving closer. Hubble called his discovery a "red shift." He noted that the further away a star or galaxy was, the greater was the red shift of its spectrum. This seemed to mean that all of the stars were moving away from the earth and the sun, and that the further away they were, the faster they were moving apart.

Einstein's relativity theory had predicted this color shift of light as a measure of the relative speed between an observer and the source of light. The subsequent measurements by Hubble and others supported the theory. Now astronomers had evidence that the universe was expanding at a tremendous rate. Galaxies at the farthest measurable reaches were receding from one another at nearly half the speed of light! The light that was coming from them had to have been traveling for billions of years. These measurements also pointed to a universe that was tens of billions of years old.

The emerging picture was one of a universe expanding as if blown apart by a titanic explosion billions of years in the past. Any event that produced this explosion (now called an Inflation) would have been the most overwhelmingly powerful occurrence of all time. If such a proposition were true, it would be the biggest surprise in centuries of scientific thought.

Facing Up to the Implications

In the 1920s scientists were beginning to accept and understand Einstein's theory of relativity. They started to apply the new analytical tools of relativity and quantum mechanics to the study of both the universe and the atom. Arriving in the midst of this scientific excitement, Hubble's discoveries were earthshaking in their implied consequences. Scientists of every persuasion subjected his data to the critical techniques of relativity and quantum physics. After much debate, the scientific community finally accepted his conclusion: The universe is indeed expanding.

The most unsettling thing about this view of the expanding universe was the tremendous amount of power that must have been involved at the instant of creation . At first scientists could not imagine any source of power sufficient to hurl all parts of the universe so far and so fast, propelling the vast mass of heavenly bodies suddenly apart. It would have had to propel them against the immense forces of gravity that tended to squeeze the pieces together when they were in close proximity billions of years ago.

The new view of the expanding universe and its earliest history became known - at first pejoratively - as the Big Bang. Then began a flurry of theoretical activity to try to imagine just what the Big Bang might have been. What caused it? How large was it? Proponents tried to imagine what the conditions of the universe were during the initial phases of the "explosion." The universe, except the hot spots around the stars that are generating energy, is very cool. What was its temperature when it was more compressed? Could this high temperature provide a clue to the propulsive power that hurled the universe apart?

The temperature problem took preeminence in the scientific investigations. When anything expands it becomes cool. Therefore the universe must have been much hotter when it was much smaller. Calculations of the new model of the universe showed that near the very beginning of the Big Bang explosion the temperature must have been many trillions of degrees. This raised several interesting questions: What was the nature of the universe when it was so hot? How small was it at the beginning? Would there be any detectable remnant of the high temperature now that the universe had expanded and cooled over the past billions of years?

It is not useful to talk about the temperature of space that is empty of any material. Rather it is necessary to see if that space contains any energy such as light or other form of electromagnetic radiation. This electromagnetic energy can then be related to a temperature. The calculations made by several different astrophysicists in the 1940s and 1950s showed that the effective temperature of space in the expanded and cooled down universe should now be about five to ten degrees above absolute zero. If true, there should be a sea of radiation corresponding to this temperature. The theoreticians had no way of investigating to see if such a sea of radiation existed, however.

An unexpected verification came not from astrophysicists but from microwave communications experts studying the noise and interference that are present at communication frequencies. Two engineers, Arno Penzias and Robert Wilson, detected persistent radiation from space at a frequency of 4880 megahertz - 4,880 million cycles per second.

Wherever they pointed their directional antenna into space, they measured the same amount of energy at this frequency.

Penzias remembered listening to an astrophysicist who had told him of his calculations of the temperature that should pervade space if the Big Bang had really occurred. The frequency of the radiation corresponding to this temperature was in the range of frequencies that Penzias and Wilson were finding in every direction in which they pointed their antenna. Wilson and Penzias refined and checked their measurements. Astrophysicists rechecked their calculations regarding the probable temperature of the universe during the Big Bang and the expected temperature of space in its present expanded state. Finally scientists agreed that the two engineers had indeed detected the cooled down and stretched out sea of radiation energy that was left over after the universe was created in the Big Bang. They called this "the whisper of the Big Bang." It was, and still is, the most convincing evidence that the universe first appeared in a single tremendous burst of energy.

Changing Our Thinking

The acceptance of the Big Bang has raised tremendous problems of comprehension. If the universe had been as hot and compressed as imagined, what was the nature of this universe? Did atoms exist? Were only the components of atoms, such as protons and neutrons and electrons, present? Were the protons and neutrons broken down into still smaller bits and pieces? Did matter even exist as such, or did the universe consist only of an unimaginably large amount of energy?

Remember that we are retracing the steps that led to the idea that matter - protons, electrons, neutrons - could be created from energy as suggested by Einstein's formula. So far in this account, there has been no hard evidence to corroborate the energy-to-matter transformation. In the attempt to develop a conception of the Big Bang, all evidence pointed to a universe originating at a "point," exploding as a burst of energy, out of which precipitated the matter that composes the universe. The intellectual path to this understanding has been long and difficult.

The first real evidence of the creation of a particle of matter from energy was found in 1937 by Carl Anderson while observing the results of cosmic rays striking metal plates. Cosmic rays are tremendously energetic fast-moving particles of matter. They consist of protons or the nuclei of larger atoms "screaming" through space. They are best observed at high altitudes before they hit molecules in the atmosphere.

When cosmic rays hit the metal plates in Anderson's experiment, he observed the appearance of a new particle which he called the positron. He concluded that part of the cosmic rays' energy had transformed itself into this new particle. Now positrons are a distinctly different form of matter: they are *anti-matter*. Positrons are also known as anti-electrons. Although having the same mass as an electron, every other characteristic of a positron is exactly opposite to that of an electron. The positron has a positive charge whereas the electron has a negative charge. A positron can exist but for a fraction of a second in our world. When it encounters an electron, the positron and the electron annihilate one another and produce a burst of energy.

Anderson had discovered a new particle, albeit an anti-particle, that had mass. Further, it was observed just as it was being created from the energy of a cosmic ray. The event established the empirical validity of Einstein's equation in the other direction: mass had been created from energy!

Duplicating the Energy-to-Matter Conversion Process

Cosmic rays are uncontrollable, unpredictable, and relatively inaccessible. It is difficult to use them for continued and detailed experiments on the nature of matter and energy. Physicists therefore like to employ particle accelerators in the attempt to duplicate the effects of cosmic rays. (A secondary task of these giant machines is to reproduce conditions as close as possible to those presumed to have existed near the beginning of the Big Bang).

Particle accelerators are machines that trap a particle of matter, such as an electron or a proton, and speed it up to extremely high velocities. This means pumping energy into the particles. In many respects an accelerator is similar to a gun. A gun speeds up a bullet. The energy then possessed by the bullet is transferred to its target when it hits it. A high-powered rifle bullet achieves a speed of about 1/3 mile per second. By comparison, particles in an accelerator reach nearly the speed of light, 186,000 miles per second!

Vast amounts of energy can be pumped into a tiny particle in such machines. For example, the proposed Super Conductor Super Collider would have been 17 miles in diameter and would have consumed more electric power than a small city. Even though the speed of accelerated particles cannot exceed the velocity of light, the effective weight or mass of the particle increases dramatically as it approaches that speed. The more energy that is pumped into it, the heavier it becomes. When such a high-energy particle collides with a similar particle, their combined energy is released in a microscopic area. In this minute space is approximated the tremendous concentration of energy that was present in the later stages of the Big Bang.

In reality all sorts of new particles are created when speeding atomic projectiles smash into a material target. Originally scientists assumed that the newly observed particles either were bits and pieces of the original particle or were bits and pieces of the nuclei of the target material. This explains the popular name for these machines, "atom smasher." When the particles produced by this "atom smashing" process were first analyzed and studied, a bewildering number of new and unknown particles was discovered. It appeared that each of the previously known and recognized stable particles - the proton, neutron, and electron - was created out of energy from scratch. Paired with these familiar particles were their newly created corresponding anti-particles: the anti-proton, the anti-neutron, and the anti-electron or positron.

New Visions of the Creation

The plethora of new particles stunned physicists and made them rethink their view of the universe as composed of just protons, neutrons, and electrons. Possibly the protons and neutrons consisted of hundreds of other particles. Possibly these bits were blasted out when atomic nuclei were smashed by high-energy particles. The crucial question became: Were these new particle species actually being created from "nothing" or were they just the constituent components of familiar nuclei that had been smashed apart?

Among the many attempts to answer this question, the cleanest and least ambiguous series of experiments was performed in 1970's in a machine dubbed the SPEAR ring appended to the Stanford Linear Accelerator. This experiment was accomplished with a design by Burton Richter and built under the guidance of Wolfgang Panofsky, the director of the linear accelerator, using concepts that were pioneered in Siberia. The accelerator itself is a two-mile long vacuum tube flanked by high-frequency electronic power generators. The generators produce electrical fields that accelerate electrons as they travel down the tube. Normally the resulting high-energy electrons are smashed into material targets. In this experiment, however, they first stored the high-energy electrons by circulating them around in the SPEAR ring, a thin vacuum tube formed into a racetrack-shaped circle. It was here that they encouraged the electrons to collide with equally high-speed positrons.

Here is how the experiment is done: The accelerated electrons are directed into the tubular ring and confined in a narrow beam as they circle round and round. While the electrons are thus confined, the next part of the experiment is set up.

Positrons are generated by having the electron beam from the linear accelerator smash into an appropriate target part way along the two-mile tube. The apparatus captures any positrons, anti-electrons, thus generated, and continues to accelerate them down the linear accelerator tube. At the far end the positrons are directed into the same ring-shaped tube where the electrons are circling, but in the opposite direction.

The streams of electrons and positrons are encouraged to collide with one another as they pass through an elaborate detector system, and the creative fun begins.

Remember that electrons and positrons, upon encounter, annihilate one another and produce a burst of energy. That annihilation energy is added to all the energy pumped into both the electrons and positrons while they were being accelerated. This added energy was experienced as an increase in the mass and the momentum of these particles.

Each electron-positron collision releases a tremendous burst of energy at the moment the electron and positron annihilate one another and disappear. **Out of such bursts of energy generated in the various types of machines have appeared every known atomic particle, every known "sub-atomic" particle, and all of their complementary anti-particles. What is pure energy following the electron-positron collision instantly coalesces into new matter.**

To be present at the SPEAR site and to view the long accelerator, its appended ring, and the particle detector apparatus gives one the feeling of being present at the creation. Here in this clean, elegant, and unambiguous experiment, Einstein's $E = MC^2$ equation has been validated in both directions. Electrons and positrons, particles with mass or weight, annihilate one another and convert into energy. The total energy of the speeding electrons and positrons then converts itself back into matter. This type of machine has produced virtually all of the different known particles of the universe!

The Stanford machine and even more powerful machines re-create the conditions of the early stages of the Big Bang within a tiny volume of "empty" space. The tremendously high energies and temperatures these machines generate result in the materialization of the building blocks of the universe. Here energy transforms itself into matter!

The Role of Energy

Not every packet of energy can be converted into matter or the components of matter. Energy is defined as the ability to do work or accomplish something. So far we have not dealt with any specific units and have talked only about tremendous amounts of energy. What units are useful when we talk about the energy we get from food or the energy required to grow a plant or to move an automobile? What other units are useful when we talk about creating matter from energy and what is the relationship between these different levels of energy?

The arrangement and rearrangement of atoms in chemical reactions involves energy taken up or given off by the electrons of the participating atoms. Such processes occur when fuel burns, when plants photosynthesize sugar, and when chemical reactions arrange atoms into new molecules. When studying these processes, it is convenient to talk in terms of the energy transferred to or from a single electron of the atom involved in the process.

An electron is an electrically charged particle. When it is not bound as part of an atom, it is attracted by positive electric fields. It picks up energy as it is accelerated by those fields. When an electron accelerates under the influence of an electric field of one volt (approximately the voltage produced by a flashlight battery), it has an energy defined as one electron-volt. Although we could use more common units like foot-pounds or kilowatts or horsepower, these do not relate readily to what takes place at the level of the atom.

It turns out that one or two electron-volts is the amount of energy transferred between individual atoms during the familiar processes of life and everyday chemistry. The sun's energy is transmitted to the earth as electromagnetic radiation consisting of photons of light and heat bearing only an electron-volt or two of energy per photon.

Einstein predicted and discovered the rule that light and other electromagnetic radiation is transmitted in individual discrete packages of energy called quanta. Each packet has an energy proportional to the vibrational frequency of the corresponding light wave. Einstein called these irreducible minimum units of light "photons." (He later won a Nobel prize for this work on photoelectric quantum theory). A bright light does not contain stronger photons; it just contains *more* photons.

One photon of light at the red end of the visible spectrum has about one electron-volt of energy. A photon at the violet end has just over two electron-volts of energy. One or two electron-volts is not much energy. However, imparted to individual atoms, it is sufficient to power all living processes in our world and to promote most inorganic chemical reactions as well.

The chlorophyll molecule in green plants absorbs photons having between one and two electron-volts of energy. This energy soon transfers to newly synthesized glucose, is stored in the electron bonds of carbohydrates and other organic molecules. This absorbed energy is eventually transferred throughout the chain of life, powering the growth and life of all living things.

Every chemical reaction involves a transfer of energy from the electrons of one atom to those of another. These energy transfers range from less than one electron-volt to several electron-volts per transaction. Higher energies are disruptive of stable arrangements of atoms. For example, ultraviolet rays consist of photons of three to four electron-volts. They can kill nearly every living cell, induce sunburn on our skins, and promote skin cancer by damaging the chromosomes of our skin cells. The higher the energy of these photons of light, the more destructive they are to complex molecular structures. A photon with six to eight electron-volts of energy can impart enough energy to an electron to enable it to skip free of almost any atom.

When electrons in atomic shells have enough energy to vibrate vigorously and to transfer that vibrational energy to neighboring atoms, we say that the material is hot. With still more energy, solid materials melt and then vaporize. The energy necessary to produce such chaotic change is about 10 to 20 electron-volts. When all the electrons have gained this amount of energy, the temperature of the material is several thousand degrees.

On the other hand, this amount of energy is puny compared to the energy needed to create an electron. To create an electron requires 511,000 electron-volts! A proton is nearly two thousand times as massive as an electron and requires 938,000,000 electron-volts of energy for its creation. These energies represent unimaginably high temperatures. Only when the universe was at a temperature of more than ten trillion degrees could protons condense from the energy that was present.

Summary: Changing Our Thinking

Recent observation and experimentation have shown that the universe originated from a large single burst of energy[3] in a process called the Big Bang. In this minute fraction of a second, this energy transformed itself into the building blocks of atoms. From thence evolved the incredible diversity and activity of our universe. Could this initiating energy be the Creator, creating the universe of and from itself? The story of the organization and reorganization of that universe is what I call, in Chapters 11,12.and 13, The Long, Long Adventure.

Chapter 2. Bibliography

Adair, Robert K., *A Flaw In A Universal Mirror*, Scientific American, 258:50-56, February 1988. Why is there anything if equal matter and anti-matter were generated in the Big Bang?

Dauber, Philip M. and Richard A. Muller, *The Three Big Bangs: Comet Crashes, Exploding Stars, & Creation of the Universe*, Helix Books, 1996. Describes momentous events leading to the creation of our planet.

Fritzsch, Harald, *An Equation That Changed The World: Newton, Einstein, And The Theory Of Relativity*, Chicago, The University of Chicago Press, 1994. How Einstein's understanding of things changed the course of history and knowledge.

Horgan, John, *Universal Truths*, Scientific American, 263:108-117, October, 1990. This article probes the origins of the universe.

Jackson, J. David, Maury Tigner and Stanley Wojcicki, *The Super conducting Supercollider*, Scientific American, 254:66-76, March, 1986. Machines like this show the transformation of energy into matter and also the reverse process.

---

[3] The most recent refinement describes an energy field undergoing rapid inflation and then transforming into subatomic particles. Other proposals involve the creation of all of the matter of the universe out of a quantum fluctuation of the vacuum energy. In both cases the source is primordial energy.

Mukerjee, Madhusree, *A Little Big Bang*, <u>Scientific American</u>, 280:60-65, March, 1999. More description of the "atom Smashing" machine that create the conditions that existed in the early stages of the Big Bang.

Musser, George, *Four Keys to Cosmology*, Scientific American, February 2004, Vol 290, No.2. The general consensus of physicists and cosmologists now centers on the assumption that the entire universe "condensed" out of a sea of energy.

Rhodes, Richard, *The Making Of The Atomic Bomb*: New York, A Touchstone Book, Simon and Schuster, 1986. A very readable and complete story of the discovery of the very real relation of matter to energy and the physical principles that allowed the physicists to understand the conversion of matter into energy in the sun and to create the atomic bomb.

Chapter 3

Forces That Control and Shape

"You can't push it with a string."
-Charles Kettering

Things happen - stars form, plants grow, the sun burns, the wind blows, earthquakes rumble and shatter the earth. The eternal questions have been "how?" and "why?" Some are content with the proverbial answer: "Because, just because." Others may seek the hidden reasons, the ultimate causes, and the means by which the events take place. The final search is for the *forces* that do the work, from whence the forces come, and how these forces exert themselves.

Although the forces of the creation are not seen by human vision, they can be measured with great precision. Scientific curiosity has defined their nature and the means by which they are transmitted. The most difficult to define, the nuclear forces, are inferred from physical processes and their strength is measured by determining the energy necessary to overcome them. Physicists have also detected the ephemeral particles that convey these forces over the minuscule dimensions of the nucleus and its particles.

Similarly, scientists have shown that material does not respond to nor does it "feel" any forces other than those that inhere within itself. Although physicists and others continue to look for new sources of motion and change, so far the four forces account for all of the action animating all the bits and pieces of our universe. Every so often a scientist may think that he has observed a new force in action, but these speculations are almost always dispelled by more careful observation and measurement.

When we look into that esoteric and minuscule part of creation called organic life, its emergent properties of self-replication and self-awareness seem to suggest a new source of cause and effect. Closer inspection, however, shows that these properties are also derived from the dynamic organization and reorganization that are a manifestation of the same inherent forces at work elsewhere in the creation.

A Saga of Unfolding Understanding

Everyone today knows the Law of Gravity, and only fools try to break it. This was not always the case. To support an early version of the theory of gravity, Galileo predicted that light and heavy objects would fall at the same speed if dropped together from the Tower of Pisa (yes, it was leaning even then). The traditionalists of the day not only opposed his theory but also wanted to prevent the experiment from taking place! It was Galileo's successful prediction, together with meticulous observations from the newly invented telescope, that spurred Newton's inference that a universal, uniform attracting force is at work in the creation. He showed how gravitation held the moon in orbit around the earth and held the planets in orbits around the sun.

Western science began to wrestle with the congruence between model and observation ever since Newton formulated his first law of motion, expressed in terms of force (F, mass (M) and acceleration (A). This "law" says that any "body," any particle or piece of material with mass, remains at rest unless acted upon by an outside force. Also any body in motion remains in motion in a straight line unless acted upon by an outside force. In other words a situation only changes when some force is exerted. This explanation still stands as one of the great fundamental discoveries of science.

In mathematical terms, the relationship is expressed as Force equals Mass times Acceleration, $F = MA$, or in another form, $A = F/M$. The resistance to a change in motion is called *inertia*. The greater the inertia or mass, the greater is the force needed to move it, stop its motion or to change its direction.

This rule can be applied with somewhat less precision to the affairs of humankind. The greater the inertia of an institution or custom, the greater is the force necessary to change the direction of that institution or custom. Things just do not happen without some force being exerted upon the object to be moved or changed. We often talk about our "mental inertia" as well: how much easier it is to cherish an old idea than to modify it or replace it!

Later in this book we will discuss the forces that are likely to generate and modify ideas. Here at the beginning, however, we investigate the simple forces that can be inferred from the behavior of particles and inanimate matter. Some forces pull, some of them push. Others harmonize and still others disrupt. Taken together, we want them to account for all change and all lack of change, all motion and all inertia. We want them to explain what we observe at this moment, and we want them to account for all the postulated history of the creation, as outlined in the previous chapter. A tall order!

Because natural forces themselves are not observable, only their effects, this chapter must present a series of interlinked inferences explaining what they must be like. We see the circumstantial evidence and measurements made of the effects of these forces. We present those explanations that have best survived the tests of consistency and predictive power. Some readers may wish to jump directly to the chapters on organization, which might be more fun, and come back to the basic forces when they want the challenge. Mental hopscotch is welcome here!

The Force Be Within You?

Stars form, plants grow, the sun burns, the wind blows, earthquakes rumble and shatter the earth. Aristotle observed it all and wrote a treatise on *cause,* the first systematic attempt to clarify what we mean when we say that one thing causes another. In modern times scientists have taken up this work in exploring the notion of *fundamental forces.* They have had great success in explaining most natural phenomena in terms of their component materials and energy. However, they always reach a point at which they must assume the presence of forces which they cannot feel or see but can only measure.

We begin with three basic questions, posed the way a person with a scientific turn of mind might pose them.

- What do these forces do?
- What are the origins of these forces?
- How are these forces transmitted?

This search is an outstanding example of the power of careful analysis and reduction of the circumstantial evidence to simpler and simpler explanations. 20th-century science has concluded that only four forces

are needed to explain all motion and change in the creation, from the smallest to the greatest phenomena. These four forces are:
- **Electromagnetic force**
- **Strong nuclear force**
- **Weak nuclear force**
- **Gravitational force**

The means of transmitting these forces and exactly how they exert their influence is not simple to explain, but we will explore those factors as we go along. These forces can be detected and measured and their effects are sufficiently well known that scientists can now make remarkably accurate predictions.

The Electromagnetic Force

As far as our daily lives are concerned, the *electromagnetic force* [4] is the principal force that modulates and rearranges what we experience. Electromagnetic forces result from the electrical attraction of positively charged protons to negatively charged electrons. This attractive force does many amazing and different things, more than any of the other three forces. When the electric force is "stationary" it is called an electrostatic force. Moving electric charges produce magnetic fields. When this force is in motion, it is called the electromagnetic force because it creates and is inexorably intertwined with a magnetic force or field.

The electromagnetic force shapes atoms into huge structures compared to the size of its component parts. It imparts strength to these seemingly frail and gossamer structures. When these electrically charged particles move or give off energy, they create traveling electromagnetic fields which we call light, radio waves, x-rays and such. These waves of energy are the means of communication as well as the carriers of energy between atoms, be they the adjacent atoms or those communicated to through the vast reaches of space.

Motion, sound, wind and waves result from forces transmitted through the bonds these forces create within materials and between

---

[4] I have introduced the term electromagnetic force since the electrostatic force of the electron's charge is both manipulated by a magnetic field and the motion of an electron produces a magnetic field. Both electric fields and magnetic fields are inexorably intertwined and are described as a single electromagnetic force.

adjacent particles of the bits and pieces of the universe. All chemistry and the structure of all chemical compounds are the result of the interaction of these forces. These forces create the bonds that tie the variously different atoms to create the millions of chemicals existing in the universe. In this role, they are the inventors of new molecules and the creators of the structures of these new combinations of atoms and molecules.

Appendix A contains a broader explanation of the role and the mechanism of the electromagnetic force. This amazingly versatile force determines the structure and the very nature of most of the creation. It is also the means of communication between the various bits and pieces of the creation and the means for transporting energy between atoms and across the reaches of space.

Nuclear Forces

Two of the fundamental forces of the universe act only within the nucleus of atoms and are seemingly never experienced by us directly. They are called the strong and the weak nuclear forces.

The *strong nuclear force* is particularly involved in the creating, organizing, and reorganizing of neutrons and protons. For example, it is the principal force involved when nuclei fuse together in the interior of suns. The strong force is what holds nuclear particles together.

(Protons and neutrons are believed to consist of sub-units called quarks. Quarks have never been seen in isolation. Their existence is implied from the characteristics of neutrons and protons and from the sub-nuclear particles that are detected for fleeting instants in high-powered particle accelerators).

The strong nuclear force is thousands of times stronger than the electromagnetic force. It holds nuclear particles together in the close confines of the nucleus, overcoming the powerful mutually repulsive forces exerted between similarly positively charged protons. This strong force has a very short range of influence and does not extend much further than the diameter of the nucleus.

Physicists have worked out various mathematical models to explain how this force might act. In one of them, the strong force is exercised via very heavy, very short-lived units or quanta of mass/energy that flash back and forth between the nuclear particles, binding them together.

The strong nuclear force plays the key role of stabilizing the heavy fundamental particles of our universe. As far as scientists have been able to observe, the building blocks that are familiar to us - electrons, protons, and neutrons - have an infinite stability. They seem to have remained unchanged for the billions of years since the creation. An apparent exception occurs when a neutron is expelled or ejected from an atomic nucleus. In this case the neutron has an average lifetime of about 12 minutes before decomposing into an electron and a proton and a minuscule ephemeral particle called a neutrino.

We say "apparently" because this decomposition does not really violate our theory. As we shall see shortly, in this instance the weak nuclear force - also an inherent force belonging to heavy particles - regularly and predictably introduces the observed instability. Further, some nuclear physicists have suggested that the protons of the nucleus might also be unstable in the long run. According to their models, protons on average may disintegrate after 10 followed by 34 zeros years! Even if this is true, for all practical purposes we say that the building blocks of the universe are stable and eternal.

A lot can be said for this kind of stability! Stability provides a platform for the continued existence of substances and materials. If atoms and their constituents were continuously flying apart and changing, the universe would be in continuous flux and would not be able to support the kind of ordered adventure that we see around us.

Complementing its contribution to stability, the strong nuclear force also facilitates the nuclear fusion taking place in the sun. Fusion not only welds hydrogen nuclei into larger and heavier ones, it also releases up a huge stream of electromagnetic radiation that warms the earth and powers the chemical processes of life. The character of the nuclear force causes this fusion to take place mostly in a slow and deliberate manner rather than in a huge explosion - a comfort to us, because the measured release of energy is a necessary condition for life on earth, including our own.

By facilitating the fusing of neutrons and protons in atomic nuclei in the heart of the sun, the strong nuclear force is a creative force as well. It produces new and novel atoms that add to the diversity of creation.

The Weak Nuclear Force

This is the other nuclear force that facilitates the break-up of the nucleus in the process of radioactive decay. It is believed that this force is also exercised via short-lived and massive quanta of mass/energy. These particles have already been detected in several different high-powered particle accelerators.

What does the weak nuclear force do for us? It promotes instability. In nuclear fission it causes an atomic nucleus to split and change into another. New, smaller atoms are produced and heat and other electromagnetic energy is given off. Most of the lead in our world has been produced in this way, for instance; lead is the major product of the decomposition of uranium into other elements.

Further, the heat produced by the radioactive decay of atoms deep inside the earth keeps the earth's core hot and fluid. It powers earthquakes and the upheaval of mountains and it drives the volcanoes that recycle nutrients into the biosphere. Of course, radioactive decay also produces radioactivity that is harmful to life! Although radioactivity generally provokes genetic changes that are destructive to living organisms, in some cases it brings about a novel and creative turn in the course of evolution.

Instability is an instrument of change. If there were no instability or probability of change or uncertainty in events, the universe would become static and unchanging and completely predictable. The instability and unpredictability that are inherent in the nucleus of an atom are part of the larger issue of the instabilities inherent in the makeup of our universe. The importance of instability to the unfolding of events is brought up again in subsequent chapters.

Gravity

The last of the four forces of nature is *gravity,* the great attractor. Unlike the other forces, gravity ties together every particle in the universe. All of the basic building blocks of matter, the ephemeral sub-nuclear particles like quarks, and the messenger photons that carry the forces are drawn toward one another by its feathery light tug.

Gravity acts in only one direction; it pulls and does not push. Like the electromagnetic force acting on charged particles, the pull of gravity diminishes inversely as the square of the distance separating any two particles. The force originates within each particle, reaching out to pull every other particle toward itself. The force is proportional to the mass of a given particle and to the total mass of a body composed of many particles. Thus large masses exert much more pull than small ones, and particles without any mass experience no gravity at all.

Gravity is such a minuscule force at the particle level that it could easily be overlooked on the atomic scale of things. Its force is 10^{-40} less strong than the electromagnetic force. Compared to this force, the gravitational attraction between any two atoms is negligible and cannot be detected.

However, gravity is cumulative; it adds up. Even the gravitational force between atoms becomes significant if there are enough of them. The cumulative gravitational force of all of the atoms in the sun exert enough force on each other to crush those atoms which are at the center. As we have seen, this crushing force causes atomic nuclei to fuse, producing both new kinds of atoms as well as the sun's radiant energy.

Gravity is not content just to squeeze and squeeze an existing sun; it adds to it. The sun's gravitational pull sucks in hydrogen and helium atoms from surrounding space. When an atom of hydrogen is attracted into the sun, the force of gravity on it increases rapidly as the distance between it and the sun decreases. This further increases its acceleration and momentum. Ultimately, of course, the atom crashes into the sun. Its energy or momentum is transferred to particles in the sun, adding to their overall heat. When the internal temperature of any large mass of hydrogen and helium becomes great enough due to the pressure generated by gravity, nuclear fusion ignites in its core and a star is created.

The "passive" force of gravity holds human beings to the spinning earth, draws water down into the lowest spots, and inexorably pulls mountains down into the sea, particle by particle. It holds the moon in orbit around the earth, the planets in orbit around the sun, and the sun within the galaxy. It pulls into the sun the thin gas of hydrogen and other gases found between the stars, adding to its source of fuel as it sweeps through the clouds of debris left by earlier exploding stars. Gravity, then, is the assembler of worlds. Or is it perhaps a slow plotter patiently putting back together the very "clay" that previously flung itself apart.

Gravity encourages other energy transformations. Recall that gravity accelerates falling objects. The larger the object, the greater the possible momentum and the possibility of harnessing it for useful work. A familiar example is a hydroelectric power plant. Gravity imparts momentum to the water as it falls. This energy is turned into electric power when a water turbine powered by this falling water is used to spin the magnets of an electric generator. Electrons are liberated in the wires of the generator and are forced out to travel through power lines, sometimes for hundreds or thousands of miles. Passive gravitational attraction has been changed into the dynamic energy of running water, then into the flexible and subtle energy of electricity - immensely useful transformations from the human point of view.

Gravity is seen and felt wherever we look, wherever we go. Although we can feel and measure the gravitational field, how this force is transmitted is still unknown. The title "graviton" has been given to the weightless particles that are presumably exchanged between bodies to convey this force. Unlike the energetic quanta or units that convey the other three forces of nature, "gravitons" are unmeasurable and undetectable except in the reality of the effects that they are presumed to produce.

In Summary

Repeated observation and experimentation has found very strong evidence for four fundamental forces of nature: the electromagnetic force, the strong nuclear force, the weak nuclear force, and gravity. These are all the basic pulls and pushes inherent in our universe. They account for all of the processes that science has ever observed.

These forces have strong similarities. All of them arise within particles of matter as an essential characteristic of these particles. Neither the forces nor the particles exist without the other. For example, the electric fields produced by the inherent electrical charge of the electrons and protons act only upon charged particles. There are no electrical fields that do not originate from charged particles. Magnetic fields originate when charged particles move. Magnetic fields do not exist other than when and where they are generated by moving charged particles. The electromagnetic field transmits energy through space from charged particle to charged particle via electromagnetic radiation such as light and radio waves.

The strong nuclear force operates only within the nucleus of an atom and arises within these particles themselves. It transmits its influence by the exchange of heavy ephemeral particles that materialize within the nucleus for only extremely brief moments of time. Whereas the strong force glues the nucleus together, the weak nuclear force causes nuclei to become unstable. It is also transmitted via heavy high-energy particles that remain within the nucleus.

Gravity is a property of all particles that have mass. Every object is shadowed by an gravitational field that surrounds it, extends outward in all directions, and creates a pull on all other objects. This pull becomes weaker with distance but never quite disappears, not even when objects are galaxies apart. How this pull is conveyed is the subject of intense interest by physicists and others.

These four forces do not permeate space waiting for the atoms and suns to be caught up and pushed around. Rather they inhere within the particles of which our universe is made. Their effects are measurable, and except for gravity, their means of transmission are known, detectable, and measurable.

To some readers this account might appear to be incomplete.[5] Nevertheless, if we wish to speculate on other forces that might manipulate the universe, we have to ask from whence they might come, by what means they might be exercised, and what their influence on the web of creation might be.

The interpretation of circumstantial evidence is always tricky, and some of the above body of knowledge will no doubt be revised and sharpened by physicists in coming years. Nevertheless, it seems certain to say that all matter, energy, and their inhering four forces appeared together at the instant of the Big Bang, and that these four forces have driven the ongoing process of creation ever since.

Chapter 3 Bibliography

Davies, P.C.W., *The Accidental Universe*, Cambridge University Press, 1982. This book contains a readable understanding of how the forces of nature work.

Weinberg, Steven, *The First Three Minutes: A Modern View Of The Origin Of The Universe*, New York, Basic Books, Inc., Publishers, 1977, chapter 4. This book includes descriptions of the forces of nature/matter.

---

[5] Some unexplained forces seem to be pushing the galaxies apart at a more rapid rate than previously expected. Galaxies apparently are shaped by more gravitational forces than produced by the celestial bodies visible within the galaxies. "Dark matter" and "vacuum energy" are names coined to explain these observations.

Chapter 4

Organization and Reality

"The only reality is organization."
Robert G. Neuhauser

The reality of anything, be it material, a thought or a civilization, is not inherent in its constituents. The reality resides in its organization. By organization I mean the plan; the *interrelationship of its constituents*. The static as well as the dynamic relationships are what really determine the nature and the uniqueness of anything. The underlying and interlinking patterns of dynamic relationships and processes that exist within the creation -- these are what define it and give it its character, in whole and in part.

Living creatures are marked by birth, constant change, growth, movement, and death. These dynamic relationships present at each stage define their underlying reality and are their animating essence or "spirit", if we wish to use these terms. On the other hand, inanimate objects often appear to us as rather static. But as we shall see, their organizational pattern also gives rise to their nature, reality, and "spirit" of themselves as well as their part of the entire web of creation and life. They may be too small or too large and their pace of re-organization may be too fast or too slow for us to appreciate them on a daily basis, but whenever we take the time to look, their essence is there in the beautiful pattern of their constituent parts. These interlocking patterns of organization proceed without a seam or break from the smallest sub-particle to the whole vastness of the universe, animating each level of being with its own characteristic essence or reality.

Organization in the World of Atoms

Look at the simple things first. Consider again the atoms that compose our universe. We have seen that the atoms are built as organizations of three basic particles, (electrons, protons and neutrons) that are in turn stable bundles of energy. The energy is organized in such a way that each particle has certain properties. These properties are not properties of all energy but belong to that particular organization of energy.

Each type of chemical element in our universe has its own unique properties. Some elements normally remain as a gas, some are metals, and others remain liquid depending on their temperature. The only significant organizational difference among these different species of atoms is the number of protons in their nuclei. This number in turn determines how many electrons occupy the different shells surrounding the nucleus. The number of electrons in the outermost shell then determines the interactive properties of that type of atom. It is as if the Creator had spent a day with Lego blocks of only three different colors and a few rules on how to put them together and came up with all of the chemical elements that constitute our world and universe.

Let's examine more closely how atoms interact with one another. Consider again, the carbon atom has six protons in its nucleus and therefore six electrons inhabit its electron shells. Other than to describe its mass and the structure of its electron shells, it is difficult to describe just what an individual carbon atom would be like if it were alone in the universe. Much more helpful is to understand how it organizes itself with other carbon atoms and with other types of atoms.

Normally, carbon is neither a gas nor a liquid, just a formless black solid like coal or charcoal. But, carbon "likes" to link with other carbon atoms, i.e. whenever the outer shells of two carbon atoms start sharing an electron, both atoms give off a photon or two of electromagnetic energy and achieve a lower energy state. Happy and more stable together! A carbon atom also finds it easy to share an electron or two with atoms of hydrogen and oxygen. Thus in nature we find thousands of compounds made up of these same three elements in a myriad of arrangements.

Carbon atoms can also achieve a stable organization by nesting together tightly - good "packing" in chemistry language. Tight packing shows up as visible crystals when enough atoms are involved. Carbon atoms are lucky: they can pack themselves into crystals in several different ways, depending on their temperature and the pressure that they are under when the crystallization begins.

An everyday encounter that you might have with carbon is the line you see on paper when writing with a pencil. The "lead" in the pencil is not lead but graphite, soft black crystals of carbon atoms. Graphite is black because the electrons in this structure absorb just about every photon of visible light that hits them. Because graphite absorbs them all, the absence of reflected light easily allows us to see the black trail that it leaves on paper. Since graphite is a soft material, bits of it are easily scraped off by the slight roughness of the paper. The material is stable at room temperature but burns if heated to about 1000 degrees.

So now we might think that we know what carbon is like, it's soft and black. But wait, there is another arrangement that is a quite different crystalline form of carbon. Carbon atoms pack very tightly together in an entirely different three-dimensional crystal when they are subjected to very high temperatures and pressures.

We don't see this rare form of carbon very often, however, except in jewelry stores and engagement rings. This crystal is called diamond. Diamond is just about as different from graphite as anything could be. It is clear and transparent, meaning that nearly all of the light photons that reach it go right on through without being absorbed. It is also the hardest material known. Scrape it across glass or just about any other hard substance and it tears out pieces of the other material while the diamond itself remains intact. It is brittle and cannot be pressed out of shape. It resists burning until exceptionally high temperatures are reached. In this crystalline form it is one of the most stable materials known.

The difference between these crystalline forms also shows that carbon atoms simply piled up together do not have a unique nature of "carbon-ness." What kind of "carbon-ness" they display on a large scale depends more on their organization than on their intrinsic nature. Their intrinsic nature - having six protons - fixes a certain range of possibilities, but which possibilities are actually realized depends on their subsequent arrangement. This is of course the pattern we see over and over again in the creation. At each level of organization an entity has a few essential characteristics - an essence, a spirit - that allow it a range of possibilities in its organization and self-organization into the next higher level. Thus the creation displays a ladder of organization, each level dependent on the previous level for its range of possibilities but not determining any one particular outcome. It is the thesis of this book that the creation has tried *many* outcomes at each level of organization, and what we experience around us is the result to date of this wonderful adventure.

Carbon atoms themselves exist in a variety of nuclear arrangements. The most common one is a nucleus with six *neutrons* accompanying the six *protons*. Six seems to be the perfect number of neutrons for carbon; this number produces an atom that is completely stable. If it is organized with fewer than six neutrons, the nucleus soon flies apart.

Carbon has been created in five different nuclear forms (called isotopes of carbon), each with a different number of neutrons. All are unstable to some degree except for the one that has six neutrons. The most useful unstable isotope is called carbon-14 because it has 14 nuclear particles, 6 protons and 8 neutrons. On average these atoms persist for several thousand years before they mutate into another isotope of carbon. Taken as a whole, these atoms mutate with enough regularity that the proportion of carbon-14 in an ancient object may be used to determine its antiquity.

The instability of the different isotopes of carbon is not related to the structures that carbon builds when it links to other atoms. The isotopes of carbon behave just like any other carbon atoms when they interact with other substances. The number of neutrons present in the nucleus determines only the stability and mass of the isotope. Again we see that the characteristics of the different isotopes of carbon reside in the pattern and the organization of the constituent parts of the nucleus. The instability of the unstable isotopes is not caused any novel or unstable parts.

Assemblies of Atoms

Let us now look at the nature of things on the next higher level. Stone is a building material. A common building stone is limestone, composed of crystals of calcium carbonate. Calcium carbonate, as its name suggests, consists of calcium, carbon and oxygen. Oxygen, which we normally think of as a gas that we breathe, is part of this hard brittle rock. In fact this rock is made mostly of oxygen, since there are three oxygen atoms to every atom of carbon and calcium. Chemists write its molecular formula as $CaCO_3$, meaning that each molecule of calcium carbonate is the union of one atom of calcium metal, one atom of carbon, and three atoms of oxygen. These three old friends combine and form a hard stone with properties greatly different from those of its constituent elements.

Now let's take our example to the next higher level of organization. When mortar cement, which includes the lime from limestone, is mixed with water and sand, it can be used to hold the stones of a house together. The water reacts with and sets up chemical links between the other constituents. The new molecules become a structural "glue" that cements the stones together into a firm wall that is nearly as hard as a single stone taken separately. Water, which is normally a liquid, becomes an integral part of a stone-like material.

Now if we put stones, cement, and water into a gigantic bag and shake it up, we would not find a house of course when we opened the bag. A house requires that the individual stones be arranged in a certain way. They must be cemented together with the proper mix of mortar cement, water, and sand, inserted in the proper amount into joints between the stones. Now suppose that another house is built next door of exactly the same materials. However, this one is designed by a different architect and built by an unscrupulous contractor who puts too little cement into the mortar. The second house does not look like the first because the architect and builder organized the stones into a different design. Besides that, the second house may fall down because the mix of the mortar was changed and the mortar does not have sufficient strength to hold the parts together under the stress of a storm or earthquake.

The reality of and the differences between the two houses lies in the design or the organization of the materials, not in the materials themselves. The comparison of the Taj Mahal and the men's room in the first chapter illustrates this principle very well.

Humans Beings as Organizational Patterns

Most of the examples we have discussed so far consist of rather fixed or stable organizational patterns. Although there is always a dynamic component -- things are always happening throughout the system -- nevertheless the system itself remains relatively constant. A regular pattern of internal activity is part of the essential nature of all systems, both living and non-living.

Most people probably balk intuitively at considering a human being to be an organization or to be defined as an organizational system. So let us first examine a living person on the physical level, as it may not be so hard to employ this concept for purely physical components. We call any living being and thus any human being an *organism,* and it is the level of the organism that biologists most frequently study the design of life.

Storing the Design of Life

One hundred and fifty years ago, an industrious monk named Gregor Mendel pioneered the science of heredity, now called genetics. Genetics describes the process of transferring characteristics from one generation of living organisms to the next. It also attempts to explain the mechanisms for transferring the hereditary information and what controls this process. In taking up this study Mendel continued a long western tradition of looking for the "essence" of living things. Prior to Mendel this study had been more rooted in religion than in science and more concerned with soul than with the body. Like Galileo and other intellectual pioneers, Mendel eventually ran afoul of the Church and had to curtail his investigations, but not before showing that much of heredity follows simple rules that do not require any fresh intervention by an omnipotent Creator.

In the century after Mendel, one living process after another came under the scrutiny of science. An amazing range of phenomena, from the contraction of muscles to the synthesis of complex carbohydrates and proteins, was explained by the method of examining individual components and how these are organized together. An intellectual peak was reached in the middle of the 20th century when it was not uncommon for scientists to describe living organisms as nothing more than complex machines whose parts and functions would soon be known. One of topics that preoccupied the best minds, then as now, was Mendel's question of how the immense wealth of subtle detail in the design of living things is so exactly transferred from one generation to the next.

A key insight into this mechanism was obtained by the microbiologist Oswald Avery in 1944. He discovered that the component of living cells responsible for transmitting hereditary information from parent to offspring is DNA. (DNA is the shorthand for deoxyribonucleic acid, a very long and very stable chain of about four relatively simple organic molecules. In humans most DNA is found in the 23 pairs of chromosomes that make up the nucleus of every human cell). Avery was able to prove by direct experimentation that DNA is the carrier of heredity data in bacteria and viruses, i.e. the stuff that determines the characteristics of their succeeding generations. Later, it was established that the DNA in every living cell performs the same function. With the discovery of DNA and its function of passing on genetic characteristics there came a revolution in biology. In 1954 James Watson and Francis Crick figured out the structure of DNA and published the first sketch of the now-famous "double helix" shape of this molecule.

Most importantly, they discovered the alphabet of life. They discovered what is now called the *genetic code,* that is, how information is "written down" in the DNA for making all of the other molecules needed by living things. In a brilliant speculation that won them a notable Nobel prize, Watson and Crick showed how the four simple subunits of DNA could act as a four-letter alphabet for writing out biological recipes. They also suggested a mechanism whereby these "words" or genes could copy themselves with exact precision to make identical DNA for the next generation. Shortly thereafter other biologists confirmed their speculations and much, much more. The mechanisms of genetic reproduction are now so well agreed upon that biologists are fond of calling this area of knowledge their "Central Dogma", an ironic reference to the rigid faith that once tried to suppress Mendel's work in this field.

The philosophical insights from biological science in the second half of the 20th century mirrored those from physical science in the opening years. Molecular biologists discovered that all living things from slime molds to humans, from elephant grass to elephants to fleas, have their unique recipes for creating a new life, a new flower, a new elephant, or a new flea. However, *each organism uses the same alphabet of DNA subunits to write its genetic code.* What is different is the arrangement or sequence of the units. What had earlier been shown at every organizational level in the physical world is now being shown to be true for the living world as well.

The information contained in DNA is sometimes referred to as a "blueprint" or a design for the creature or organism. A *recipe* is a more appropriate description, as proposed by the evolutionist Richard Dawkins. A recipe for a loaf of bread does not describe the bread's characteristics. Instead it prescribes the ingredients to be secured, the sequence in which they should be mixed and kneaded. It also specifies the conditions: the time allowed to rise, the conditions and timing of the baking process, and the atmosphere in which these conditions are to be maintained. When the recipe is followed faithfully, a proper loaf of bread is created.

Similarly, when a fertilized egg is provided with the proper environment and nutrients, its DNA is able to mobilize surrounding molecules to carry out its construction program. It "instructs" the proper chemicals to be assembled within and by the cell at the proper time and in the proper sequence. The new molecules in turn cause the cell to grow and to replicate its DNA, in preparation for the cell to divide into two new daughter cells. The daughter cells then continue the same process of chemical synthesis and cell division, each new generation receiving its own exact copy of the first cell's DNA. Soon the DNA directs newly dividing cells to specialize their function. Different types of cells appear, cell types that will later develop into the different organs and structures of the body. All of them however, carry the complete DNA code for the whole organism.

As we have seen, the DNA alphabet is a simple one of just four letters. These letters are strung into chains of "words" called genes. In our bodies about 100,000 genes are arranged into a few continuous DNA chains, each one having the shape of a spiral ladder or helix. These are the chromosomes found in the nucleus of each cell.

Our chromosomes contain a tremendous amount of information. The amount of information stored on 23 pairs of human chromosomes is greater than the information stored in several sets of encyclopedias! If this genetic code is damaged or altered by radiation or chemicals, new cells or new offspring may develop incorrectly. Many "birth defects" are known to originate right from the moment of conception, when the defect is already present in the DNA of the fertilized egg.

The DNA storage mechanism has provided us with a splendid example of the importance of organization or design. It is fascinating to look at some of the other key structures of the human body in the same light.

Differentiation

When cells with the same DNA, let's say our own, develop into different cell types or tissues, we call this *cell differentiation*. By week 3 in the life of a human embryo there are already the forerunners of muscle cells, white blood cells, nerve cells, bone cells, liver cells, and so on. Yet we know that all of these cells carry the identical DNA recipe in their chromosomes! What has happened to make them suddenly grow differently?

Rather as in real estate, the earliest signals lie in location, location, location. Cells on the outside of the embryo experience a slightly different environment from those on the inside, cells near the point of attachment to the womb are bathed in a slightly different nutrient soup from those further away. Such environmental factors interact with the DNA program stored in the center of the cell, causing some parts of the program to be turned off and other parts to get turned on. In the case of a developing embryo this leads to the establishment of separate cell lines or tissues as component parts of a single organism. Following birth, other environmental factors will turn off and on the sections of the DNA that regulate the activity of these tissues.

Before DNA and its regulatory mechanisms were understood, the development of embryos into adult organisms was a major mystery. Now it too has been explicated in terms of the very precise organization of key molecules at the right place at the right time.

Chemical Communication

In plants and simple animals it has long been obvious that the different cells must be sending signals to each other via chemical messengers. In humans, too, there is a complex communication system based on molecules that carry a message. Many of these molecules fall into the class of "hormones", i.e. they regulate something and that is the only job they do. Their action begins when a hormone "key" fits into a receptor "lock" on the surface of the right kind of cell and alters the process going on inside. Very often the structure of the hormone is exquisitely precise for its job. For example, the molecular structure of progesterone, the female hormone of pregnancy, is different from testosterone, the principal male hormone, by only one carbon and a few hydrogen atoms! In this case very precise size and shape count for everything.

This precision is carried onwards by messenger molecules *inside* the recipient cell. Another pair or two of lock-and-key molecules transmits the message to the heart of the cell, generally to the DNA in the nucleus. The message switches one DNA recipe on or another recipe off, which either promotes or inhibits the assembly of a key cellular product. At every step of the way it is the exquisitely precise organization of these molecules - within themselves and with each other as locks and keys - that allows this system to work so exactly and efficiently.

Nerves and Muscles for Fast Responses

No matter how precise, chemical messaging is slow over distances. It is pushed to the limit by a plant such as the carnivorous Venus Fly-Trap. This flower closes itself over any insect that gets stuck in its fatally attractive opening. It has flexible cells that contract under the influence of chemical messengers and shut off the victim's escape. To our eyes they appear to contract slowly and deliberately. On plant time, however, they are surely moving at breakneck speed! This system would be much too slow to control the muscular responses of an animal.

More advanced living organisms have an electrochemical network, nerves and brain, that for many purposes has superseded chemical messaging because of its greater speed. The brain is the body's main switchboard for incoming and outgoing messages, and that is the organizational aspect we describe here. Of course the brain is also the home of the thinking, conscious mind. The final section of this chapter takes up the now-familiar theme of essence and organization in accounting for some of the simpler phenomena of perceiving and thinking.

Most incoming messages to the brain come from our sensory organs of eyes, ears, nose, tongue and skin. Most outgoing messages go to our muscles, transmitted as electrochemical impulses along a chain of outbound nerve cells. At each junction between nerves and at the final junction between nerve and muscle, communication depends on the sudden release of messenger molecules, "neurotransmitters," by the transmitting cell that fit into matching receptors on the recipient cell. In a muscle cell this triggers a contraction or relaxation and causes movement. Within a fraction of a second our sensory apparatus reports the motion, and another fraction later our brain sends a wave of revised instructions to adjust and perfect the intended movement.

What levels of complexity in this picture! The essence of our neuromuscular system is that it offers a fast response to changes in our surroundings or inner state. This is accomplished by a tightly organized system of sensory, nerve, brain, and muscle cells. Each of these cell types has essential characteristics making it distinct from the others. Nerve cells, for instance, can almost instantly transmit electrochemical impulses from one end to the other. This quality depends in part on having highly specialized teams of transmitter and receptor molecules. In turn the most important quality of these molecules is that they have a complimentary shape and the transmitter molecule uniquely fits the shape of the receptor molecule and they even seek each other out.

Feedback

Our complicated system of communication and regulation is not a one-way system. It contains feedback processes. If a cell produces a chemical needed elsewhere in the body, the producing cell often is stimulated by a hormone that is secreted by the cell that needs it. If the cell overproduces, the receiving cell has a different mechanism for producing a second chemical messenger. This one gives negative feedback to the producing cell and causes it to slow down its output.

Later we will examine negative feedback in some detail, as it is a crucial mechanism in maintaining the stability of many dynamic systems, both living and non-living. This feature of inner control, even self-control, is important to our understanding of the creation's great adventure. As we shall see, it plays a major role in making some systems successful and long-lived while others spin out of control and disappear.

Feedback as a characteristic of dynamic systems was first elegantly described by the philosopher-mathematician Alfred Whitehead and subsequently elaborated by systems theorists such as Norbert Wiener. At this stage of our argument it is sufficient to say that even the regulation and control of the dynamic processes found in nature do not require the outside intervention of any new force. Processes speed up and slow down according to inner relationships already built into the system, and the principle of the primacy of organization is reaffirmed.

Linear and Nonlinear Systems

Organisms are often compared to machines, especially if their functions are considered one at a time. As we have just seen, *any* organism is a more complex type of organization than a simple linear machine. A linear machine is one in which there is an input, an operative mechanism, and a resulting output. A can opener is a simple machine. It has a mechanism that pushes the sharp edge of a wheel through the top of a can. It also has a knob that turns a separate rough wheel, and this second wheel causes the sharp wheel to roll along the lip of the can and cut out the can lid. One process leads to another in a straight linear manner.

A gasoline engine is a more complicated machine. It has some feedback in its design. The rotary motion of its crankshaft runs a system of shafts, cams, and valves that controls the flow of fuel into the engine and times the spark that ignites the fuel. The resulting confined explosion pushes a piston which turns the crankshaft. The cams attached to the crankshaft "receive information" or "get feedback" about how far the crankshaft has revolved, i.e. they are again pushed at just the right instant. Their up-and-down motion is again passed along to the components that control the input of fuel and the timing of the spark that ignites the explosion that turns the crankshaft. The engine keeps running. In this case "feedback" refers to a secondary motion produced by the motor that feeds back the exact timing for the engine's next inputs, allowing it to perform efficiently.

Very few things in our universe are like simple machines. Many involve multiple, complex, interacting feedback systems. Living organisms, for example, succeed because they are able to employ a great number of feedback systems. They in turn are immersed in a larger system, their local ecosystem, which has even more checks and balances.

One of the first and most perceptive ecologists of all time, John Muir, observed, "When you pull on anything, you find that it's hitched to everything else." Living organisms have succeeded not only because they have built-in feedback networks but also because they are embedded in the larger organization called the biosphere, that interconnectedness of all living things so aptly described by Muir. Organisms exist not as isolated discrete physical entities but as organized dynamic systems exchanging energy, matter, and information with the wider biosphere. Their elements and molecules - and the elements and molecules of *our* bodies as well - flow through this living system, again and again!

Intangibles

After so much biology, let's look into a less physical and more symbolic realm by examining the role of organization in language, words, and speech. Language is composed of individual words. Each word is intended to convey a meaning, to define an object, to specify its action, or to describe its characteristics. The spoken word is a combination of sounds in a particular order. Sounds are complex combinations and sequences of different frequencies of vibration in the air that can be detected by the ear of another person. There is no direct relationship between these vibrations and the object or action represented by that word. A very elaborate organization of auditory equipment in the ear and brain and a complex system of assigning meanings is required before sounds make any "sense."

It is fascinating to watch an infant acquire the power to discriminate between sounds - first between human speech and noise, then between its mother's voice and just any speech, then the context in which it hears the different words of its care givers, and finally the meanings of individual words themselves. In language, as in everything else in the creation, the constituent parts make little sense until we understand how they fit into a context, a higher level of organization.

Further, long after the use of sounds evolved into language, writing was developed to preserve or record the ideas conveyed by language. At first stylized pictures were used to describe the object or action. In early attempts at writing languages, the different squiggles that were originally inscribed with charcoal on bark or hides probably had no direct relationship to the sounds of a word but only to the visual representation of a person or object. Later, symbols were given to *sounds,* and these symbols were arranged in sequence to represent the sounds in a spoken word.

What is interesting to us, if the sequence of sounds is altered or reversed, the word has either no meaning or possibly an entirely different meaning than that intended by the original speaker or writer. Similarly, if the sequence of the individual squiggles that we call letters is scrambled or reversed, they lose their meaning. If they are all run together and not marked off from one another, they are also difficult or impossible to understand. This is as true of modern alphabets as it was of the early forms of writing.

In written English all words are built from our 26-letter alphabet. When we assemble letters and words into a sequence, the intent is to convey a certain meaning or perhaps a feeling. It is an imperfect system of course. No matter how precisely a sentence is composed misinterpretations and faulty communications may occur. These sometimes occur because an individual letter has been wrongly chosen or badly written, but far more common are errors of organization, poor choice of words, inappropriate sequence of ideas, and so forth. Like architecture, meanings depend as much on good design as on good materials.

So far it is easy to see that the essential factor inherent in speech, writing, and words is really its pattern. It doesn't take a Shakespeare to know that words cannot just be strung together in any old sequence and still convey the same meaning. Language also requires a detailed set of rules for putting words into their proper order for conveying a particular meaning. And further, the different languages of the world do not use the same set of rules. When we translate a sentence of English into another language, we not only have to translate the words, we also have to rearrange their sequence in accordance with the new grammar. Otherwise the meaning would be lost or obscure.

Language is not always intended to be a precise transmission of facts or ideas. Words are also used in an evocative way to stimulate thinking or recall an experience. The context of the words helps bring up the associations stored in a person's memory. In this case the same words may stimulate very different thoughts in different listeners, depending on their previous knowledge and experience.

Brain, Mind, and Soul

Any explanation of "reality as organization" must apply across the board. It must apply to the perception, knowledge, consciousness, memories, and emotions held in the brain. This is an area of notable technical difficulty. In part scientific research is only now elucidating the structures associated with mental phenomena.

Our individual brain began with the codes on the original set of chromosomes that initiated the embryo that developed into our body. This part of our DNA also supplied the recipe for the development of our brain and its neural networks. Nerve cells are built from the same constituents as other cells; it is their internal organization that gives them their character of electrochemical signaling and their organization with each other that gives them their collective character of enabling perception, memory, emotion, consciousness, and reflection.

Modern science has recently appropriated an old word to encompass all these system-wide abilities of neurons connected together: *mind*. In a notably succinct definition, "The mind is what the brain does." Our mind is simply the total collective functioning of all the neural cells of our body and brain.

Many readers will wish to include an animating spirit to explain such sublime characteristics as consciousness, ethics, and love. But the animating spirit is there! It emerges right from the neural networks themselves, just as an electric charge emerges from the arrangement of condensed energy in an electron or a magnet emerges from an appropriate metal subjected to the appropriate conditions. The qualities associated with spirit also inhere to the matter and energy of our body and brain when the latter are appropriately organized. Thus these qualities too are subject to our consideration and reflection. Such reflections and arguments make up the second part of this book. It is indeed a Great Adventure that we are launched upon!

The Physical Structures Supporting the Mind

The brain structure with its billions of complex nerve cells and trillions of possible interconnecting pathways starts to develop during the early stages of embryonic development and continues throughout early life. The nerve cells themselves develop early, but the interconnection of the cells continues throughout life.

The physical structure of the brain is akin to the silicon chips of a computer and their wired connections. The brain is built of units organized and interconnected so that they accept simple input signals and compare them to other information coming in from other pathways. Each unit either passes the signal on to another part of the brain or allows it to terminate. The brain, like the computer, also has a structure that can store the signals, and this information can be retrieved later.

In addition to chips and wires, computers need processing instructions called software. Software is "soft" because it can easily be changed to instruct the hardware to perform different tasks, depending on the situation. The mind too includes a kind of "brain software," but this grows and develops within the brain and is integral to it. Certain patterns of interconnection develop among the trillions of possible pathways. When these interconnections are used repeatedly they apparently become relatively fixed, an aspect that is very helpful for performing useful tasks time after time.

"Genetic Memory"

In the history of human evolution, some neural pathways have remained essential to all human beings at all times, for example, the timing of the heartbeat. These pathways are essentially hardwired into fixed arrangements of designated neurons. The DNA recipe for human beings always includes a chapter on how to set up these fixed regions of the brain. No new fetal brain has to learn these tasks; these tasks were "learned" long ago in the course of evolution and "remembered" by the genes that carry the code for the appropriate structures. This is why we may use an enchanting metaphor and say they are part of our collective "genetic memory" of what has been found to be successful.

Genetic memories allow the newborn infant to respond to its environment by crying, to sense its need for air by breathing, to sense its need for nourishment by nursing from its mother. Other genetic memories are less precise: perhaps the need for human affection is a general instinct that can be satisfied by a variety of experiences and behaviors. The human brain contains enough genetic memory to produce the necessary nerve and chemical control messages to keep the body functioning and growing. It also has the genetic knowledge necessary to produce reflex actions that protect against some types of accidents, such as blinking the eye when an object approaches rapidly or closing the eye to cut out bright lights.

Memory and Reflection

A more important characteristic of the human brain is that many of its neurons are *not* prearranged by the DNA development blueprint at all. Whereas other creatures are endowed with a large amount of genetic memory, the human brain is in large part left open to self-arrangement depending on individual experience. This means we have an enormous capacity to *learn,* i.e. interpret sensory inputs, acquire new behaviors, store knowledge, make associations. These learning processes feed back to the mind's software that monitors and directs the functioning of the brain. From repeated cycles of mental action-feedback-action, we slowly see the emergence of more complex notions like personality and emotion, in which hardwired tendencies and individual life experience both make contributions.

The mind correlates bad experiences with their associated sights, sounds and other sensory inputs. When these sensory inputs are encountered again, it channels these sensory impressions into memory pathways where they will alert the conscious mind to danger. Thus the brain makes use of some nerve interconnections to establish memory patterns that become nearly permanent. The mind cannot forget these memories. Fortunately favorable experiences can be remembered in a very similar way!

The most familiar functions of the mind are thinking, decision making, motor control, and creative thought. Some of these functions are reflexive functions, i.e. responding to inputs from itself. The mind organizes the brain so that it compares memories to inputs from the sensory systems. The mind then refers to these stored memories and reflects upon them by comparing these two or more different pieces of information. It might ask, for example, is it a new thing that I'm seeing or an old one? Then it can make a decision based on memory whether a proposed action is desirable or not. From there it can send out impulses via motor nerves to muscles to carry out movements such as running or smiling.

Creativity

Creative thought involves the process of comparing learned memories and organizing them into new patterns. The new patterns are culled into one or two new ideas, a new organization of facts and impressions. (As we shall see, not all of this process necessarily takes place consciously). This organization of facts and impressions is then stored in the memory of the brain, available as starting material for another creative cycle. Creative thought can take place entirely within the brain without additional outside sensory inputs, or it may make use of fresh sensations.

It is instructive to know that an infant who is not allowed to interact with its mother or another nurturing person develops with a severely distorted and diminished mental capacity. In an extreme case the infant dies for lack of adequate sensory input and stimulation. Such inputs are apparently required for the correct development of the brain and its normal functioning. It is a clear demonstration that brain organization is only partly complete at birth; there is a lot of software organization that depends on learning. And of course it emphasizes once again that essential properties do emerge from organization. If you prevent a favorable organization from being formed, the desired properties cannot appear.

Consciousness

Different parts of the brain are dedicated to different functions. Some are devoted to speech, others to sight, creative thought, motor control, memory or thought, and the organization of thought. Apparently the brain contains a system of interconnectedness that "makes the rounds", periodically checking on the recent inputs and deciding which ones to discard and which ones to remember. We do not remember every sight, sound, touch, or taste input but selectively remember and analyze only certain ones. If a given input alerts the system to something significant, that input is referred to other parts of the brain for reflection or action. Unlike many mental activities, this activity is aware of itself. We call it *conscious thought*. Consciousness has not yet been associated with a special part of the brain, and perhaps never will be. For now we may say that conscious thought is the total interrelated analysis of inputs and stored memories that the mind performs.

In the course of human history there has been an immense amount of speculation about the mind and its nature. Some thinkers have looked upon it as something bestowed upon the body at birth. Others have endowed it with properties of communicating with and being a link between the brain and some other "spirit" world. Others have declared that there is a qualitative difference between the human brain and the brain of other creatures. This difference endows it with the unique ability to think and to have emotions and plan ahead in time.

The notion that the mind is an independent entity residing in the head or that the personality is an entity residing in but apart from the brain is refuted by the experience of people who suffer physical damage to the brain. This author's aunt suffered a stroke that greatly reduced the blood supply to a part of her brain, disrupting important parts of her network of communication channels. She remained in a coma for months until the damage began to be repaired or bypassed. She gradually regained the function of consciousness. However, the disruption of the normal organization of the brain altered her personality substantially. From the physical damage stemmed a sequence of intellectual and emotional damage, changing her into a much different person.

There are many degrees of consciousness, ranging from self-consciousness and self-awareness to merely responding to or acknowledging external stimuli. We next explore some of these different levels of consciousness.

Animals

Anyone who has lived with pets can tell us that an animal is not an automan without emotions or the ability to see and think ahead, or to understand some language. When one of our family members mentioned the word vet in a conversation, our dog, who normally jumped into the car when anyone opened its door, had to be dragged into it for his visit to the veterinarian! This happened repeatedly. When the dog saw camping equipment piled in the hallway for our camping trips he went into a sulk and refused to obey normal instructions and lay around in a funk until we returned.

Animals can also have human-like emotions such as vindictiveness. When our cat was unceremoniously dumped out of the hammock so that I could read my paper in comfort, I caught it urinating in the shoes that I had just removed. This is not to say that animal brains are the same as human brains. In their organization and functions they have quantitative differences in many respects because their brains are smaller in many regions and larger in others. The olfactory centers of a dog's brain are huge compared to those of a human. This contributes to a dog's far superior ability to detect and discriminate between scents.

The qualitative differences between the more advanced animals and humans are few. 98% of the genes in a chimpanzee's DNA are identical to human DNA. That two percent deviation makes the difference between chimpanzees and humans and between chimpanzee and human brains. Humans have evolved centers for speech control and the sense of numbers and mathematical relationships that animals apparently do not have. These centers in the human brain can then develop the ability to control speech and perform mathematical manipulations that are beyond the capability of animal brains. Nevertheless, the individual brain cells and the chemistry of the brain functions are nearly identical in advanced animals and humans. The differences in the organization and the extent of the interconnections in the human brain allow the development of a mind that allows humans to become composers, scientists, mathematicians and philosophers.

The Ghost in the Machine

Some might agree with the view expressed so far that the reality of things are their organization. On the other hand, they may have an uneasy feeling that there are other realities that cannot be examined in this way, or fall into a realm that has no relationship to any type of organization.

Ideas or thoughts are realities that have no physical content. Though they originate in the brain, are interpreted by the mind and are stored in the brain, they do not have to reside there. An idea is immortal. Once it is expressed it can exist indefinitely and persist long after the mind of a person who formulated it has died. It can exist in books, in recordings and in the brains of others. What is an idea but a unique combination of impressions, feelings, facts, and conclusions? Change the relationship of the components of the idea, and its nature changes. Its uniqueness lies in how these components are interrelated, and not in the components themselves. Then there are some of those least understood areas of the process of the human mind, such as inspiration and imagination. We will touch on these areas now.

Inspirations

Many people, and here I cautiously include myself, place a high value on inspiration or revelation. Let us look at a few theories about our sudden and unexpected insights.

Some thinkers have reasoned that there is a collective unconsciousness that all humans share. They conclude that some mysterious or ethereal communication pathway exists outside of people's physical beings and connects them together. They affirm that humans possess some as-yet-unknown means of sending out and receiving these messages and images, and that these messages are experienced as revelations when they are received by individual minds.

As we have seen, it is plausible that there are collective mental images or scenarios that almost all humans share. Behaviors and feelings that proved essential to human evolution may well exist as instincts or "genetic memory" hard-wired into our DNA program. It should come as no surprise to us if our brain has ways of thinking imbedded in it that include common responses to common inputs from the outside world.

One such common response might be the feeling of "awe" in the presence of very large or very powerful natural phenomena, a feeling related to fear but definitely not the same as fear. We can understand how the sudden onset of this feeling, perhaps brought on by a sunset or rainbow, might be interpreted as an inspiration, especially if this feeling stimulates strong associations held in one's individual memory. Nonetheless the feeling itself is in all probability a genetic memory or instinctive response rather than the manifestation of some ethereal communication. In a different vein, sometimes ideas or solutions "just come to us", apparently without conscious effort. Could it be that these are communications from an outside source?

We might look for the possible sources and routes of these communications, but a more obvious explanation is at hand. A good deal of the activity of the mind is done *subconsciously,* below the threshold of self-aware thought. Take the example of driving a car. We can drive down the road while conversing with a friend or thinking of the day's activities and be completely unaware of the actions that our body is taking. Later we realize that we drove for miles "without thinking." But were we really "not thinking", or was it thinking that was so routine that it remained unconscious of itself?

Many people report that they do much of their creative thinking at the subconscious level. At first they may wrestle with a problem consciously and find no satisfactory solution, so they "put it out of their mind" and do something else. Later, the problem resurfaces in their consciousness and a new approach presents itself. Could it be the result of a revelation given from the outside? Probably not. More likely it is the result of the brain experimenting with new arrangements of its memories and data, working away below the surface. When it finds something new or promising, it breaks back into consciousness and shouts, "Eureka!" If this moment is particularly sudden or thrilling, it is easy to see how it might be interpreted as a deliberately sent communication.

One philosopher, when asked about the secret of creative thinking, summed up his advice in three words: "Only make connections." Apparently the mind working in a subconscious way is able to do this very well. Although new ideas are sometimes the result of new experiences and inputs, more often they arise from rearranging mental elements that are already present.

Human Enterprises

When we come to complex human organizations, however, we have to sharpen our analytical tools. Cultures and civilizations are the most visible and complex of human organizations, and they seem to be constantly in flux. Not only do they have built-in rhythms and repeated cycles associated with their structure, but the structure itself often appears to change, bringing in fresh rhythms and altered cycles.

Despite these complexities, human institutions may also be analyzed to show how their organizational pattern determines the essence of their reality. The crucial test comes when part of the organizational pattern changes. When this happens and the system then ceases to function as it had before, even though all of the same people are present and working, it is clear that the cause of the change in the organizational pattern caused the decline. This shows clearly that the organizational pattern is the essence of that institution. It has been replaced by a new reality, a new system, even though every individual person in it has remained.

Social systems have a certain degree of stability that allow them to function. On the other hand, things are never in complete harmony in all sectors of a society. Changes take place because of external circumstances or because the system is out of balance. When changes take place slowly enough for the social patterns to readapt, society evolves into something slightly different. If the reorganization takes place very rapidly, we experience a revolution.

In Summary

In the physical world, clearly the reality of anything is its organization, be it simple or complex. Indeed the physical world itself is a unique organization of energy, a unique organization that facilitates further organization. This organization of the physical world determines the reality of everything up through the greatest structures, the most complex plants and animals and the human brain. When the non-physical world is examined, it will be found that the reality also resides in the organization, whether the subject be thoughts, music, art or literature.

Organization is both static and dynamic. It can be a simple geometric pattern or it can define a linear cause and effect relationship. In organisms it exhibits a complex relationship of interacting processes that form these dynamic living organisms. Those dynamic and convoluted interrelationships continuously change and they generate new realities.

Chapter 4 Bibliography

Kauffman, Stuart, *At Home In The Universe:* Oxford university Press, New York, 1995. The Search For The Laws Of Self-Organization and Complexity.

Mullins, Kary B., *The Unusual Origin Of The Polymerase Chain Reaction*, Scientific American, 262:56-65, April, 1990. A simple system that shows how DNA replicates itself. This system is now used in all DNA analysis work.

Dennett, Daniel C. *Darwin's Dangerous Idea*, Simon and Schuster, New York, 1995 This book shows how at each stage of the evolution of the universe, different forms of organization create the new realities.

Chapter 5

Stability and Instability

"Nothing is permanent except change."
-Heraclitus

"The art of progress
is to preserve order amid change
and to preserve change amid order."
-Alfred N. Whitehead

Stability or permanence is an illusion. Although "solid as a rock" implies permanency and solidity, even a rock is far from solid. Its atoms have an electron shell and a small nucleus and are otherwise hollow. And permanent? Most rocks of the world are in their fourth or fifth incarnation as rocks. They've been worn down, dissolved, melted, and reconstituted several times in the 4-5 billion years since the earth first formed.

"A diamond is forever" sounds catchy, but in fact nothing is forever. The closest things to being forever seem to be protons and electrons. Although even they can be created and destroyed under the right conditions, left alone they seem to have been stable and enduring since the creation and will endure forever, although that prediction is questioned in the latest theoretical models. (See Appendix B for more on this subject.)

Stability As The Preserver

Here we'll start at the beginning. Protons and electrons are permanent and stable. But not all matter is so lucky. Nearly half the mass of most atoms consists of neutrons. Neutrons are as stable as protons as long as they are within the nucleus of an atom. When neutrons burst out from their nuclei during radioactive decay or nuclear fission, however, the resulting free neutrons are far from stable. Rather quickly some of them split into a proton and an electron, half of them doing so in the first 12 minutes.

And the others? Half of the remaining neutrons split apart during the second 12 minutes, leaving only one quarter of their original number. Half of this group in turn decays during the next 12 minutes, and so on, until finally there is only one free neutron left and then it too splits apart. Because the time for half of any number of free neutrons to decay is always the same, we say that their *half-life* is 12 minutes.

Since neutrons split into protons and electrons, the proton and electron assemble themselves into a hydrogen atom. a permanently stable form of matter. In this case an unstable neutron has rearranged itself into a stable one, a configuration which now offers a stable platform for building more complex structures such as molecules.

Stability also applies to the forces acting on and between these particles are consistent and unchanging. We have already identified the four fundamental forces: the electromagnetic force, the strong and the weak nuclear forces, and gravity. As far as we have been able to observe, these forces are indeed constant and unchanging, both over time and over the breadth of space.

Stability As The Foundation

We have all noticed how things in nature work and work well. Indeed, they often seem to have been carefully *designed* for what they do. Thus many people believe that the Creator must also be the Architect and Designer of our universe, consciously and deliberately guiding each step of the evolution of the universe.

On the other hand, our new view holds that the Creator and the creation are the same and that we are part of it. The wonderful design we see all around us is the result of endless experimentation (change) followed by the retention of what is good (stability). Further, a characteristic organization or design is the essence of each part of the creation. That essence inheres from within and does not result from any outside force. Thus matter must be imbued with a strong tendency to stabilize itself, preserve its organization, and make itself permanent.

If this were not true, if everything was continually moving and breaking apart, there would be no opportunity to evolve the structures and creatures of the world and the universe. Stability provides a platform on which structures can exist and modify themselves. The endless experimentations of nature require such stable platforms. From atoms to galaxies, from sugar molecules to living creatures, the evolution of the creation is an unceasing process. None of these structures or organisms is assembled all at once. Each improvement takes place on a previously evolved foundation that is reasonably stable. If a new structure proves to be slightly more stable, it becomes the next platform from which further complexity can evolve.

As Richard Dawkins has aptly said on the question of design, "There is zero probability that a whirlwind going through a junk yard could assemble an airliner from the parts that it sweeps up." An airliner is built of parts that have the proper strength and heat resistance. The shapes of its wings are derived from the successful designs of smaller airplanes. Those have in turn were developed from the design of glider wings modeled after the shape of the wings of birds. Each component, from the wings and body and engines to the control mechanisms and electronic communication system, has been built on the experience gained from the successful, stable, aircraft that were previously designed.

Instability, the Creative Process

The creation is characterized by both stability and instability. Instability promotes change and destruction, creation and death. Change is the process of reorganization or the creation of a different or a more complex organization. Stability provides the continuity that preserves a successful change.

Let us start near the beginning of creation to see how stability and instability have always been characteristics of our universe. In the earliest part of the Big Bang, all of the different possible subatomic particles, each with its own combination of properties, "condensed" out of the initial energy. Most of these subatomic particles can only be temporarily created in particle accelerators today. Of all those particles, only protons, neutrons, electrons, and neutrinos were stable enough to persist and participate in the molding of the observable universe. The unstable "exotic particles" all disintegrated, leaving the more stable particles bathed in a sea of re-released energy.

After billions of years and after the stars had begun to form, hydrogen nuclei started fusing into helium and subsequently into heavier atomic nuclei. At that point a new type of instability appeared, the instability of radioactive isotopes.

Instability in the Nucleus

Our old friend carbon, we may recall, always has six protons in its nucleus, but it can exist as isotopes of carbon with differing numbers of neutrons in the nucleus. The unstable isotopes are called *radioactive* because they tend to disgorge high-energy particles and radiation as they alter themselves into another isotope.

Taking all elements together there are 337 stable isotopes and 54 unstable isotopes occurring naturally on the earth. Radioactive isotopes may seem insignificant at first glance, but they are a major factor in change or instability of the creation. Some convert into different atoms. Others bombard surrounding atoms with ejected neutrons. These can cause the neighbors to split or to become radioactive. Much of the energy released during this radioactive disintegration ends up as heat, and this heat has major effects. The center of the earth is kept molten by the radioactive decay of certain long-lived isotopes. The radioactivity of unstable isotopes also has a profound effect on the organic world. Radiation damages the chromosomes of living cells and causes cancer and birth defects. On the positive side, in low doses however radiation can promotes beneficial changes as well as harmful ones.

Radioactive decay is also the alchemist of nature, because one element may change into another during this process. The goal of ancient chemists, who called themselves alchemists, was to create a new element, preferably gold, from the less valuable elements. They inevitably failed because the chemical reactions in their furnaces and cauldrons could only manipulate the electronic bonds of elements and compounds. They had no tools to disturb the number of protons in the nucleus and change the type of atom.

The Paradox of Quantum Physics

Radioactive isotopes nicely illustrate one of the paradoxes of quantum physics. That is, observers have absolutely no clue, nor can they ever know, when an isotopic atom is about to disintegrate or decay. But we can follow in Madame Curie's footsteps and learn about the *collective* behavior of such atoms. If we have a large quantity of an identical isotope and know how many individual atoms we have, we can predict quite precisely how many will decay during any given period. In fact, the rate of radioactive decay can be measured with accuracies not obtainable by most other measurement techniques. With proper instruments we can count the number of individual disintegrations, and counting is the most precise of all measurements.

The paradox is that having a full knowledge of the collective behavior still says little about the individual behavior of a single atom or nucleus. The best we can do is to calculate the *probability* that an individual nucleus will decay in a given time period. Such uncertainty is typical of most events occurring at the atomic and subatomic levels.

Other instabilities are also associated with unpredictability. Electromagnetic radiation such as heat and light easily breaks certain chemical bonds between atoms, especially those in which electrons are being shared among carbon atoms, as occurs in most organic molecules. But a blast of light or heat never breaks all the bonds, only some of them, and no one will ever know in advance which individual molecule (or gene!) will be altered.

In short, not only does the creation change due to inherent instabilities at the level of its fundamental particles, but individual events involving these fundamental particles also become unpredictable. As we shall see, this holds significance for our understanding of how genetic change takes place from parent to offspring and in biological evolution as a whole.

Everything In Flux

A fascinating motion picture was made of the images produced by an ion microscope. The microscope is examining the extreme tip of a sharp metal needle as it is being heated and cooled in a vacuum chamber. As the movie opens the microscope shows images of fuzzy-looking balls. These are the atoms of metal lying in tidy little rows, tightly organized in the crystal structure of the metal needle point. Occasionally a little ball pops off the structure. This means an atom has gained enough energy from its neighbors so it is able to break its links and skip free, vaporizing off the surface. More surprisingly, other atoms suddenly reappear on the crystalline structure, condensing out of the "atmosphere" surrounding the needle point. But no anarchy here: when they arrive, they line up in proper order!

As the temperature of the needle is increased, the atoms become more animated. The fuzzy-looking images pop off and reappear more rapidly. At maximum heat they are quite frantic indeed, vaporizing and condensing in a frenzied, spontaneous, unpredictable dance. Later, as the metal cools down, the activity slows but does not cease. At all times the quantum paradox applies: at any given temperature we can count with some precision the rate at which atoms gain enough energy to boil off the surface and then return, but we are never able to guess which individual atoms in the picture will be the next ones to skip free.

All linkages between atoms result from the interaction of their electron shells. All of these linkages can be broken by nothing more potent than heat. Although the bonds holding metals and minerals together are the strongest, even they are subject to breakup. The bonds of organic compounds are more easily broken. Because they are formed using the small units of energy delivered by photons of sunlight, they are subject to being damaged by comparable units of energy.

When molecules are held together by quite weak bonds, even room temperatures and sunlight are enough to break a link here, a bond there, until the substance loses its important characteristics. We have all many times read, "Keep this medicine in a cool dry place." There is usually good reason for this, because the medicine will eventually decompose and turn into a different chemical as some bonds become broken and the atoms reorganize themselves into new chemicals. The medicine then becomes ineffective and possibly even dangerous. Storing such chemicals in a cold place retards this decomposition but does not stop it.

There are still other forces that break electron bonds, the glue that holds everything together. Ultraviolet rays are very effective for weakening and breaking down most plastics, which is why they should be kept out of prolonged strong sunlight. Heat eventually melts and vaporizes everything. X-rays and gamma rays destroy tissues deep within a human body. Microwaves heat water molecules, which is why they are an effective cooking agent for wet foodstuffs to change their chemistry.

Despite these disruptive hazards, the tenacious bonds between electron shells still provide stability for the molecular basis of life, while sometimes destructive levels of electromagnetic radiation and atomic decay provide the means for change and force the changes to occur.

Processes Leading To Stability

A process is a dynamic and moving thing, a sequence of events, matter and energy obviously driven by change. Processes get started because of instabilities, and instabilities keep them rolling. Yet, as we look around us, many processes seem to stay within a narrow path and reach a predictable conclusion. We might even say that they *create* a stability at a higher level of organization. Let's see how.

The universe, the broadest organization of the physical world, contains processes that are "linear" and others that are circular or cyclical. Linear processes are those that lead from one situation or organization to another one, then they stop or go forward again. They generally do not go backwards or sideways or return the first situation. For example, the first sudden crystallization of energy into matter was a linear process, as was the assembly of this matter into stable electrons, protons, and neutrons. Another linear process is the production of heat and light from the sun. The construction of permanent buildings, roads, railways, and dams are linear processes carried out by human beings.

But just as important are the processes that "go around" and come back to the same state or situation. The motion of the earth as it spins on its axis is the simplest possible kind of cyclical process. As a result of this motion, the sun appears to rise every morning in the east, cross the sky, set in the west in the evening, and reappear the following morning in the east. Always, every day, on the same course, at the same speed. If we lead an average life, we experience this daily cycle about 25,000 times. Because we are so used to it, it is hard to imagine that this rotation was once initiated by great instability and cataclysmic change, but it was. In our perception this rotation is now the essence of stability.

Moving up one step in complexity, we can trace the process whereby water evaporates from lakes and oceans, becomes water vapor, falls as snow over a polar region, compacts into a glacier, creeps down to the sea, and breaks off as an iceberg. When it floats into warmer seas, it finally melts and becomes part of the ocean again. At each step there is continual instability and change. Nonetheless we realize that none of the steps are new and that they will always lead to more of exactly the same steps. Therefore we think of the whole process as a stable one that allows many other processes to flourish.

Cycles in Living Processes

Now we turn to the most important cyclical process in the world of life: the carbon dioxide - oxygen cycle. Living plants derive most of their food from carbon dioxide. What they really need is the carbon, our old acquaintance from other illustrations. Chlorophyll molecules in plants absorb energy from sunlight and use this energy to pry carbon away from oxygen. Oxygen, released as a waste product, goes back into the air. The carbon is immediately combined with water in a second reaction to form sugar molecules. This is the food that the plant needs and uses to build its structure and power its life processes.

When the plant dies oxygen, the gas in the atmosphere that is most eager to form compounds, reacts with the carbon in the plant -held in sugars and fibers and many other molecules- to make carbon dioxide, generating some heat in the process. The same thing happens if an animal digests the plant. The animal breathes in oxygen, the oxygen combines with plant-derived food in the animal's tissues, and the animal enjoys energy and heat. The animal breathes out carbon dioxide as a waste product, which is taken in again by plants as a starting material.

Two cycles are at work here, one of energy, one of carbon and oxygen. Energy from the sun arrives as photons of visible light which are trapped by chlorophyll and used to turn carbon dioxide into complex carbon compounds. We might think of the resulting sugars and fibers as a kind of energy storage, waiting to be used by the plant to grow and reproduce, or used by a grazing animal as its supply of fuel, or released as heat into the atmosphere when bacteria cause the plant to decay. In most of these steps the energy released by one process becomes the starting energy for another. Ecologists use the terms "energy flows" and "energy cycle" to describe how energy from sunlight drives a whole chain of life processes once it has been captured by photosynthesis. Of course some of this energy eventually leaves the earth again as photons of heat or light, but not before it has passed through many different organic molecules and many different living things.

Similarly carbon and the oxygen go round and round in a circular process. The endless cycle of carbon and oxygen, linked to a corresponding flow of energy, is a fundamental characteristic of life on our planet. Looked at in this way, the processes of life as a whole seem very stable, even if any single process may be unpredictable or unstable.

Stability at the Level of the Organism

Though any given organic molecule may to be ripe for early destruction - from sunlight, from digestion, from decay, from being consumed by fire - living organisms as a whole, like plants and animals and you and me, possess an amazing stability. We may be fragile, but we tend to outlast any particular molecule or cell of our body. The same thing is true at the level of human society. You and I may return to the creation, the fecund earth from which we were formed, but our children and subsequent generations continue in the communities and social organizations which we leave behind.

This kind of stability - based on underlying changes that are continual, repeated, predictable, and cyclical - is of an especially fruitful kind. We encounter it often as we analyze the long-long journey that brought us here. It is one of the most important mechanisms whereby the creation is able to add to the complexity of its organization over and over again, without ceasing and without destroying previous foundation work.

At the level of the individual organism, the chemicals of life - the nutrients, the building blocks of its tissue, the foods that supply its energy - all flow through its living structure. It is the *organization* of this structure that is persistent, even though the building blocks of nutrients, cells, and fibers come and go. The molecules making up the cells are oxidized and move on. One by one most of the cells die. The body replaces them, building new cells from the nutrients that flow in, guided in this process of replacement and growth by a stable functioning system.

As long as the organization of its parts remains intact, the organism continues to live. When important links of this organization are disrupted, it dies. Living organisms are the supreme example of organization being the *reality* of a thing, not only of its structure but also of the process and the life that emerge from it. Not only does the organization define the single life of a single organism, it also provides the stable platform for repeated, predictable, and cyclical change that allows the slow accumulative process of evolution.

Stability of living things and their the DNA Recipes

The stable cycles found in living beings require a great deal more explanation than the simple example of water - water vapor - water- ice - water. As we have seen, organic molecules and organisms come and go, matter and energy pass through them in a constant flux, yet somehow the overall organization persists. We might say the organization *remembers* or *records* what to do despite the changeover and replacement of its components. How this recording is accomplished was something of a mystery until the middle of the 20th century, when the recipe molecules were discovered, those lovely spiral chains called DNA.

The stability of a living organism resides in a plan that is mostly written out in DNA. We'll take a look at the stability of these molecular chains themselves, then a more detailed look at the different processes that are written down in the DNA code. Remember that DNA specifies almost *everything* about an organism, what it is and what it does. It carries the plan for the whole structure, size, and shape of the living being, for its interactions with other beings, for the cyclical flow of materials and energy in and out of the organism, and finally for its reproduction. If we are impressed at the apparent stability of living processes and wonder how so much detail can be remembered so accurately, then DNA is a big part of our answer.

We have seen that the chemical bonds holding organic molecules together are not especially strong. They commonly have energies similar to those of photons of visible light. Higher energies, notably photons of ultraviolet light, can break these organic bonds and rearrange molecules. This introduces a strong element of instability and unpredictability into otherwise stable organizations and processes.

Marvelously, DNA is protected from much of the hurly-burly surrounding other molecules in a living cell. First, its double strands of code molecules are at the center of a spiral structure, a helix. The outside of the helix is formed of two robust fibers of sugar and phosphate groups whose chemical bonds are relatively strong, thus offering some protection to the more delicate code chains inside. Then the whole helix is wound extremely tightly around itself, sort of like a woven rope being wound tightly into a ball. This densely wound structure is visible under a microscope and is called a chromosome or plasmid. Finally, in all organisms higher than bacteria, the different chromosomes are packed together tightly into a single package in the cell nucleus in the center of the cell. Under very adverse conditions of heat or ultraviolet exposure, the DNA molecules would obviously be the last ones to be destroyed. For further insights into the structure and stability of DNA, see Appendix B.

Social Activity

Human activities, including governments and societies, also exhibit stability and change. As we have seen, "stability" does not always mean the absence of change. Especially in human affairs, it also means the kind of regular, repeated, and predictable change that brings us back close to our original starting point. Stability is frequently associated with feelings of security, even confused with it. The forces of instability can come from outside human society: disease, drought, or earthquakes for example - or from within the human community itself, or from both.

Human society seems to need the reassurance of cyclical change and the kind of stability that it provides. Cyclical changes lead to cultural and personal traditions that emphasize historical continuity. Paradoxically, it is these that offer the stable base from which change can be demanded and fought for. Every revolution looks backwards as well as forward, hoping to glimpse a moment when stable social rhythms once walked hand in hand with human happiness.

In general customs and traditions are not consciously formulated; they simply evolve from previous behaviors and beliefs. In this regard human and animal societies are alike. Migratory snow geese don't know why they migrate en masse to their nesting grounds, but they do. We can theorize that it neatly meets their conflicting needs for nutrition and reproduction, but we cannot be sure of that either. What is safe to say is that both snow geese and humans seem to enjoy an annual cycle of movement and change that is regular, repetitious, and predictable.

In the case of snow geese, fledglings seem to "remember" how to migrate even in their first season! Their species navigating ability has been stable for so long that it has become an inherited instinct, written down in the DNA code together with everything else about snow geese. We have seen how the integrity of this code is fiercely guarded, yet at the same time a certain safe degree of variation is guaranteed.

In humans a quick explanation of repetitious, "traditional" behavior is rather different: it is *learned* during each individual's lifetime from family and peers, and later it is transmitted to the next generation of sons, daughters, nieces, and nephews. In this case "stability" and "change" operate over a considerably shorter time than in the case of snow geese.

Stability and Change in Human Ideas

In the realm of human activity, stability and instability are everywhere evident. In theory simple things like ideas could exist forever. However, if new information diminishes their importance, in practice they are abandoned. New facts or insights may be added to change an old idea into a new idea. The persistence of the original idea may provide insights for building new ideas.

An example is simple grade school arithmetic. The manipulation of numbers to represent real events or to record the passage of time provides the base for more advanced mathematics. Pupils are taught to use the results of other person's mathematical discoveries. If every new mathematical technique had to be developed by each individual from scratch, there would be precious few innovations!

The same applies to the sciences. Each new idea is accurate to a certain degree and within certain boundaries, but it is always incomplete. The bright side is that each new idea provides a framework on which other advances may be built. For example, after years of trying, Newton finally deciphered the effects of gravity and its role in the motion of planets and other physical bodies. To do this, he had to develop new mathematical tools to explain the astronomical measurements of his period. His work was based on earlier observations that established the planets' movement around the sun and on the earlier mathematical tools available to him. Then came Einstein. He upset Newton's somewhat simplified scheme and showed that masses change when bodies move with respect to one another at high speed. Einstein's concepts and predictions held up remarkably well until they were applied to individual electrons and subatomic particles. Then the new quantum physics and its distinctive mathematical tools modified both Einstein's and Newton's ideas.

Stability and Instability: A Summary

There are other factors inherent to our universe that favor either stability or instability, but we do not have time or space to describe them all. Without the stability offered by the stable (successful) organization of components, there is no platform from which progress or coherent change can appear. Without the instabilities that are characteristic of all levels of organization, change is almost impossible. Instability is the factor that forces change, and this instability is an inherent characteristic of all existence. At the same time a successful organization is able to incorporate the change and build it into a new reality, a reality that is subject in turn to the hazards and the opportunities presented by the inevitable change that it undergoes.

Imagine a complex organism such as yourself. Imagine food and air flowing through it. The physical parts of your body erode away one by one while new parts form themselves to take their place. Visualize your memories embedded in well-worn paths through your brain. Think of them remaining intact as those pathways in your brain are rebuilt, atom by atom. You may be struck by the centrality of the organization that defines *you*. You can then appreciate the stability that is achieved when the design of the organization of your component parts cooperate in this highly complex manner. This interrelated organization is much more durable and dependable than a perishable structure relying on mere chemical bonds.

I remember the first time that it really struck me that the reality of something was not in its constituents but in the organization of its component parts. It was the day I was waiting to photograph a landscape of serene fall colors. A cloud cast a shadow over most of the landscape. Looking up, I could see the bottom of the cloud moving rapidly away. At the speed it was moving, it should surely clear the scene in a few minutes. Twenty minutes later I realized that its shadow had not moved. Then I took a closer look at the cloud. The cloud itself was hovering stationary over a low mountain. On the windward side, bits of moisture condensed and joined the cloud and moved rapidly over the mountain, and on the lee side, the cloud eroded away.

It hit me with the force of revelation: this cloud was not a lump of condensed water vapor moving across the sky. It was, instead, a cool section of the sky. The cloud became visible when moisture, sweeping up over the mountain, encountered the cold region and condensed. The cloud dissipated into water vapor on the other side as it was warmed by its descent. The moisture flowed *through* the cloud, became visible droplets, then vaporized again. For some time I watched numberless constituents of this cloud come and go, yet it was always the "same" cloud that hovered over me.

The Cosmic Deity

Chapter 5 Bibliography

Atkins, Peter William, *Creation Revisited:*, New York, W. H. Freeman & Company, 1992. A Distinguished Scientist Looks At the Origins Of Space, Time, And The Universe

Cassidy, David C., *Heisenberg, Uncertainty And The Quantum Revolution*, Scientific American, 266:106-112, May, 1992. Describing the revolution in knowledge of activity at the particle level revealing its indeterminate nature and giving a clue to the fundamental instability of thing.

Chapter 6

Affinities

"Ah, sweet mystery of life At last I've found thee
. . .
This the answer, 'tis the end, 'Tis all of living,
For it is love alone that rules for aye."
- Sigmund Romberg

We said at the outset that reality is the organization and self-organization of matter and energy. It is time to take this further. It is not enough to say that the creation is self-organizing, which it is. We should also explore the *principles* of this self-organization. What guides it? How could those four fundamental forces have arrived at a creation that includes me?

We need to understand the principle of *affinity*. Affinity is the propensity of things to associate or join together. Affinity is an inherent tendency to draw towards one another, to link to one another, or to unite with each other. Without affinities the universe would be just a cloud of atomic particles or an expanding sea of energy. But it is not, and in fact our universe is driven by different affinities at all levels of its organization.

The organization of matter and energy and its corresponding affinities are indivisible. As an egg becomes a chicken, every structure comes about through the action of forces that are affinities, and every organization in turn exerts affinities and is moved by forces and affinities. No thing, non-living or living, can be considered separately from the forces that make it happen. The same principles apply to non-material entities such as ideas and emotions.

It gets exciting now. The "sweet mystery" may be that all matter, from the moment of its conversion from energy, seeks to associate itself with other matter. There are rules for this: the four forces. The forces set the pattern for organization and self-organization. The affinity principle appears and reappears at every succeeding level of organization until it leaves its imprint on the full cosmos, including you and me.

Particle Affinities

At the most fundamental level are those sub-nuclear particles called quarks. Quarks are the bearers of the various properties of nuclear material: mass, spin, charge, and so on. They apparently cannot exist alone and have never been isolated because of their strong affinity for other quarks. These quarks combine in different combinations to form all of the stable particles of the nucleus of atoms. The compelling affinities of quarks become the strong nuclear force as they form protons and neutrons. As we have seen, the strong nuclear force of proton binding is much stronger than the electromagnetic force tending to keep protons apart.

The strong, attractive nuclear force is one of the four fundamental forces. The other three forces are also concerned with attraction, repulsion, and the tendency of matter to come together. We may generalize to say that all matter and energy are propelled by affinities. We can also turn it around and state that each force is an expression of one unifying principle, that of affinity.

Atomic Affinities

In our daily lives we experience the weaker forces of electromagnetism and gravity. Both are affinities. Without these attractions, the universe would consist of electrons and atomic nuclei bouncing around in an amorphous hydrogen-helium soup forever -- a pretty sterile broth compared to what the creation has actually managed!

A key display of the electromagnetic force lies in the propensity of atoms to join with one another. When atoms are free of entanglements and loose in space, we describe them as a gas. Much of the universe consists of gas, particularly the space between the stars, which has only a few atoms of gas in every cubic meter. Importantly, however, even in this state most atoms exhibit a mutual affinity for one another.

An atmosphere of gas surrounds the earth. Here nitrogen atoms pair up with other nitrogen atoms. Oxygen atoms have a powerful affinity for other oxygen atoms, as well as an affinity for almost any other element. Virtually all of the atmospheric oxygen atoms link with another oxygen to form an oxygen molecule, and this molecule exhibits most of the same properties and reactivity as the oxygen atoms alone. As we now know, these properties are due to the number of electrons in the oxygen shell.

Single electrons repel each other because they have the same negative electric charge. But as soon as electrons are organized into shells around an atomic nucleus, then as a group they attract other electrons into the shell. That is, atoms attract other atoms, depending on whether or not they can help fill each other's outermost electron shells. If they do, they make shell-to-shell links and form molecules. These new materials have new properties. They are all made from preexisting matter - the familiar story of organization and self-organization "from below."

We may note that atoms with their outer shells already filled are usually indifferent to other atoms. Only under the most extraordinary conditions will some of them unite with atoms of a different breed, or even with atoms of their own kind. These are called noble gases or noble metals. In today's world we might call them bigoted atoms! Noble metals such as gold and platinum have an affinity for atoms of their own kind and only reluctantly form compounds with other elements.

Another display of molecular affinity is the propensity of similar molecules to pack together to form crystals. When water containing a dissolved mineral deposits the mineral onto a growing crystal, the new molecules join and line up in a regular three-dimensional pattern to form an enlargement of the crystal. There is a very strong affinity here of like molecules for like molecules. Foreign molecules are generally excluded, although those having a similar structure in their outer shell of electrons may sometimes be included to form a more complex mineral.

Electromagnetic forces in the electron shells determines the structure of all the physical things that we see and hear and touch in daily life. An affinity produces both the accumulation of atoms of matter and the reactions that create new substances from these atoms. It creates the hardness of diamonds, the strength of steel, the flexibility of rubber, and the warm light of a summer sunset. It permits our consciousness and our wonder at this adventure of which we are an eternal part.

Gravitational Affinity

The "Great Affinity" is gravity. Gravity is the attraction of everything with mass for every other thing; even the paths of photons of light are pulled and bent by gravity. It has the most powerful influence on the evolution of the universe. Paradoxically, however, gravity is also the weakest of the four forces, far weaker than the electromagnetic force that holds our immediate world together. It is the least well known force.

How is such a weak force so potent and influential? It becomes strong because it builds up with the quantity of matter. Everything having the property of mass or weight has a gravitational pull toward every other particle having mass. The larger the mass, the greater the pull. John Muir expressed this type of process poetically. He described the process of glacial erosion that produced Yosemite, the most magnificent of all mountain valleys: "Nature chose for a tool, not the earthquake or lightning to rend and split asunder, nor the stormy torrent of eroding rain, but the tender snow flower noiselessly falling through unnumbered centuries." The weight of those "tender snow flowers" crushed the underlying rock and gouged that deep and beautiful valley.

Gravity forms the stars, the planets, the galaxies. It ignites the nuclear fires that produce the warmth for our planet and the variety of atoms that populate and form our world. It powers the waterfalls, brings down the rain, levels the mountains, and pulls water together to form the oceans. This inexorable force, gently tugging and relentlessly pulling over immense distances and for all time, began its work and exerted its affinity from the first moment of the appearance of matter. Initially the immense expansive forces of the Big Bang overpowered gravity and flung matter apart. When that force had largely spent itself, gravity patiently and continuously began its slow and persistent task of forming our universe. As it drew the far-flung bits and pieces toward one another, the other fundamental forces came into play.

The creation has experienced billions of years of universe-building. At the grand level of size and distance, only one force was able to bring things close enough together to allow the other expressions of attraction to operate. That force is gravity.

On a larger scale, the affinity of gravity slows the expansion of the universe and may ultimately determine its destiny. If there is enough matter in the universe, its mutual attraction will sooner or later stop it from migrating further apart and it will begin to draw back together. Astronomers in later aeons will detect the suns and galaxies of space coming toward them with ever-increasing velocity. These will proceed to a tremendous implosion. The entire universe may plunge in upon itself with unimaginable fury and speed. Gravity, the weakest of all of the forces, will have triumphed as the master of the destiny of this universe.

On the other hand, if there is not enough matter in the universe for the tug of gravity to stop its outward expansion, then the universe will die a slower, colder death. Nuclear fires in the hearts of the suns will wink out. One by one the lights of the universe will be extinguished, and gravity will embrace the ashes in its relentless grip as the dead stars drift forever outward into the void.

Affinities in the Living World

In the living world, affinities are not only essential to simple biological function, they also give it its purposefulness and enchantment. The behavior of living beings is based on more than inherent imperatives to grow and reproduce. It is also based on inherent tendencies to associate and join together.

Two simple examples. The assembly and replication of large biological molecules like DNA and cellulose fibers works by finding exact fits for complex shapes and electron charges, sort of like fine cabinet work. Here we find that the basic electromagnetic force giving rise to a higher level of mutual attraction.

Another example is the striking specialization that we see everywhere in nature. Such specialization is always accompanied by association and cooperation. It is easy to see why. Since no bit of living plasm can "do it all", it must depend on others to do what it cannot do. Although it is not uncommon to find cooperation of the signaling-at-a-distance kind, it is far more common to find the direct exchange of food, energy, genetic material, immune information, and so on by two bits of plasm that are in full contact with each other. This means affinity. This means working in cooperation between organelles, cells, tissues, organs, individuals, and communities, each with its own set of affinities.

Affinity allows biological specialization. Growth and development could have meant just the replication of more and more cells, or larger and larger cells. In some cases this did happen. But the more successful route proved to be the specialization of cells and the development of organs with specialized functions. If single cells just replicated and remained in the nutrient soup on their own, photosynthesizing or scavenging, as some single-celled organisms still do, they would have to forgo the opportunity to form more complex organizations. When they began to attract one another and associate that they began to forge larger structures. Later as multi-celled organisms they specialized, making those new multi-celled creatures better predators or better able to survive the vicissitudes of life than their single-celled predecessors.

Or creatures can become co-dependent while remaining structurally independent. Many unrelated organisms found close affinities to be desirable. The Portuguese man-of-war is a small colony of different organisms that live together and share the functions of capturing food and fending off predators. If any one of them is absent the Portuguese man-of-war would can exist in its current form. We humans and most other complex organisms harbor colonies of smaller species on or within themselves. For example, we keep countless bacteria in our intestines. If they are unintentionally cleaned out and kept out, say by an antibiotic treatment for a disease, we may "starve" because they play a very crucial part in the digestion of food. This type of mutually beneficial affinity, leading to intimate association and even co-evolution, is called *symbiosis,* and nature is everywhere full of its fascinating examples.

Termites live by the millions in colonies. They live in "cities" that they build to house their tribe. Termites cannot survive outside of the colony. The termite eats wood but cannot digest it. A colony of protozoans living in its intestine are voracious digesters of wood fibers (cellulose) and are able to separate the cellulose fibers from the lignin that glues them together. Little fin-like parasites called spirochetes are attached to the outer "skin" of each protozoan. They push their host around in their search for food. Inside the protozoan are little bacteria-like self-enclosed structures called organelles. These structures contain the enzymes that help break down the cellulose and convert it into sugars and starches. The glue-like lignin left over from this digestive process is excreted to build the termite house in which the termites live as a protected colony. In short, these different creatures have developed an affinity for one another and make a comfortable living at it.

Most living organisms have a sense of themselves. They recognize the cells of a different species and even a different individual of their own species. When coral polyps are broken up into individual cells and mixed with cells of other types of coral, the cells recognize cells of their own species and join to form new polyps while excluding cells of different species.

A very complicated example of this is the human body's immune system. Our bodies are equipped with several defenses for expelling and killing internal predators such as intruding cells, viruses, or bacteria. The system recognizes "self" and vigorously attacks anything that it does not recognize as having the characteristics of itself. If the immune system loses this ability to tell the difference, it may busily go about destroying itself. If a patient receives a transplanted heart or kidney, one of the biggest risks is that the immune system will reject it and make it impossible for the new organ to work.

Lewis Thomas has pointed out that many cells that have been isolated from their original organism lack this sense of self. This happens, for instance, when a cell line is cultured in test tubes in a laboratory. We might say that these naked cells have "lost their self-respect." Under the right conditions they will promiscuously join up with other cells from a widely different organism and fuse together to form a weird new cell. Most of these wind up as junk food for other organisms, but occasionally, just occasionally, one survives and prospers to start a new line of evolutionary development. It is just this type of generalized affinity of cell for cell that was probably crucial for the creation of the first multicellular organisms.

We also harbor inner cellular's strangers. All of the cells in our body contain little subunits that seem to have evolved separately before finding a home and moving into the ancestors of all animal cells. Here these little strangers developed a symbiotic relationship with the cell and continued to be passed along as an indispensable portion of the cell as the host organism evolved.

For example, little organelles called mitochondria reside inside each of our cells and perform indispensable functions. Among other things they convert food into energy. The mitochondria have their own DNA chromosomes, separate from the chromosomes in the nucleus of the cells. These organelles also divide into a new generation each time the host cell divides. They have no father, since they do not reproduce by a sexual union. (They are supplied from the mother in her egg cell and are not fertilized by any part of the father's sperm cells). They are independent passengers enjoying the ride, but they are also necessary passengers. Their indispensable work is the fare they pay for gaining security and near-immortality.

We find a mirror image in the plant world. The first organisms to use sunlight energy to make food from carbon dioxide were a kind of tiny blue-green algae, lone rangers in the ocean that had a profound cumulative effect on our earth's atmosphere. Somewhere along the way, one of these alga fused with and took up residence inside another bacterial cell. These become the organelle called a chloroplast. Chloroplast contain green chlorophyll and carry out the work of photosynthesis. The new hybrid consisting of the host plus chloroplast evolved to become the ancestor of all sun-powered plants. Having chloroplast residing inside gave these plant cells a tremendous advantage - they could directly tap the power of the sun. Plant evolution and development took off with great speed and vigor.

Affinity for one's own species may imply dis-affinity for certain other species. Plants, which are anchored to the ground, cannot move toward one another. Many of them have developed a strategy of excluding other species from their territory and tend to live in a colony of just their own family. We pull weeds and grass from our garden not only because they steal nutrients from the vegetables that we want to eat; but some of these weeds also put out poisons that stunt the growth of their competitors, the vegetables. The slow-growing black walnut tree on the corner of my lot secretes a very potent poison into the soil. This poison prevents most trees or plants - except black walnut trees! - from taking root or thriving in its shade.

As I write this, the calls from a flock of wild geese taking off from the creek below the house reminds me that birds and animals of a common species show an affinity for one another in their life and travels. Of course the affinity of the complementary sexes within these groups is decisively important for the propagation and continuation of any species. Not only do these different types of affinity promote the survival and perpetuation of individuals and species, but they also contribute a sense of well-being and pleasure to the individuals who possess them. Observe the antics of a flock of mallard ducks on a pond or the play of a couple of kittens and you will realize that this social affinity produces sheer pleasure.

Social Affinities

The history of the human race is the history of its social structures and the interrelations between these structures. People are found clustered in groups, be they a family, tribe, village, nation, a religion, trade group, craft, or profession, and their lives are patterned and enriched by these bonds.

Only the rare individual can survive or prosper isolated from all others. Certainly a lone individual cannot propagate. Lacking the information and experience that others can give to help cope with the world, the isolated hermit or castaway has a diminished life which would be enriched by interactions with others.

A significant result of these social affinities is the inevitable formation of social and economic structures. These organizations soon begin to take on a life of their own. Individuals find that they can be more effective performing one or two activities that they do well and relying on others to do the other things for them that the others can better perform. In a very small social affinity group, this is a simple back-and-forth type of interaction.

As a group grows in size, specialized groups of individuals develop. Communication and traffic between individuals and groups and between differing groups becomes quite complex. Communication and interaction are no longer just a back-and-forth operation. They involve the entire emerging system. Further, as the organization of the system becomes more complex, it has a multiplying factor built into it. People become more efficient by specializing. The sum of their productive activities is greater than if each individual tried to do, by themselves everything that is necessary for life. Then the products of society increase not only in quantity but in quality. The individual artisan, scholar, or healer advances their art and adds it to the shared heritage of society.

Affinity as an Agent of Creation

Affinities are an inherent characteristic of creation. They are a guiding factor in the dynamic organization and reorganization of the universe. They operate at all levels, from the sub-nuclear to human societies as well as the vast cosmos. At certain levels these affinities are obviously those of the four basic forces of the universe. At higher levels of organization the active affinities continue to mimic these basic forces, although the clear line of evolution from one to the other is not obvious.

What most of us are really concerned with is ourselves as humans and the human society in which we survive. This basic concern extends to the web of life that we are a part of, in which we are inexorably entwined. What accounts for the affinities that operate at the levels of all this organic life? The easiest answer is that without these affinities, there is no survival and no replication. Unproductive processes are not repeated and are not built into the processes of life. They are not remembered and passed along as DNA instructions or as the lore of a tribe or family. These affinities were built into the living world as soon as the more basic forces of matter began to assemble the first replicating molecules of life. That account is the subject of a later chapter.

This is a good point to remember the continuities between the physical world and the realm of life. In both, any reality is its organization, *including the forces and affinities that brought it into being in the first place and are responsible for its replication.* This is the most powerful tool we have for understanding the vast diversity and community of the creation and, we may add, for understanding ourselves.

Affinity as Love

This chapter started out with a quotation from the lyric of a Sigmund Romberg operetta. It makes the point that "*Love -- 'tis the answer/ 'tis the end/ 'tis all of being.*" It is the "*sweet mystery of life.*"

Love is an awesome creative force. It is an affinity that binds individuals to one another, to their family, to a tribe or nation. Love is not a luxury. One powerful form of love is the bonding that develops between a mother and an infant. It begins and develops even before birth, during the pregnancy. The human maternal/child love that reaches peak strength during the child's early years is perhaps the strongest of human affinities.

Love is the force that pulls humans together into couples, families, clans, and fraternal groups, and ultimately in entire societies. It is a creative force that produces harmonious relationships, engenders sacrifices for the good of others, and provides a foundation for the construction of these human institutions and associations. It also supplies the affinity between two members of different sexes that produces offspring and holds the two persons together in an enduring nurturing unit that cares for the young. In these aspects love is a creative affinity that results in stability as well as new creations. It produces joy and rejoicing. Life, literature, and poetry offer eloquent testimony that the search for and the finding of love is the most sought-after goal of human existence.

Love is not confined to the human world. Those other species whose development requires parental nurturing and education generally show a parental bonding that is hardly distinguishable from human love. The geese that raise their young along our creek mate not just for the season but for life. They exhibit affection and protectiveness toward their young and grieve when a mate dies.

Anyone who has raised a pet can tell you that a bond as strong as human love can develop in both directions between a human and an animal. These bonds are not only ones of mutual dependence for companionship and dependency, but also a love develops that shows affection and caring.

As we wander back down the evolutionary path, where does love fade out and the four forces of the universe take over? Perhaps love is merely a different expression of these affinities. Surely these creative and conserving forces that shape and preserve successful creations *are* the basis of our existence, the very ground of all being. The energy that coalesced to form the tangible universe manifested the first of these affinities as it organized itself into those enduring minuscule bits of which everything is still composed. The entire universe can be considered as "love" made visible.

Chapter 7

Replication

The creation of a large housing development consisting of hundreds of essentially identical homes is an example of economic efficiency. Of course, a large house nearby didn't get pregnant and have a litter of "pups," but replication is an efficient means of construction in both the housing industry and in the creation itself. The creation usually does things efficiently.

Self-replication is a characteristics of this universe. We're all aware of the ability and the necessity of each living species to replicate itself or it will die out. Those with a sexual method of reproduction have a particular urgency to replicate themselves. Death is built into the life cycle of every individual. The more primitive organisms that simply divide into two also replicate themselves. There is no defined death of any one generation of these creatures, since the cell lines themselves are essentially immortal.

We normally do not consider the inorganic realm as "living." Yet replication does also takes place among non-living things. In some aspects, particularly in its ability and propensity to replicate structures, the inorganic realm shows some significant similarities with the realm of the living.

The replication processes in the universe are mostly self-replicating processes. Unlike the methods that produce a housing subdivision or a run of the daily newspaper, these processes proceed on their own without outside control or direction. They are part of the ongoing process of creation, the process of organizing other bits of reality into a new reality. The hundred or so different species of atoms are not created by a self-replicating process. "Factories" in the deep interior of dense stars produce the conditions that force the smaller, less complicated bits to join together into more complicated ones. The heat and pressure of a sun's interior are the necessary conditions. Once the process gets going, it continuously produces many copies of similar atoms.

Self-Replication

Self-replication begins when these atoms coalesce under the influence of different fundamental forces and affinities. As atomic nuclei escape from their "factory," they cool to the point where their electron shells can form stable bonds with neighbors. One of the first tendencies is to link (or "pack") with identical atoms into unique three-dimensional structures. Metals, mineral, and sulfur crystals are some of the more familiar examples.

Atoms of dissimilar elements, with different electron arrangements in their shells, do not generally fit well into this structure. If they do attach themselves temporarily, it is with a tenuous grasp. They are readily displaced when the proper atoms come along and take their place, because these fit neatly into the structure. When the few atoms necessary to form a basic three-dimensional structure have assembled themselves, they are ready to self-replicate their little organization by recruiting new members. Additional identical atoms pack in all around the central core and a structure called a crystal begins to grow. No matter how large it grows, the initial shape remains the same, whether it be four, six, or eight-sided, square-ended, or pointed.

Almost all atoms have an emerging property in common: a priority to satisfy their need for a completely filled outer shell of electrons. In addition to linking with their own kind, they also link with appropriately different atoms to form molecules of new materials. Molecules are then free to link with either other similar molecules or different ones. Molecules can also form crystals and start the self-replicating processes just as atoms do. They pack into three-dimensional structures and form characteristic crystals with characteristic spacing between the molecules. When bits and pieces of these crystals are broken off, each piece begins the task of replicating itself and building a new and larger crystal, much like the bits of the broomstick shattered by the Sorcerer's Apprentice.

The solid crust of our earth consists of such crystals. They organized themselves into the rocks and minerals that we take for granted. They are an example on a grand scale of the power and significance of the self-replicating process. From the mighty monolithic rocks of the mountains to tiny grains of sand and soil; from the lava solidified from molten material in the depths of the earth to the salt deposits left over from dried up bygone seas; these beautiful precise structures are a major part of the reality of this planet.

The "living" rocks continue to grow wherever the proper atoms or molecules present themselves to the surface and pack themselves in. The rocks never lose this ability to continue to self-replicate. As children, many of us grew impressive mineral gardens by adding several chemicals to water. The next morning, to our fascination, intricate chains of crystals had formed and grown up out of the solution and over the edge of the bowl. Not all crystals are just larger versions of smaller crystals. Crystals themselves may produce additional intricate structures. The faces of two similar crystals can link together and start growing out at odd angles to one another, producing very intricate and beautiful chains and interlocked patterns. We often find enchanting results of this in our mineral gardens.

We all know what happens when a few molecules of water pack closely together in air at sub-freezing temperatures and form a unique pattern, the nucleus of a snowflake. As other molecules of water vapor join in, the pattern replicates itself and branches out in all directions, repeating the structure of the molecules at the center. Water molecules link in an amazing variety of basic patterns, and it is difficult to find any two snowflakes that are identical. The unique three-dimensional pattern of each individual snowflake is repeated symmetrically over the entire snowflake.

So far we have described simple replication processes. These processes are accretion processes. Additional atoms pack in to continue to enlarge the existing three-dimensional array of the parent group. When bits and pieces get broken off, a true replication process begins, since these small new crystals will begin to grow as well.

The previous descriptions of the replication process has been in the inorganic realm. Sand, rock, soil, ice, and the like are not incorporated into any living creatures, but of course the individual atoms found in these inorganic structures may be expropriated by living things to build their own organic molecules.

Organic molecules, even complex ones, can form crystals and grow in size by the accretion of similar units. Even the most intricate organic molecules, the DNA chains of life, can nestle together and crystallize when removed from a cell. Indeed, it was by studying a DNA crystal that Rosalind Franklin, a colleague of Watson and Crick, was able to guess the helical structure of its units. This led to the Watson/Crick hypothesis of how DNA replicates itself and to the theory -- soon to be confirmed -- that DNA embodies the instructions for stringing together amino acids into all the myriad proteins of life.

Whereas the replication of crystalline structures is by simple accretion, replication in the organic realm means making fresh exact copies. At the most complex it means the appearance of a whole new individual organism. Self-assembly by following good packing rules is useless at this level of complexity. As we have already seen with proteins, *instructions* are required for this kind of replication.

Replication by Instructions

The DNA in the cells of all living things control their own replication, the replication of the cell, and the replication of the whole organism. This is a "nonlinear" process, involving interdependent activity between different parts of a system. (The crystallization of metals and minerals is a "linear" process because there are no outside instructions, nothing other than their characteristic patterns of electrons determines the shape). In the living cell, DNA and the other constituents of the cell are inescapably bound together. Each part depends upon all of the other parts to function.

The secret of DNA replication lies partly in its elegant simplicity. The cell starts the replication by using an enzyme to force the two spiral DNA strands to unwind. This exposes the code portion of the molecule, consisting of protrusions on the string of subunits, each protrusion corresponding to one of the four characteristic letters (bases in the biologist's language) of the DNA code. These bases normally face inward toward the center of the spiral where they match up with complementary bases on the other strand.

[A reminder: There are four types of subunits in a DNA chain. Each has a distinct base designed to match with a base on the other strand. They are like letters of an alphabet. A group of three letters is a code or codon. It is an instruction specifying exactly one specific amino acid from among 25 amino acids. A long string of codons is like a word, called a gene. The gene is an instruction to the cell to assemble a specific protein consisting of a precise sequence of amino acids.]

Each single naked DNA strand now replicates a partner strand. An enzyme does this by attaching a complementary DNA base to each one of the unattached bases on the naked strand, one after another, until both chains are once again double chains from top to bottom. These two double chains separately twist and coil themselves up extremely tightly, making the protective packages called chromosomes which are visible under a microscope. (In higher organisms chromosomes start out as pairs, so that after replication there are actually four double chains, each with roughly identical DNA instructions). A cell ready to duplicate its chromosomes has already built up a good supply of raw material, i.e. the four different DNA bases. When the assembly enzyme gets down to work it is able to go surprisingly fast, matching up bases and tying them together end-to-end.

As we've seen, at the end of DNA replication there are twice as many chromosomes as at the beginning. The next step is to separate them into two near-identical sets. Custom-designed enzymes separate the duplicated pairs, tugging half to one end of the cell and half to the other end. Then the cell membrane constricts in the center till it touches and closes the channel between the two cell halves. Imagine squeezing a long balloon in the center until it closes. The two halves split apart to make two separate daughter cells. The two new cells now spend time growing in size and stockpiling the materials required for another replication. When they are ready, they start the process all over again. Could the replication process go on forever like this? Yes it can! It does so regularly in single-celled organisms such as amoebae and the like.

The nonlinear or circular processes so characteristic of organic life become evident in these steps of replication. The DNA first transfers information to the rest of the cell, telling it what enzymes and chemicals are needed in order to grow and function. The rest of the cell assembles these molecules, including the chemical bases and enzymes required to replicate the original DNA that started the cell off in the first place.

In such circular patterns of replication as occur in living creatures, we can no longer find simple causes and effects. Any change at any point has an effect all around the circle. The entire web of life - within a cell, within an organism, within the biosphere of living creatures - consists of these interrelated circular processes, "wheels within wheels." One fascinating aspect is that the information embodied in DNA can be thought of as modifying the very physical world that it depends on. It builds agents - cells and organisms - that manipulate the environment to their advantage and to the advantage of cooperating organisms.

DNA's emerging property of self-replication has long ago stabilized and extended itself. Now DNA also helps to forge the best terms and conditions for its own survival and replication.

The replication of DNA information in living creatures promotes continuity and stability, a platform from which the forces of change can experiment to create additional realities. It is also a profligate process. Originating from that single fertilized cell in which each of our lives started, there are trillions of copies of that unique original set of chromosomes, one set in every cell of our bodies.

In organisms more complicated than a single cell, the DNA instructions specify that the simple replication process of grow and divide is repeated only four or five times after fertilization. Thereafter the "grow" instruction for these "stem" cells becomes different for different cells and they start to produce proteins and enzymes that are different from one another. These cells grow up to look different and act different. (Not surprisingly, biologists call this "cell differentiation"). Having replicated enough times, the differentiated cells become the various specialized structures and organs of the body: muscle, gut, nerve, liver, bone, and so on. Early on, a chemical message originating in the DNA even changes the female sex to male in about half the embryos. (Every human fetus begins its early development as a female).

The dichotomy between male and female brings us back to those chromosome pairs visible at cell division. Simple addition shows that we cannot receive all of our mother's chromosomes and all of our father's chromosomes, for then we would have twice too many. Evolution has solved this problem in an elegantly simple way. The final cell division that leads to two unfertilized eggs or two sperms does *not* double the chromosomes . These cells finish with only single set of chromosomes. At the moment of fertilization the two sets of single chromosomes from the egg and the sperm fuse together in the egg cell. Each chromosome has received a mate! Together they form one new set of paired chromosomes, eager and ready to replicate and launch the new life on its course.

The emerging property of self-replication is at the heart of all living things. Viruses are probably the most primitive, stripped-down kind of living entity. Since they are unable to replicate themselves their only function is to make sure that their DNA is replicated many times by a host cell. Viruses usually consist of a short DNA chain surrounded by a protective coat. They invade a cell and take over its apparatus for DNA replication, usually wrecking the cell in the process. Other viruses contain only short RNA chains (a sort of mirror image of DNA) as does the HIV virus which is believed to cause AIDS.

DNA Chains: Knowledge and Memory

Our survey of replication has found some common characteristics in the different "species" of matter in the universe, in living and non-living materials alike. These characteristics are inherent in their individual patterns or designs. The property of replicating their organization emerges in molecules that achieve greater stability by packing themselves tightly together in crystals, or stringing themselves into long chains, the macro-molecules of life.

The property of replication also illustrates the role of the "information" contained in organizational patterns. A successful design embodies the information for making it, with the structure itself acting as a memory for storing it. Mineral molecules "know how" to form rocks. Oxygen atoms know how to form oxygen molecules. Carbon atoms know how to form diamonds or graphite, and human chromosomes know how to form a fully functioning individual when they themselves are reproduced in a human cell.

The creation is awash with such information. As each higher level of organization appears, the new structures quickly find out what their emerging properties are. They experiment, trying to build organizations which are still more complex. Some are successful and stay around, others are unsuccessful and disappear. The successful ones embody more information than the ones in the level below. By trying out variations the creation learns. By replicating its successful structures it remembers.

In the case of DNA a staggering amount of information is written by millions of DNA molecules into "words" - genes - strung along its chromosomes. This kind of genetic writing appeared several billion years ago and has been greatly developed since. Some genes are one-word instructions for making one protein, but most genes work in concert produce several words that specify several proteins. That's because it is very rare for one protein or enzyme to do a job alone. Usually they work in groups. Pushing the analogy one step further, genes also work in collaboration, to get the right products made at the right time. We might call a group of genes that work together a genetic "sentence." With all these letters, words, and sentences, there are infinite possibilities, an infinite number of recipes that could be written. In fact, genetic sentences, orchestrating the development and functioning of all complex organisms, are continually being composed, recomposed, and remembered.

In recent years we have begun to learn the molecular chemistry of how animal behavior is remembered in the genetic sentences too. In birds, for example, genetic knowledge and not training is used to assure that they mate with the right species. This knowledge also instructs birds on how to make a suitable nest, when and where to migrate to find food, and how to recognize a safe breeding ground. In humans, it perhaps tells us how to live and act in more situations than we would like to admit. Our preferred myth is that our actions are done from our own volition or are conditioned by our own experiences. Research in the genetically influenced patterns of human behavior shows, however, that many types of action and individual personality characteristics have a strong genetic base. Left-handedness, manic-depressive mental illness, and certain kinds of creative genius are examples of traits which are strongly influenced by our genes.

As we have noted, the creation is profligate in its reproductive processes. Not only does it replicate DNA in every cell of every creature, it is profligate about its specialized cells for reproduction. Ferns produce millions of spores on every leaf. Human sperm is distributed in hundreds of millions of copies, fish lay hundreds of thousands of eggs, and trees produce seeds by the hundreds of thousands each year. Each of these agents of reproduction is a replication of an individual's entire unique pattern. They are broadcast widely so that the memory and information contained within them have a good chance of being replicated into a full new individual. If all goes well, this individual in turn reproduces and the remembered information is perpetuated.

These circular, interlocking, and intersecting patterns of cause-and--effect allow the creation to remember and perpetuate the web of life. We see that the creation learns, remembers, and carries forward the creation process to the next generation, where more capabilities are perhaps revealed and remembered. Such a process of accumulation suggests that replication may indeed have ultimately created intelligence and intelligent creatures.

Summary

Of all the endless experiments of nature in hooking atoms together in molecules and chains, only those patterns that could survive in their environment did survive. Those patterns became the creation's knowledge, carried onward to further generations by replication, with the pattern itself representing the memory of success. When self-replication finally occurred, the accumulation of new successful patterns speeded up greatly. Still later, with replication following DNA instructions, the DNA rather than the organization as a whole became the store of remembered successes. Living things had set out on their special journey toward exquisite specialization, awareness of their surroundings, consciousness, self-consciousness, and, we will affirm, moral reasoning.

Chapter 7 Bibliography

Radman, Miroslav, and Robert Wagner, *The High Fidelity Of DNA Duplication*, <u>Scientific American</u>, 259:40-46, August, 1988. Replication allows the continuity of life.

Chapter 8

The Scale of Things

"Don't write naughty words on walls
... that you can't spell."
-Tom Lehrer
"On a clear day you can see forever."
-Burton Lane

To talk knowingly about anything, you need a fairly good understanding of what you are talking about. In this chapter, I want to encourage you to think about the whole of creation and the scale of creation. Unless we make the effort to stretch our mental perspective, our views will be largely limited and provincial.

The aim is to stretch your view three ways:
1) toward the infinite
2) toward the infinitesimal and
3) over all three-dimensions of space.

If we are going to try to understand the Creator, we should first understand as much as we can about the creation.

When we are small children, the entire world revolves around us. Other people are beings that drift in and out of our sight. The images of other people and things surrounding us are only tangentially part of our life. We have no conception of the world and how it works, nor of its extent. Later, as our perceptions mature, we become familiar with our home and neighborhood but as yet do not really comprehend what is beyond it. As we become aware of the rest of our world, it usually seems unreal or just like a picture in a magazine or an image on the television set.

Most people of the world have a horizon of only several miles beyond their immediate community, an area that they understand intimately. Everything else is just hearsay, a rumor, or a static picture.

Let us go on an exploration and look at the creation on different scales. We are located right near the middle of the scale of the universe, so this journey will go in two directions. First, we will start our journey in the direction of larger things.

We'll start with ourselves. If we think we know something in intimate detail, it is usually our self. If we stretch out our arms and twirl about, we occupy a space roughly six feet high and six feet across. We are going to take this journey in jumps of ten. Each view will take in an area ten times wider than the previous one. The area covered will be 100 times as great and the volume will be one thousand times as great as the previous view.

The first jump takes us to the size of a small house and lawn. We are familiar with that so we'll move on. The next jump takes in an entire neighborhood. We're reasonably familiar with what goes on there, so we'll take the next jump. Now we are looking at an area the size of a small town. Well, we usually know what goes on there but we don't have much control over it. However, it has a familiar feel and we are comfortable moving around in it.

Now we take another jump and we're looking at a moderately large city. Above it is a blanket of air, but at the top of the cubic volume we're looking at the air is pretty well thinned out. We can't stay up here unless we are equipped with a pressure suit and a supply of oxygen. Down on the ground things are pretty scary. Here and there we see neighborhoods where they don't speak our language, and the people's customs are different. So far we've taken only four of the twenty-five jumps we'll take in this outbound direction of our journey. There's much more to see!

The next jump takes in a moderate sized state or a very small country. As far as the state (or province) is concerned, it isn't much different from a large city. People are spread out a little thinner and mainly lumped into cities and towns scattered near the places where water, food, and transportation are available.

Another jump takes in a medium sized country or a lot of ocean, depending where we were when we started this journey. This country looks a lot like the state and functions in pretty much the same way, so we'll take our next jump.

Now we see the entire earth, its continents and oceans, polar ice caps and many of its countries. A sobering thought intrudes when we realize that everything we'll ever need for ourselves and our progeny, forever, will have to be found on the thin skin of the earth. We don't understand the workings of the different nations in the community of earth and that frightens us. So far, those nations haven't worked out a good organization to keep things going smoothly and equitably. Almost every country now has in its power the ability to spoil it for all the rest of the world. All the water and the air we see are all we will ever have. In its soil all of our food must be grown, as well as the trees for our houses and paper. The minerals and metals we use in our homes and factories must all be found in the thin top skin. The only thing arriving from outside this earth is the radiant energy that powers it and keeps it warm enough for life to flourish. If we have any sensitive perception at all, we feel awesome to the core when we see this blue, sun-drenched planet floating in the black void.

Our next jump takes us further out into space. The only thing we see in the next cube of space is still the earth, appearing to be the size of a soccer ball. It looks much smoother, though. Almost all of the roughness of mountains and valleys is smoothed out. The highest mountain on this soccer ball-sized earth protrudes upward only the thickness of a postage stamp. The deepest ocean is no thicker than a good coat of paint. All of the atmosphere appears to be no thicker than the leather hide of the ball.

With our next jump, the earth appears as small and as smooth as a marble. That little speck circling it about 240,000 miles away (a distance of thirty times the diameter of the earth) is the moon.

On our tenth jump we may feel somewhat lonely. Our new cube of space contains only a little bright spot where the sun's light bounces off the nearly invisible earth. We also notice that in the empty space around us, all that we can see are light rays, which we can see only if we look in the right direction. X-rays, ultraviolet rays, gamma rays, and heat waves also flow through our space, unseen by our eyes. Neutrinos in copious swarms speed through everything but leave precious few tracks. A few atoms of matter occupy each cubic foot of this realm.

If we do it at the proper time, the next jump will bring the planet Venus into our space. This planet is orbiting closer to our sun and is considerably hotter than our earth, much too hot for our type of life to exist or thrive.

With the next jump we take in the sun and its five inner planets. The

The Cosmic Deity

planets are nearly invisible from this distance and the sun is only a small speck brightly shining near the center. With the next jump, we've included even the outer planets but we couldn't possibly detect them without a telescope. Sizes are now getting beyond our easy comprehension. Our slice of space this time is over 10 billion miles across.

The next three jumps do nothing but make us feel more isolated. Only the sun is visible in these new chunks of space. The distances are so great that light requires two years to travel from one side of our space to the other. Since it's rather inconvenient to talk in terms of tens of trillions of miles, we'll use the measuring stick of light-years, the distance that light travels in one year. If we had a telescope powerful enough to look back to planet earth, we would now see what was taking place there a year ago.

Our next jump brings another star into our space, so we feel a little less lonely. That star is just about the same size as our own sun so we haven't discovered anything particularly new. Our next jump brings a goodly number of stars within our reach. But now, because of the vast distance from our sun, we can no longer see it without a telescope. Perhaps we feel a pang of homesickness for its steady reassuring warmth amidst all this cold emptiness. Our nineteenth jump shows that our star (sun) is in a small cluster of stars floating in much more empty space.

Step number 20 brings the biggest surprise so far. Now billions of stars and star clusters are our neighbors. They fill our view like a cloud, strung out in gossamer strands. It is the Milky Way - the same great cloud that we can see on a clear night from our back yard. We might be tempted to think that all of space is populated with these clouds of stars. We stop here to wonder how many of those stars have planets circling them. How many of those planets are large enough to maintain their atmospheric gases? How many of them are just far enough away from their sun to allow water to condense into oceans but warm enough so that those oceans aren't frozen? On how many of these have the processes of affinity and replication conspired to organize those self-replicating structures that evolve into living creatures? On how many of them have the creatures evolved to the point where they are making telescopes and looking in our direction to see if they are alone in this vastness of creation? Are there planets where the passions of their inhabitants have overwhelmed their reason and caused them to despoil their fellow creatures and the web of life that sustains them?

Jumping again, we have a startling show, something only astronomers are privileged to see. There, in the center of our space surrounded by a few star clusters, is a swirling mass of stars. It resembles a flattened disc, shaped like a pinwheel with its blades swept back. In the center, hidden by clouds of gas and dust, strange things are taking place. The speed of rotation shows that there is a huge mass, located in the center, tugging the stars in toward the center as they whirl faster to resist this pull. We can not see the center, but we know that the instruments of astronomers on earth would show hints of neutron stars, those burned-out giant stars where matter has collapsed to about a millionth of its previous dimension. There are also hints of black holes, where shrunken giants are so dense that their gravity sucks in all neighboring matter and pulls back any light or radiation that might betray their location and size.

Looking closer at this galaxy, we also see stars in the process of being born in the denser clouds of gas. We see the whole range of different sizes of stars. We see stars in all of their different phases of life, including those that are dying out and turning cool again. Here and there we may be fortunate enough to see the expanding cloud of debris and gases blown off by a supernova that exploded earlier. In these clouds we might see suns such as our own, still in formation, assembling their satellite planets by gravitational attraction. Numbers become nearly meaningless as we attempt to count the stars in this galaxy. At best we can estimate that we see a hundred billion. How many others are hidden from view, or are unseeable by our eyes, we can only imagine.

Another step outward and we find that we and our galaxy are not alone. Nearby are several other galaxies, some spiral-shaped like our own and others fatter and more round. The next step brings in many more galaxies clustered in the dark void, so small on our scale now that they appear like individual stars themselves.

Our next-to-last jump makes the whole place look like a snapshot of a snowstorm. Fuzzy clusters of galaxies inhabit space everywhere. Although they appear to be close together, many are millions of light years away from their nearest neighbor.

Our twenty-fifth jump makes us think that we are again looking at a section of the Milky Way. Clusters of galaxies are reduced to appearing as individual stars making a thin cloud, like drops of mist above a waterfall. The scale of distance is hard to encompass in our minds. If we lived in one corner and wanted to signal to another corner of our newfound space, it would take several billion years for our radio signal or a flash of light to travel one way. We would then wait another several billion years for an answer.

We could probably make another jump of ten. Then we would see only a faint haze fading off into nothing. The light from the furthermost reaches would take more time to reach us than the age of the universe. Those furthermost galaxies, if we had sufficiently powerful instruments, would show us the formation of the first suns and galaxies near the beginning of space and time. We would see events that probably occurred nearly 15 billion years ago.

We have finished our exploration of the creation going outward toward the infinite. Now we'll go back home and start our journey in a different direction, this time toward the infinitesimal. Each one of our next jumps will take us downward in size by a factor of 10. The area in view will be smaller by a factor of 100 with each jump. The volume of space will drop by a factor of 1000.

Our first jump downward will take in only the face of the person with whom we began the first part of our journey of exploration. We're familiar with that so we'll jump forward again. This time we are so close that we are conscious of the hairs sticking out from our friend's face and the alligator texture of the skin, something we don't particularly like to acknowledge.

For the rest of the journey we need some instruments. Our eyes are not up to the job of seeing such small things without assistance. After the next jump we see under our microscope the scales of worn-out skin cells about to flake off. If we are fortunate, we might see a delicate colorless mite, a tiny creature that often lives in the detritus of shedding skin cells. Jumping inward again, our microscope shows us the individual cells of skin. It also shows us some unexpected little spots: bacteria that find a home in our skin, resisting our vigorous efforts to wash them off and challenging our attempts to achieve better sanitation.

To progress further requires more sophisticated instruments. Our next tool is a scanning electron microscope. It scans the scene with a fine beam of electrons and displays what it encounters as a television picture. The new instrument is detecting electrons that are bounced off the specimen we're examining. The bacteria are in clear view, showing their different regular shapes, some with protuberances. These protuberances are a kind of virus, a still smaller living thing called a bacteriophage which preys on bacteria.

If we shift our view to look inside one living cell deep in the skin, we see a whole community at work. Sequestered inside the cell nucleus is the master of ceremonies of the surrounding activity, the chromosomes of

DNA. Elsewhere in the cell, organelles called mitochondria generate the needed power by "burning" small food molecules, turning them into carbon dioxide, water, and energy.

A new instrument is needed for the next jump downward in size. A transmission electron microscope is our new tool. Viruses, the smallest living things, which consist of single strands of DNA or RNA and a thin protective sheath, can now be seen clearly.

The next jump takes us to the limits of instruments that can produce an image. Up close, the surface of the cells that the viruses are attempting to break through appears incredibly rough. Beyond this point in our journey we can obtain no more direct observations. Now we have to rely on reconstructions based on information that has been painstakingly gathered by many scientists over many years of careful work.

After our next step, such a reconstruction allows us to "see" tiny, fuzzy images of individual atoms, arranged in recurring patterns in the macro-molecules that make up the cell surface. One macromolecule fills our entire field of vision.

After another step or two we might expect to see individual electrons in their atomic orbits. But electrons are not like little particles, even though they tend to behave like them sometimes. Instead we have to be content with having them be represented as a vague wavy cloud smeared around the atom, forming a shell.

After our next jump the electron shell of the atom completely fills our view. The individual electrons we hoped to see avoid being tied down to a shape and size, however.

Now we duck inside the electron shell and search for the nucleus of the atom. We know it's there, but it is too small to be "seen" yet. Two more jumps through seemingly empty space, and now in the center is another tiny speck, barely visible. Another jump and we see a small indistinct fuzzy ball, the nucleus. We know what's in there but we can't really visualize it or know how it is organized.

Another jump and the nucleus fills our view. This nucleus that we are exploring turns out to be our old friend carbon. We know it has six protons and six neutrons and is held together by the strong nuclear force. This force wields its power by transforming itself into short-lived sub-nuclear particles that are tossed back and forth between neutrons and protons, alternating between energy and matter. A strange world indeed.

Still, we cannot guess at any shapes inside the nucleus, because scientists have no evidence yet about how the protons and neutrons fit together. When the next generation of atom smashers are built, maybe these Rolls Royces of science will help us to construct an image of the nucleus and show us how these particles arrange themselves. Hopefully this multi-billion dollar wager will also give us some understanding of how the quarks that carry the various properties of matter are assembled into protons and neutrons.

Here in the nucleus we are at the heart of matter. Our carbon nucleus contains more than 99.9% of the weight of the carbon atom and the number of its protons determines the nature of the atom. But these protons are very far indeed from their electrons, which exert their influence only by their mutual electrostatic attraction to the electrons. The nucleus is otherwise isolated and lives a life of its own. It isn't bothered or changed by the gyrations of the electrons far away in their shells and by their myriad activities.

Now we have come to the end of our inward jumps. Probably there is one more that could be made, right into the protons and neutrons themselves, but again we can only guess what that view would be. Already it is hard to imagine how infinitesimally small a single proton is. We would have to line up one trillion of them, touching each other, to add up to a single centimeter. Looked at another way, if we were to change the scale of things so that protons were to become the size of grains of sand, we would find that our human bodies now stretch more than two thirds of the way around the earth.

What an immense journey in distances! Our 40 steps outward and inward changed the scale of view by a factor of 10^{40}. This means that the diameter of the visible universe is 10^{40} times larger than the diameter of an atomic nucleus. If we write it out, it means 10,000,000,000,000,000, 000,000,000,000,000,000,000 times larger. The change in volume is 10^{120}, written as the numeral one with 120 zeros trailing after it, which we won't write out! This is the scale and the scope of the creation. This is that changing and evolving, seething and growing network of organized energy within which we exist. It was launched from the energy and power of the Creator and organized and reorganized by the forces that reside within its constituent parts.

We will take another tour of the creation soon. That journey will take place in another dimension, the dimension of time.

Chapter 8 Bibliography

Boeke, Kees, Cosmic View: The Universe In 40 Jumps, New York, The John Day Company, 1957. A lucid view of the Universe from the sub-microscopic to the extent of the cosmos.

Sagan, Carl, Cosmos: New York, Random House, 1980. A tour through the Cosmos in picture and prose.

Dyson, Freeman Infinity In All Directions, Harper and Row, 1998 This great thinker explores the universe in both directions of scale and the as well as in direction of the great diversity within the creation.

Chapter 9

The Small, the Weird, the Wonderful

Quantum, Relativity and Time

"Anyone who is not shocked by Quantum theory has not understood it."
- Niels Bohr

*"If a man does not feel dizzy when he first learns of the Quantum
. . . he has not understood a word."* - Werner Heisenberg

*" The theory of Quantum Electrodynamics describes nature as absurd
from the point of view of common sense . . .
So I hope you can accept nature as she is; absurd."*
-Richard Feynman

We think that we live in a reasonably predictable world, made up of atoms that we can expect to behave fairly well and predictable. We live in houses supported by pillars and walls composed of linked-up atoms. We're reasonably sure that they will continue to be linked up to form a structure that will not fall on our heads in our sleep. Time goes reliably by, measured by the ticking of our clocks. Gravity reliably holds us to the earth, and the stars show up night after night in their same positions in the sky. When we take a closer look, however, "It ain't necessarily so."

Shaking the Faith

Four revolutions in thinking about our world have occurred in the past 500 years. Galileo is credited with drawing a line through history separating philosophy (the why of things) from science (the how of things). Philosophy is based on logic and arguments. The results of philosophical thinking are only as good as the ideas or premises on which they are based and the precision of human reasoning ability. Galileo substituted observations and measurements for ideas and confined his reasoning to the logic of mathematical proof.

Newton created the second breakthrough. He developed the understanding and mathematical tools to calculate and explain the planetary motions and force of gravity that were observed and measured by Galileo. In doing so, he also uncovered some basic laws of cause and effect that had nearly universal application.

Another revolutionary view of time and space came about when Einstein speculated on how the world and the universe would appear to a traveler traveling close to the speed of light. He discovered that time and other events must be looked at in a relative perspective. From this discovery came the revelation that time cannot be divorced from space and that matter and energy are transformable into one another.

The fourth revolution in scientific thinking came when physicists tried to apply Newton's physics and Einstein's relativity to the prediction of the movement of atoms, electrons, and protons. They found that it didn't work. Instead of regularities they discovered probabilities. Instead of the commonplace effects of our everyday world, they found sudden jumps and discontinuities, but always of a discreet size or quantum. That is why the "New Physics" pioneered by Heisenberg, Schrödinger, Bohr and other intellectual giants became known as *quantum physics.*

Things aren't always what they seem nor are they as predictable. Indeed, some aspects of this universe may seem downright weird and absolutely contrary to common sense. For instance, even the size and shape of things are not always what they were measured to be a moment ago -- not if we're down at the quantum scale. The idea that everything in our universe has definite dimensions of height, width, and depth and is located at a certain position at a certain time -- this idea becomes somewhat fuzzy. What we see instead is that these dimensions are all relative and in some respects interchangeable with one another.

On the universal scale of things, as we have just seen, we are located somewhere in the middle. In size, in position, and in time, we are midway between the atom and the most far-flung reaches of the galaxies of the universe. We are far from the beginning of time. For us, most daily events are predictable, from the speed of falling objects to the orbit of the moon around the earth. From the strength of a bridge girder to the effects of fertilizer on crop growth, things go along a predictable path.

It is when we consider the smallest objects, the electrons and nuclei of atoms, that the rules change. We go from the rules developed by Newton, those that precisely predict the direction and speed of billiard balls after a collision, to the rules of a dice game, where events are determined by chance and probability.

Similarly, when we consider the large scale, the landscape gets somewhat rubbery and strange. The tremendous relative motion of the galaxies, and the intense gravitational field around massive celestial bodies, stretch time and warp space. Space bends and stretches. Time and space are inexorably linked.

Galileo is usually remembered as the genius who defied the dogma of the established Church and showed that the planets revolve about the sun. He is revered in scientific history as the man who replaced philosophy with measurement and mathematics as the means for understanding what was going on and predicting future motion. Before his time, science was primarily a thought process. Galileo began to tie things down by making measurements of his observations. Then he developed mathematical models that allowed him to describe and predict events in a regular way. Newton took these techniques and applied them to the force of gravity and the motion of planets.

By 1800 it appeared that these two geniuses had developed methods that could predict everything and anything in the physical world. If we just made the right measurements and used the proper mathematical tools, then our ability to predict was limited only by the precision of our measurements and the number of calculations that we could practically make.

In Newton's view, if one could know the weight, speed, and direction of every particle and the forces acting on it, then one could predict all future motion and action. The mathematics might be gargantuan, but in principle every event could be calculated and known in advance. This view asserted that the universe was on a fixed course and that everything would happen according to a plan. That plan could be figured out with enough study and mathematics. The theologians of the time had a mixed view of this assertion. They liked the idea of a fixed course and grand plan. They were less enthralled that the scientists were the ones who would discern the plan and know the future.

Newton's laws of motion, governing change of position and speed and forces acting on any part of the universe, were once thought to determine everything from the way billiard balls collide to the behavior of electrons and protons to the orbits of comets and planets. Now we know, not quite!

Time Flies, But Not As We Thought

Einstein first shook up the thinking of scientists with his revelations of relativity. These insights apply primarily to large objects and things which are moving fast; they also apply to our concepts of time and space (or distances and dimensions). Shortly thereafter, Heisenberg, Schrödinger, Pauli and others dropped another bombshell with their quantum physics. Quantum physics primarily explains how little things, such as atoms and electrons and subatomic particles, behave.

Many aspects of Quantum Physics and Relativity are incomprehensible without the help of sophisticated mathematics. Nonetheless, some conclusions derived from these principles must be incorporated into any comprehensive view of the creation. These phenomena are real, they are operating right now, and they help define the creation.

First let us look at time and space as Einstein did. We usually think of time as something that is ticking away and always was and always will be ticking away at the same rate. Einstein showed that in fact the relative speed of objects profoundly effects time. So does gravity. Time is relative to both of these factors; there is no thing such as absolute time. Einstein showed conclusively that in the long run we cannot think separately of space and time. Instead, we must think in terms of space-time.

When objects move rapidly relative to one another, their dimensions shrink, their time slows, and their mass increases. These were the conclusions of Einstein's thought experiments. They have now all been proven by observation and rigorous tests. Gravity distorts and bends space, and what we perceive to be straight lines may not be all that straight after all. Instead of perceiving the universe as expanding, we should instead think of space itself as expanding and stretching. It is *space-time* that is stretching, neither time alone nor space alone.

Let's look at the implication of gravity affecting time. If a clock starts running here on earth and then is taken out into space, it speeds up. Scientists have proved this by using two exceedingly precise timekeepers, atomic clocks. When they were run side by side in the laboratory, for years they agreed precisely on elapsed time. One clock was then taken high above the earth on an extended flight in a slow-flying airplane. When it was returned to earth and compared to its reliable companion that had remained on the ground, it was found that the high-flying clock had moved ahead of its companion.

On the surface of the sun, with its much more powerful gravity, a clock would run significantly slower. In a black hole it would run even slower still. Stephen Hawking, the famous wheel-chair-bound physicist, has said that when the universe was infinite in density at the occasion of the Big Bang, there was no such thing as time. In an infinite density universe, gravity would be infinite and "clocks" of any description would stop. Dimensions or space would also not exist in an infinitely small universe. Time or space-time originated together with the universe at the instant of the Big Bang.

We might argue that it is only clocks that are altered by speed or gravity. We might assume that clocks merely try to keep track of time. If something causes the clock to run slower, it does not necessarily have an effect on time itself, it just slows the timekeeper.

This raises the question, "What is time?" Time is a measure of change. If nothing changed, if nothing moved with respect to any other thing, time would have no significance. If nothing changed, there would be no light, because light travels. Electrons would not move about the nucleus. No chemical reactions would take place, and nothing would fall under the pull of gravity.

We measure or keep track of time by the movement of things. A day is the interval between the start and the end of a complete rotation of the earth around its axis. We break this down into smaller units when it is desirable or convenient. The earth's rotation is a crude measuring stick because its rotation is slowing down, and the earth wobbles a bit too. The most stable references are certain atomic vibrations, the light given off by the electrons of excited atoms, or the pulses of radio waves from certain pulsars. These references are our most reliable and stable clocks.

They tell us that the relativity observations are not caused by some quirky clock whose speed gets messed up by difficult conditions. On the contrary, these different indicators of motion and time are all slowed down or speeded up by their velocity relative to one another. They are all influenced by gravity. All of these time standards agree when they are used to verify the relative nature of time. They all agree that time actually changes under these special conditions, that time is not absolute.

This forces us to the inescapable conclusion that time had a beginning. Further, under the right conditions, such as the final stage of a collapsing universe with gravity increasing toward infinity, time could also have an end. With all of the matter in the universe converging to a point in this possible collapse of the universe, space would also shrink to nothing and both space and time (space-time) would cease to exist.

Can We Believe In Uncertainty?

At the other end of the dimension scale, in the realm of the infinitesimally small, things get really quirky. Electrons have certain definite properties and characteristics, such as a negative electric charge that draws it to a positively charged nucleus. It has a weight or mass that can be measured with good accuracy and repeatability. Once it was thought that we could predict how an electron would behave under any circumstance. We could do this if we knew its weight, charge, position, velocity, and the forces that were acting upon it. Even if the mathematics were too complex for a person to make these calculations, the electron would always perform predictably and there would be no room for chance.

This is a very important juncture of philosophy and science. The action of electrons upon one another results in the physical structure of most everything that we call matter in our world. The physical communication that they exchange, in the form of photons of energy, are the means of transporting power and energy throughout the cosmos. If the future course of every electron is in principle determinable, the universe is on a predictable course. If it is not, any non-predictable action of an electron results in an unpredictable change in the arrangement of the universe. It influences in some manner all future changes in the creation.

Quantum physics has learned that it is not possible to know everything about a single atomic particle. This is not because we are not clever enough or not able to make critical measurements with the required accuracy. It is because certain key bits of information are unknowable simultaneously. If we know one piece of information very precisely, then another crucial bit of information has to be unknowable at that moment. The consequences of this limitation are that the action of subatomic particles is *not* predictable. At the smallest scale of the universe, atomic and subatomic events happen unpredictably. As a result, the structure of the universe and its parts, and information and energy that are exchanged, are not completely predictable.

Consequently it is apparent that the universe is not on an inexorable course where every thing is predestined or where the future is completely fathomable. Rather, future events are only probable, not certain. As we shall see in the next chapter, it is more like an adventure than a journey.

Initially Einstein could not accept this concept. He pronounced, famously, that "God doesn't play dice with the universe." At the grand celestial level where his new physics operated, there was no room for unpredictability

The Strange World of the Small

The subatomic world is weird. It turns out that electrons, protons, neutrons, and photons all have a dual nature. Sometimes they behave as particles and at other times they behave as waves. It even appears that they display their nature on request. If we test for their particle nature, they show their particle nature. If we test for their wave nature, they act as waves. It is a bit like the joke where the tailor whispers to his partner to turn on the blue light because the customer wants a blue suit. This dual nature is also impossible to visualize. How can anything be a particle and a wave simultaneously?

This enigmatic aspect was revealed in a series of simple tests. The wave nature of light was first demonstrated by passing light through several closely spaced parallel slits and allowing the light to fall on a photographic film. The resulting picture shows zebra-like stripes of light and dark, proving that there were overlapping waves interfering with each other. However, when only one slit is used, the pattern on the film corresponds to that of a multitude of tiny particles! When electrons are put to the same test, they behave exactly like light photons. They show both a wave and a particle nature.

Later someone realized it would be interesting to send a beam of protons or neutrons toward the parallel slits. (Remember that protons and neutrons are "heavy" particles with a well-defined mass). No difference; they too behaved exactly like waves! When they were passed through a single slit, they once again behaved like particles. Previously, it had been thought that the bits and pieces of atoms were well-defined particles and that light and other types of electromagnetic radiation were energy waves and nothing more. Quantum physics showed us that light, which presumably has no weight or mass, behaves at times like a solid and weighty thing. At the same time it showed us that solid bits and pieces of our physical world - protons, neutrons, and electrons - can behave like light waves.

One aspect of this paradox is trying to visualize how a little ball can go through many slits at once without breaking into smaller balls. A second conceptual dilemma is how a wave that can go through many slits simultaneously can cram itself through a single slit at other times. A third dilemma is how seemingly heavy, measurable, and tangible atomic particles can behave like waves. Still other absurdities show up. The electron spins, but it has to spin around twice to get back to its original position. But as Feynman says, we have to accept nature as it is -- absurd.

The issues raised by the unpredictability and the apparently absurd paradoxes of nature are not trivial. They compel us to explore one of the main issues of existence and philosophy. The issue is the predictability and the predestination of the universe, or, contrariwise, the unpredictability and the adventuring nature of the universe. Although the action of a single electron cannot be predicted, the action of a large number can be predicted with great accuracy, not as a certainty but as a probability. We cannot know where any single electron goes when it is unleashed in a television picture tube. However, when we generate an electron beam consisting of billions of electrons in the tube, they arrive at the screen in predictable ways that cause the tube to display a television picture in great detail. In a large group, their path is perfectly predictable.

The same unpredictability and probability apply to the events that take place in the nucleus of an atom. All radioactive isotopes of atoms are unstable. There is an absolute certainty that every unstable isotope will disintegrate or partly fall apart sooner or later. The moment when any particular one of them will disintegrate is absolutely unpredictable. However, if we observe a sufficiently large number of unstable atoms, we can learn to predict with some precision how many will disintegrate in any given interval of time.

Once again, on an individual basis the predictability is zero. On the collective scale the probability of events comes close to a certainty. An individual atom has great freedom. When a great many atoms are involved, their freedom and unpredictability almost seem to vanish.

Feeling Dizzy, or Feeling Adventurous?

These are some of the seemingly weird and absurd aspects of the creation: the expansion of space, the creation of space-time, the different time scales of different observers, the bending of space by gravity, the wave-particle nature of the basic building blocks of creation, and the unknown ability and unpredictability of some of the basic events that shape the creation. These phenomena all suggest that the nature of the creation is a seething, moving dynamic association of its bits and pieces, where every part is moving in ways that are not always familiar. This is a universe with no absolute time or space, a universe that bends and contorts itself in the process of endless creation and re-creation.

The conclusions are that time is not infinite, that space and time were created together. The trajectory of the organization of the universe is not predetermined but is modified by chance. Atomic events are not certainties but are only predictable with a degree of probability. Large accumulations of matter are more stable and predictable, producing the variety of creatures that make up the universe. The unpredictable instabilities and quantum effects force the changes that allow new creatures to form, to evolve, and to change again.

These effects complete our survey of the underlying forces and characteristics of the creation. Altogether they make up an adventure on a grand scale. We now see a vast multitude of actors - including ourselves - forming the whole rambunctious play, each driven by internal tension between stability and instability and the need to find affinities. It is time to see how the play is getting along.

The Cosmic Deity

Chapter 9 Bibliography

Calder, Nigel *Einstein's Universe*, Viking Press, 1979. The implications of Relativity on time, space and motion.

Englert, Berthold-Georg, Marlan O. Scully and Herbert Walther, *The Duality In Matter And Light*, Scientific American, 271:86-92, December, 1994. How all matter and energy has a dual nature; as particle and as waves.

Gilmore, Robert, *Alice In Quantum Land: An Allegory Of Quantum Physics*, Springer-Verlag New York, Inc., 1995. A popular easy to read explanation of the consequences of the Quantum Physics.

Chapter 10

An Adventure, Not A Journey

*"When you are on a journey
and the end keeps getting fuzzier and further away,
then you realize that the real end is the journey."*
-Karlfried Graf Durekheim

So far we have been exploring what has been going on in the universe and not examining why. Maybe we'll never know the why but we can at least examine the process for clues. Unless we ground ourselves in the facts and observations that we discern in the creation, we will fall into the role of "armchair philosopher."

The premise of this work is that the Creator and creation are one. The inescapable questions that arise are, What is the Creator up to? Is there a purpose, a goal, a final destination?

Modern thought is predominantly preoccupied with goals and objectives. We tend to endow every thing and every activity with a purpose. Indeed, we seem to *need* some feeling of purpose in our activities just for mental well-being. The need to have a purpose is thoroughly built into our thinking and perhaps even into our very nature.

We dream, we plan, we scheme to organize our life and our surroundings. We blend our planning and our spiritual views together. We perceive a Creator and attempt to divine the Creator's plan. If we are devout, we may try especially hard to attune ourselves and our lives to what we think is the Creator's grand plan.

Having a Purpose Means a Journey

The highest goal of many people is to find a purpose in their lives. They visualize a desired objective and try to decide what path leads to that goal. Then they devote considerable effort to achieving the goal and walking along the path that they have chosen.

Sometimes the route to achieving an objective is a pain and a nuisance. Mark Spitz was a winner of seven Olympic Gold medals in aquatic events. When he was interviewed after one string of five victories, he reportedly said that he didn't want to get into another swimming pool as long as he lived! Apparently his goals were simply to gather Olympic Medals and not to be a great swimmer or to enjoy the power and grace of swimming that his training produced. If we believe him, the hard training work was just a trial, a trial that he was willing to go through to get to his real goal.

This view of life is akin to that of a journey. We know where we are starting from, we know where we want to go, and we plan our journey accordingly. We may have to overcome obstacles and suffer privations or detours. Maybe we realize at the outset that our goal may never be achieved. Nevertheless the destination is the desired prize, not the process of getting there.

Contrast this to an adventure. When we start on an adventure, we have no objective in mind but to explore and enjoy the discoveries that await. We are prepared to experience them, be they sublime or dangerous. Some lead to dead ends or even to tragedies. Others lead to delightful revelations. The unknown is the lure and the trip is its own reward.

Did the Creation Have Humans As A Goal?

Many have argued that we humans are the ultimate purpose of the Creator, the culmination of its work and its highest achievement. But are humans -- and the human mind and intellect -- really the goal and purpose of the creation?

On the evidence it hardly looks like it. The creation has taken some tens of billions of years to come this far, and there is no sign at all that it has stopped or even paused. Human life only appeared in the last tiny fraction of the immense lifetime of our universe. From a scientific viewpoint it looks like hubris to suppose that the entire universe was created to support and nurture the development of one species and one kind of mind, our own!

Let us go back and look at the facts, from the Big Bang to the present state of the cosmos. The scientific evidence does not support the view that the planet earth sits at the top of a pyramid of development, a crown jewel amidst all the wild and woolly reaches of space. Even on our own planet there is no clear single path of development that leads inevitably to humans. Rather there are many paths leading to a great host of living creatures, some of which are very specialized and/or very intelligent. Many of these creatures lie far from the human lineage. The development of humans can hardly be the purpose of the marvelous evolution of all of life.

Nor are humans at the apex of an evolutionary tree. A more factual view positions them as one twig of a huge shaggy bush that displays an enormous diversity of life forms. The realm of living things seems to have explored every possible avenue of shape, form, and function in adapting to its environment. We might say that the appearance of a naked primate ape walking on two legs was an accident, or we might say it was practically inevitable sooner or later, given the creation's penchant for experimentation.

Equally we might say that the appearance and continuance of the human line was just plain luck. In geologic time many other invertebrate and vertebrate creatures died out in the periodic catastrophes that overwhelmed our earth. It is only by happenstance that the thread of evolutionary development leading to human beings was not snipped early on by collisions from space or by ice ages or by epidemic disease. These and similar catastrophes have caused the extinction of many major and interesting families of life. It was by unhappy chance that these families disappeared and it was by happy chance that our own ancestors and those of our fellow living species made it through.

Certainly humans are neither the largest living beings nor the strongest. They are neither the most agile nor the most enduring creature populating this planet. Yet for their size they have become by far the most numerous. What distinguishes humans that allows them their steady growth in numbers and domination over others? It is not because they are uniquely well adapted to a particular ecological niche. It is because our intellect and mental capabilities allow us to modify practically all environmental conditions to meet human requirements. We have a powerful mind, and it is our mind which has given us our recent evolutionary success.

Is this human mind, then, the obvious goal of the creator and the ultimate handiwork of the universe? The human mind is certainly a product of the ongoing creation, but there is no evidence that it is an end or culmination of creation. As far as we can tell, the other processes and forms of creation continue on their paths in both the near and far reaches of the universe. Others did not abandon their own creativity when the human brain emerged. Thus it is possible that right now other forms of mind are developing somewhere in the universe, perhaps have already evolved to be more powerful than ours. Nor is it likely that the present human mind is a final destination, the ultimate in intellectual development. The same kinds of slow evolutionary experimentation that led to the present human mind will no doubt lead to the future human mind.

Journeys and Adventures

Let's explore further the idea that the Creator/creation is on an adventure instead of a journey. A journey is like the trip of a drop of water in a river system. The raindrop that falls on a particular rock on a particular mountain has a near certainty of reaching the ocean. The river system that connects the rock to the ocean inexorably carries our raindrop to its destination. At every juncture, from the first trickle leading away from the rock to the last river, the water drop goes downward via larger and larger streams till it discharges into the sea. Once in the ocean, its journey is done.

And once in the ocean, its adventure begins. If the water drop evaporates, there is no guide to bring those individual water molecules back together and coalesce them into the original drop of water. Nor will the new raindrop fall on any particular rock on any special mountain. It is off on an adventure. The most powerful calculations cannot tell us when or where that raindrop will fall.

Now let's look at what happens if we imagine the water drop traveling in reverse, trying to go upstream from the ocean to the rock. If the drop had no map nor memory of its previous journey, it could finish up on almost any mountain rock. It would certainly have an extremely low probability of landing on the rock where it first started. At every junction of every stream it would have to make a guess as to which branch to take. Its upward trip would be an adventure and not a journey.

What about the single salmon that can instinctively return to the small tributary where it hatched? That salmon has retained an important piece of information, the unique smell of the water from its hatching environment. At each branch of the stream this smell guides it in its choice of direction, and it unerringly returns home to its spawning ground. This is a fish that wants nothing to do with adventure. It's on one of the most crucial journeys of its life, and only one destination will do.

Scientific Hindsight

It is a famous saying that science is a better historian than a prophet. Science excels at uncovering the unpredictable path that the creation has already taken. It is only just warming up for the far more difficult business of prediction.

The traditional scientific viewpoint is somewhat akin to looking down the stream toward the river and the ocean. The scientist watches the water flowing downward at each stream juncture. After a few simple observations she or he predicts with great accuracy the direction that the next drop of water will take and what its destination will be. After a little time the scientist also discerns the rules guiding the flow of water. When the water drop in a stream reaches another stream, the rule is: go down. The tug of gravity makes this decision. Any other drop of water entering the river system follows the same rule and arrives at the ocean in the same way.

In the 19th century, as we have seen, scientists dreamed that soon they would be able to explain all these phenomena as being fully determined. In the 20th century a new generation of scientists realized that the creation is not determined in its details at all. For instance, the water-course in our story may follow an alternate route down the mountain from time to time. Not all the water molecules follow the flow-down rule all the way to the ocean. Because of quantum physics, we now say that there is a great probability that most of the molecules will reach the sea, but here and there an individual water molecule meets a different fate.

The river system was chosen for these examples because of an uphill similarity to the history of the universe. The universe began all at once in the Big Bang and has been streaming outward ever since. Again and again it has forked by chance and created a multitude of side branches.

Another way to appreciate this is to pay a visit back in time and observe and understand the processes that brought us to where we are today. Now it is easy to see that there were many points where the creation tried different paths before settling on the one where we are now. We can try to extrapolate this unpredictable progress a short distance in the future, but we cannot predict the fate of even our own lives. The forward motion of the creation is always an adventure for us.

To test this idea, you may want to look at your own life. You can take a journey over known ground and trace your genealogy back many generations. By studying the lives of your ancestors and those who molded them, you can understand your own heritage and makeup. You can study the genetic influences that are helping to shape your physical and mental characteristics right now. Your ancestral lineage certainly looks like a clear path that leads straight to you. Then, when you turn around and look into the future, you see only a fuzzy adventure of many paths. You cannot predict the lives of your children or your grandchildren or guess the life situations which will shape them. You see only a myriad possibilities and a thousand forks in the road.

Not everyone is happy with this prospect of course. Many people desire a sense of certainty and security about their future, and they work mightily to make their lives secure. In their hearts they long for predictable outcomes that are ordained by a Plan.

But what does this imply? Suppose we could arrange our lives and the world about us so that every action and reaction is known and predicted. Our goals in life would be assured and we would never have to make any choices or decisions. In fact, individual decisions and independent action could not be allowed, since this would disturb the predicted outcomes laid out in the Plan. Then everyone would live happily ever after -- or would they? This might be some people's vision of a Heaven. I suspect, with human nature what it is, that after a short spell we would call it Hell.

A Model, Or A Building Kit?

How does the Creator manifest itself so that creation is an open-ended adventure? Maybe a simple analogy from our own experience sheds some light. Children like to build things, and many toys and kits of materials are offered to satisfy this want. The toys come in two different categories. One of them is a box of parts which children can assemble into a particular toy such as a car, an animal, or a house. We'll call this a model kit. Each part is numbered and fits together with the others in only one way. The kit also comes with instructions to explain where each part goes. If the sequence of operations is properly followed, we obtain the desired finished product. If we try to put the parts together in a different way, they don't fit properly and they don't make a satisfactory toy.

The other kind of toy is a kit of parts that fit together in lots of different ways. In my childhood these kits were tinker toys and erector sets. Today they are Lego and similar construction sets. The kit consists of dozens or even hundreds of parts but only a few different kinds. Every piece is identical to the others of its kind except perhaps in color. Each kind is ingeniously designed to fit together with ones similar to itself and with others in many different ways.

Children put these parts together as they choose, following only a few simple rules. The rules are determined by the shape of the parts, not by a master plan. The child can create as many different houses and bridges as she likes, and daddies and chocolate cakes and windmills, or she can put them together at random to see what happens. No instructions are necessary, only the simple rules for joining any two parts. By trial and error and steady improvement, marvelous edifices and mechanisms come into being. The grand sweep of the child's creation is made possible by just two things: the imagination of the child and the handful of simple shapes that fit together in an orderly way.

How different from the model kit! With the model kit, only one result is intended and only one result emerges. And it comes about only if all the instructions and plans are carefully followed.

The model kit is analogous to a universe created according to a plan. There is a plan, a destination, and a journey. This idea of a carefully designed universe is an old one, and it is still argued by some. The second concept, that of the tinker toy set or Lego, is analogous to a universe with no plan but only internal rules. This universe builds and rebuilds itself, testing all kinds of designs, capable of going on a creative adventure. This is the new paradigm for thinking about the world around us, and it is one of the central arguments of this book.

Fitting In The Final Pieces

Our physical universe is not composed of special pieces that fit together to make one jigsaw puzzle. All our experiences and observations tell us that this is not true! The Creator has rather manifested itself as a set of simple building blocks with a few rules about how they fit together. The fitting-together rules are written right into the pieces themselves, just like the Lego blocks or tinker toys.

These rules turn out to be the four fundamental forces that guide all the interactions of the universe. These forces operate under the overall principle of affinity which says that any part or particle always seeks interaction with other parts and particles. Affinity may be thought of as an inherent characteristic too, an inner need to find others, make associations, and exchange energy. No bit of the Creation, not even the smallest bit, has ever wanted to be alone!

Even a superficial view of creation suggests that it is an open-ended adventure rather than a journey to a predetermined goal. Our creation is rich with worlds of seemingly infinite complexity based upon a foundation which is elegant in its simplicity. It spans incomprehensible reaches of space and time. It reveals many dead ends, spectacular achievements, and shrouded secrets.

With this beautiful adventure in full swing, why have human beings sometimes tried to impose a journey on the Creator? Why have they believed the Creator initiated a journey when an adventure is the more obvious alternative? Isn't our chance and unpredictable universe a marvel of beautiful design after all? Is there any reason to think it has stopped its restless search? As the sailors say, "When you are sailing, you're at your destination." Clearly the Creator, manifested as the creation, is off on an adventure. We are privileged to be a part of this grand adventure, to share in its wonder, and to be awed by its wonderful diversity.

Chapter 10 Bibliography

Atkins, Peter William, *Creation Revisited:* New York, W. H. Freeman & Company, 1992. A Distinguished Scientist Looks At the Origins Of Space, Time, And The Universe.

Dennett, Daniel C., *Darwin's Dangerous Idea: Evolution And The Meanings Of Life,* New York, Simon & Shuster, 1995. The author shows how all phases of the universe evolve in an unpredictable manner.

Barrow, John D., *The Origin Of The Universe*, Basic Books, 1994.

Ferris, Timothy, *Coming Of Age In The Milky Way*, William Morrow and Company, Inc., 1988.

Hawking, Stephen, *The Universe In A Nutshell*, Bantam Books, 2001.

Chapter 11

The Long Long Adventure

"... Deep in the sea
all the molecules repeat
the patterns of one another
till complex new ones are formed.
They make new ones like themselves
and a new dance starts
Growing in size and complexity
living things, masses of atoms
DNA, protein dancing
a pattern ever more intricate.

Out of the cradle
onto the dry land
here it is. standing:
atoms with consciousness:
matter with curiosity.
Stands at the sea,
wonders at wondering:
I a universe of atoms
an atom in the universes."
-Richard Feynman
Nobel Laureate

In the beginning? All peoples have a story to explain how the world began. Creation legends are innumerable; many have focused on a Creator who is not unlike a human being. Allow me to tell a new creation story. Allow me to take you to the beginning of time. In our imagination, we'll accompany a different perception of Creator/creation as this manifestation unfolds into our wild and wonderful universe.

We've previously touched on a lot of the things that will be happening in the course of this adventure. Now we'll try to put it all together in a coherent way and in its proper sequence. Significant things happened pretty fast in the first couple of minutes of time. In this short interval occurred the transformation of energy into every one of the stable and enduring parts and pieces of the entire universe.

We have to say here that Energy was primordial. Out of it originated space-time and all matter. The energy manifested itself suddenly and just once, as a *singularity*, a one-time event of incalculable force. Theologians and scientists alike sometimes refer to it as the moment of creation.

That moment of creation, the *transformation* of energy into space-time and matter, is the Big Bang. Scientists are reluctant to speculate about the instant itself, because they cannot test or create the conditions of "time zero." However, they talk about the universe as it existed a very small fraction of a second after time zero. They do talk about the happenings in this interval of time because they think that they can replicate these conditions in the very largest particle accelerators.

Thus the singularity is where our story begins. Space-time and all else began its existence out of this singularity. The singularity left behind no clues about any antecedents, only that it existed. Infinite power is one of the few attributes of the singularity that we can comprehend. It is that power that we may call the Creator. It is that power which became the creation, and ultimately ourselves.

Come along on this adventure. Re-live your past, since every part of you was present at the creation and participated in this long, long, adventure. The adventure contains mysteries and unanswered questions, but those hidden parts cannot obscure the reality of the creation of which we are a part.

Time Zero

Stephen Hawking is one physicist who has thought about the initial conditions at time zero itself. He conceives the start of the universe as having zero dimensions, an infinite temperature, and no boundaries. (It was Hawking who named it a "singularity").

Imagine we are there. The singularity seems to be infinite in its energy or power and without form or structure. There exists a single super force and this super force alone. It exists before the creation of matter. There are no particles or forces as we know them, no rules or laws of physics, and no time.

Then * * * * *

And then the singularity instantly becomes an unimaginably vast burst of energy and primordial particles. In that explosive rush some of its energy changes into a swarm of ephemeral wave-particles. Although few of these proto-particles last beyond a thousandth or a millionth of a second, they represent condensed energy. The big bang starts to cool down from an infinite temperature to one where recognizable sub-particles of matter appear and sustain themselves. Akin to drops of mist that form in cooling air, particles of real matter and anti-matter start to condense out of that expanding rush of energy.

Within a fraction of a second after time zero, infinite power has transformed itself from energy into matter. This matter is imbued at the instant of its birth with the forces that govern the subsequent interaction of all matter and energy. The Creator has become the creation.

Right from the start the universe shows a characteristic that it still exhibits today: infinite creativeness. As Wolfgang Panofsky says," At these high energies (temperatures), any particles that can be formed will be formed." In fact hundreds of different kinds of sub-nuclear particles and their anti-matter complements are formed. Only a very few of these particles are able to survive for more than a fraction of a second before they disintegrate. A few, with an apparent infinite lifetime, survive to form the matter of the present universe.

When energy transforms itself into matter, it obeys its own internal rules. For instance, the creation is frugal. It does not allow any loss of energy. When energy is transformed into subatomic particles, the universe cools down. If an unstable particle appears and subsequently disintegrates, it pays back the amount of energy that was needed to produce it. The universe heats up again slightly.

The Conundrum of Anti-matter

When the expanding universe cools a little further, pairs of familiar particles materialize, such electrons, neutrons, and protons. But these are not matched pairs but complementary pairs! Each pair consists of a particle and its anti-particle. The appearance of a particle of matter always means the appearance of an anti-matter complement.

Matter and anti-matter are incompatible, however. If they touch, they annihilate one another and release energy equivalent to both of their masses. Now that the universe is cooling enough so that no new particles are being condensed, neutrons and anti-neutrons and protons and anti-protons are busily annihilating one another. By some estimates, only one in a billion remains! The survivors are all matter particles. (Note, an anti-matter universe would work just as well as a matter universe).

But here presents one of the great mysteries of the universe. If equal numbers of particles and anti-particles are always formed, and if they exactly annihilate one another when they collide, why is there any matter left over? This process of annihilation should continue until every particle of matter and anti-matter are converted back into energy. This is what always seems to happen in high-energy particle accelerators. There seems to be a slight a symmetry in the process that results in a very slight excess of matter over anti-matter, one of the great remaining mysteries of the creation!

Back we go to the main story: As the universe continues to cool, it drops below a critical threshold temperature. Below this temperature no new neutrons and protons are formed. The rapid expansion has thinned out and slightly cooled the photons that carry most of the remaining energy.

Nonetheless the temperature is still several billion degrees. Some 12 seconds after the creation, our universe consists primarily of photons, electrons, and their anti-matter companions called positrons, together with the much-diminished number of neutrons and protons.

The next significant milepost takes place at about 14 seconds. Things have cooled to about one billion degrees. Now it is the fate of the electrons and positrons to gobble one another up. Apparently all of the anti-matter positrons get eliminated, and the number of surviving electrons equals the number of remaining protons. Our universe is now set to be a matter universe, not an anti-matter one!

I've taken several pages to describe these momentous events of the grand adventure, the creation of the stable building blocks of the universe. These pages are way out of proportion to the true expended time. In fact the initial process happens in just a few seconds

But now that the building blocks are built, we are ready to come to a more familiar subject, the birth of atomic nuclei. We find that the neutrons and protons which survived annihilation are not idle. Some protons persist as the future hydrogen nuclei. Some neutrons combine with protons and form substantial numbers of helium nuclei. By the end of just four minutes nearly all the neutrons have been incorporated into helium nuclei. The remaining free neutrons start to decay into protons and electrons. In several hours virtually all of the free neutrons are gone.

The universe is now a little calmer and in general does not undergo such wild and rapid transformations again. Its realm has become that of atomic nuclei and clouds of electrons; but still at energies too great to allow them to settle into atoms. The major changes to come are in the infinite organizational patterns that these pre-atomic particles can make.

The Ascendance of Gravity

For the next several hundred thousand years the universe continues its immense outbound rush of expansion and cooling. The gravitational tug is trying to slow down this rush as each particle exerts a minuscule pull on every other particle. For now, though, gravity's weak little tug is no match for the internal pressure and outbound velocity of the particles.

After hundreds of thousands of years, our cosmic fireball cools down into the 10,000-degree range. Electrons settle into orbits around hydrogen and helium nuclei, forming complete atoms of hydrogen and helium. As matter calms down, so too does energy. Photons of visible light - far less energetic than the cosmic rays which dominated before - establish communication among those electrons that are bound to atoms. The universe is organizing itself into tangible things that we can see and feel.

What has happened to the photons of energy released in the annihilation processes? This sea of ultra-high-energy photons stretches out and loses energy as space expands. Do you remember those communication engineers back in Chapter 2? This is the cool radiation that they discovered. It has been called the echo or the whisper of the Big Bang, electromagnetic energy that has been stretched and cooled off to an effective temperature of just a few degrees.

After such a prolonged expansion, one might expect the universe to become cold, slow, vast, and dilute. Indeed, the universe does go into a dark and apparently static phase for perhaps a billion years. To a human observer, who can see only visible light, the universe would appear to darken and go red as the temperature approaches 1000 degrees. The light fades out as the temperature drops slightly lower.

The universe might have cooled indefinitely, had it not been for gravity, that minuscule force imbued into every particle. Slowly but surely gravity begins to slow down the expansion of the cosmos. Slowly but surely matter is drawn in to itself, accruing ever-larger masses of matter, setting the stage for the next grand act of creation.

The Birth of Stars

In the spreading clouds of helium and hydrogen are countless regions with a slightly higher density of atoms than in the surrounding space. Gravity begins to pull the denser pockets of gas more tightly together. As atoms crowd toward the center of the denser area, the whole cloud begins to rotate, just as an ice skater rotates faster when her arms are pulled in tightly to her body. This results in a sort of flattened disc, often with spiral arms trailing back. In the core and in the denser patches of surrounding gas, creative possibilities abound.

Gravity's pull is relentless. More atoms get sucked into the center of the cloud. The gravity becomes stronger as each arriving atom adds its pull to the ones already there. The atoms pile on, producing pressure on the ones already in the center. Further, the arriving atoms have a considerable velocity. As they plunge into the surface of the cloud, their momentum is turned into heat. The assembled mass of atoms becomes hot.

At 1000 degrees the mass begins to glow as a red ball. After another million years of growing and heating, the temperature in the core reaches several million degrees. Now electrons are stripped off atoms and bare nuclei are once again forced into proximity with one another. For these long-lived entities, the return of heat and pressure must seem like a journey backwards as well as forwards! A crushing pressure builds until hydrogen nuclei begin to "ignite" and fuse together, releasing tremendous amounts of new radiant energy. A sun is formed. The universe begins to light up, as star after star ignites.

Not just one sun appears but uncounted billions of suns, inhabiting every reach of the universe. Every corner of space is filled with dramatic new manifestations of creation and the power of the Creator. The pace of creation quickens, especially in the variety and number of transformations taking place. The new stars attract others to their neighborhood. They perform a swirling and weaving ballet as they dance in and through the gravitational fields of neighboring suns.

The largest stars form where the density of hydrogen and helium is greatest. Even as they heat up and start to burn, their gravity pulls in more gas from surrounding space. It is the ultimate size of a sun that determines what nuclear processes occur inside its core. The very small red dwarfs, for example, are just barely able to sustain the nuclear fusion that causes them to light up.

Larger stars burn furiously and rapidly. One sun may expand into a huge "blue giant" star; another may develop an instability that causes it to flare up and wane in a regular pattern. Still another may explode in nature's most creative and spectacular event, a supernova.

Heavy Atoms Forged in Nature's Crucible

A supernova is a giant star that gets "out of control." First, a nuclear fusion frenzy combines the helium and most of the hydrogen into slightly heavier atoms. This causes the star to swell up to thousands of times its normal size. Suddenly the heat-producing process in the core comes to an abrupt end and gravity pulls the entire immense fireball back towards the center in a grand implosion. As the material crashes back, the pressure becomes overwhelmingly intense. In a brief instant all of the remaining small nuclei fuse into carbon and other, heavier nuclei, releasing an unimaginable amount of energy. (It was recently estimated that in the first 10 seconds of a supernova explosion, as much energy is radiated as from all of the other visible stars and galaxies combined). When the Tycho Supernova exploded in our galaxy in 1574, it was bright enough to be seen as a daytime star.

Supernovas produce the nuclei of atoms that are heavier than carbon and which are not produced in the hearts of other stars. The extreme heat and pressure of the great implosion acts as a titanic hammer, forging the lighter elements into heavier elements. The resulting outward explosion then belches these heavier elements out into space at nearly the speed of light. Glowing with fantastic colors, the bursting bubble swells up and even seems to engulf the nearby stars.

From this cloud of super-hot debris new stars eventually begin to coalesce. These second-generation stars now contain the heavier elements that we find everywhere in ourselves and in our world. The inescapable truth is that most of our personal atoms must have gone through this violent but creative part of the Creator's adventure. We were once at the heart of a supernova!

Turning up the Gravity

This is a good moment to rewind to an earlier stage of creation. Sometimes the gravitational forces present at the birth of a star are so great that electrons are pushed directly into protons, forming neutrons. Such a neutron star is so dense and so heavy that it may become a "black hole," a super-dense hole from which gravity allows nothing to escape. Even nearby stars get sucked in. But before these stars disappear into the black hole, they emit the fiercest waves of electromagnetic energy to be found anywhere in the universe. These huge sources of radiant energy are called quasars, exceeding the energy output of hundreds of galaxies.

Quasars are not only the most energetic things that have ever been discovered, they are also the most distant things that we can detect. We are able to see them at the most vast distances because of their tremendous radiated energy. Ordinary stars that are as far away are too faint to be seen with our present instruments and telescopes.

Equally fascinating phenomena are to be found closer to home. With ordinary instruments we can appreciate the diversity of the heavenly creation: pulsars, black holes, red giants, blue giants, white dwarfs, and a plethora of other celestial bodies. None of these are permanent and each has a cycle of formation and dissolution, similar to the other forms of creation that surround us in daily life.

Looking closely at certain suns, we see planets circling around them. Planets form when blobs of heavier elements rotate like halos around newly formed stars. Whereas lighter elements get sucked in or are blown away, the heavier particles continue swirling in a solar orbit. Eventually their mutual gravity brings them together and they merge into planets. If a planet then receives sufficient energy from newly arriving matter or from the radioactive decay of its heavier atoms, it may melt and become quite round, like our own earth.

The Conundrum of Seeing Backwards in Time

So far we've looked at the variety and immensity of creation. We haven't yet looked at the *dimensions* of creation, its vast spread and its existence for billions of years. Dimensions that we usually think of, for instance miles and meters, are minuscule compared to the entirety of creation. Our sun is 96 million miles away, and the nearest other sun is so far away that to talk of its distance in miles becomes very difficult. One convenient measure is the time it takes for light to travel such a distance at its speed of 186,000 miles per second. It takes the light from our sun about six minutes to travel to us. The light from the nearest star takes several years. The light from the nearest galaxy to ours takes millions of years to reach us, and the radio signals we detect from the furthermost quasars require billions of years to travel to our planet. When we look at the heavens, we are literally looking backwards in time.

We do not see the stars and galaxies as they are and where they are today. We see them as they were and where they were when their light started to travel toward us. They have been expanding, changing, exploding, shrinking, moving, and evolving in many unknown ways during the millions or billions of years since they first launched their electromagnetic photon messengers in our direction.

What we see now are slices of time somewhere near the midpoint of the process of creation. Except for the microwave radiation emitted in the first million years of creation, the earliest clues we are receiving now are not more than seven billion years old. As the Big Bang occurred some 15 billion years ago, more than half of the cosmic record is hidden away, closed to our direct observation.

What is overwhelming clear is that all the physical evidence we have points to a common origin in that first Big Bang. Thereafter the four fundamental and inherent forces have done the rest. The first three forces maintain a dynamic local creation, while gravity, that grand affinity, in the end has the final word for the universe as a whole.

Gravity is the forge whereupon are created stars, heavy atoms, and such glorious displays of power and diversity as galaxies, supernovas, neutron stars, and quasars. It blows stars apart and gathers the dust into new stars, planets, asteroids, and comets. It takes a planet and wraps it around a sun to supply it with warmth and power. Gravity bends and twists space, and in the end it decides the ultimate fate of the universe. If the universe contains sufficient matter, gravity will halt its expansion and bring it crashing back in on itself. If not, the universe will expand indefinitely, gradually becoming ever colder and more dilute, until in the end all light dims and finally goes out.

Bringing the story down to earth

We won't finish with such a cold and cosmic scene. In fact it is time to open up a new phase of the adventure. As you may have noticed, we overlooked something rather important as we watched the formation of solar systems. Perhaps it didn't seem important at the time because of the grand and immense displays of power going on elsewhere, but it *is* important, at least to us. Let's go back there again.

Somewhere in mid-universe, in the outlying arms of one of the more common types of galaxies, there lies an ordinary second or third-generation star that ignited about five billion years ago. Less ordinarily, orbiting around it is a medium-size planet that appears to be an anomaly, an unusual creature in this part of the cosmos. It has both an atmosphere and a thin skin of water covering most of its surface. A closer look shows that there is a minute scum of organic matter on its surface, only a few grams per square meter on the average, but quite unlike anything encountered in our journey thus far.

In the next chapter we shall take our exploration of the creation to this thin-skinned and curious planet. It will be a love story because it is about our Mother, the planet earth.

Chapter 11 Bibliography

Brimhall, George, *The Genesis Of Ores*, <u>Scientific American</u>, 264:84-91, May, 1991. How the process of earth formation separates out its components.

Disney, Michael, *A New Look At Quasars*, Scientific American, 278:52-57, June, 1998. A description of the most violent processes going on in the universe.

Kirshner, Robert P., *The Earth's Elements*, Scientific American, 271:58-65, October, 1994. The significant atoms that compose and drive the evolution of the earth.

Reinking, Gregory F. , *Cosmic Legacy*, New York, Vantage Presse, New York, 2003 A complete and lucid history of the evolving cosmos extending from the Creation up through the advent of humans and the technological revolution.

LoSecco, J. M., Frederick Reines and Daniel Sinclair, *The Search For Proton Decay*, Scientific American, 252:54-62, June 1985. Are the building blocks of the universe eternal?

McCrea, Sir William, *Arthur Stanley Eddington*, Scientific American, 264:92-97, June, 1991. One of the great minds that elucidated and explained the discoveries of the past century that led to our current understanding of the universe and its creation and evolution.

Shaham, Jacob, *The Oldest Pulsars In The Universe* , Scientific American, 256:50-56, February, 1987. These celestial bodies allow us to study how the universe existed in the era of the birth of stars and galaxies.

Taylor, S. Ross, and Scott M. McLennan, *The Evolution Of Continental Crust*, Scientific American, 274:76-81, January, 1996. Our dry land floats on a mantle of denser material and has been changing and "disappearing" throughout the ages.

Wheeler, J. Craig and Robert P. Harkness, *Helium-rich Supernovas*. Scientific American, 257:50-58, November, 1987. Computer modeling suggests that supernovas result when the denuded core of a massive star collapses. These "peculiar" supernovas are close cousins of this year's bright event. These events produce the elements that allow life to evolve.

Chapter 12

Getting Down To Earth

"Teach your children what we have taught our children,
that the Earth is their Mother. . . .
This we know, the Earth does not belong to us;
we belong to the Earth.
All things are connected like the blood which unites one family.
We are all connected."
                                                                    -Chief Seattle

This will be a love affair, our love of our "Mother" the earth, our home, of which we are a part, from which we have sprung and to which we will ultimately return. This part of the adventure actually started a long way back. To look at it unfolding, we'll rejoin the adventure when the planet earth begins to accumulate from the dust of a super-nova explosion. This dust and debris is circling about a star that began to form within the Super Nova's cooling bubble of debris.

Planet Earth has settled into a nearly circular orbit around this sun, fortunate because such an orbit maintains a rather constant distance from its source of heat and power. Gradually its gravity competes with the sun's pull and nearby flying chunks we call asteroids, meteorites or small planets are pulled crashing into its surface.

This heats up things. Inside, three other heating processes are taking place. First, the increasing pull of gravity on all of this material increases the internal pressure and raises its temperature. Secondly, some of the atomic nuclei are radioactive, and give off heat as they disintegrate. These two sources of heat eventually melt the entire planet. In this molten mix, atoms seek one another and join into more complex molecules, releasing more energy in the process. This "chemical reaction" heat is the third source of energy. The molten mix now assumes a spherical shape slightly bulging at the equator. The heavier material consisting primarily of iron and nickel sink to the center and the lighter elements rise toward the surface.

The warmer the material gets, the more chemical activity increases. Atoms of different types begin to link up with companionable types, forming the minerals we see in the rocks. By now the planet is a seething boiling mass. Bubbles of newly formed gasses such as water vapor, carbon dioxide, nitrogen, carbon monoxide, hydrogen sulfide, methane and other volatile gasses pop to the surface and start to form an atmosphere. Comets bearing more water crash into the globe.

Fortunately, by this time the mass of the planet is large enough that its gravitational pull prevents most of these gasses from flying off into space. This thin blanket of gas covers and surrounds the molten ball in a seamless blanket.

Eventually most of the free chunks of material that are in the dust cloud orbiting around the sun, are either pulled into the sun or swept up by the planets. Heating from in-crashing chunks of material decreases. Most of the vigorous chemical activity begins to subside as the materials get well mixed. Then this source of heat also subsides. The heat from disintegrating radioactive nuclei with half-lives shorter than a billion years also diminishes. Earth's surface is all the while cooling by radiating energy back to space in the form of heat waves that are radiating from the hot blanket of gas.

Eventually, parts of the surface material cool enough and crystals of mineral compounds and metals form as these new molecules exercise their affinity for one another. They link up to one another in crystalline form, forming a solid crust of stone. The heat still being generated within the molten interior causes gigantic volcanic eruptions that squirt molten material up through breaks in the crust.

Sometime in this interval a large asteroid strikes the partially molten earth a glancing blow, knocking a molten blob into an orbit around the earth, The moon is born!

The flowing semisolid mantle under the crust of rock heaves these newly formed rocks up into mountain ridges. The "boiling" action from below also pushes these islands of crusts about, smashing them into one another and pulling some parts back into the molten interior where they are re-melted.

In another several hundred million years the surface cools enough so that some of the gasses in the high reaches of the atmosphere form clouds of minute drops of liquid. These begin to fall towards the surface, only to be re-evaporated before they reach the ground below. Eventually the lower atmosphere cools to the point where these drops can fall on the surface. The first ones evaporate as soon as they hit the hot rocks below. Eventually as the rocks cool enough the drops that land can run down the upthrust. Parts of the rocks are dissolved by the liquid and carried along. Other rocks are abraded away by the rush of the flow of liquid and the particles of rock carried along with the flow.

These torrential rains continue for millions of years, wearing down the mountains and sculpturing their slopes. They wash away particles and dissolved chemicals, depositing them in the pools that are forming in the low spots. New types of rocks and mineral deposits begin to form at the bottom of these bodies of water.

By now, most of the water in the atmosphere has condensed into the seas, lakes and rivers. The sky slowly becomes transparent, and the sun's rays once again reach the surface. Higher and higher concentrations of dissolved elements and minerals are now accumulating in these oceans and lakes.

During this age of storms and rain, the waters in the atmosphere drench the land, re-evaporate and drench it again. All the while lightning storms are sending bolts of electric current through this strange mixture of gasses, forming new and previously unseen compounds of the lighter elements.

Some of these chemicals are caustic or acidic and help to eat away the rocks. Others are curious chains of hydrogen, oxygen and carbon with other lighter elements stuck on here and there. These are more fragile molecules than the minerals. The temperature of the surface of the land and the seas is now low enough that the more fragile bonds holding these compounds together are not destroyed by the heat. Today, these "organic" molecules would be rapidly eaten or absorbed by the creatures and plants of the sea. But in this epoch there is nothing to gobble them up and they continue to add to the increasingly thickening soup in the oceans and seas and ponds.

These new molecules are a different breed than the ones that form the crust of the earth. The ones that form the crust, its rocks and its minerals are very disciplined. They form precise geometrical crystal patterns when they link up with one another. These new molecules are different, They often twist and spiral, sometimes turning around on themselves, forming circles. They form long chains and often link up end-to end. Whereas minerals usually show an affinity for only their own species, these new chemicals have many hospitable sites along their structure, where other similar or even different molecules can comfortably hook-up. We call these newly appearing strangers, organic molecule. Not surprisingly, among these are the molecules that we call amino acids and nucleic acids. These are the building blocks of the structure of all living creatures, the "tinker-toys" of life.

Now we come upon one of the last great mysteries of the adventure of creation. How do these molecules ever arrange themselves into the living organic matter of this planet earth? Although it is a mystery today, the range of mystery is being narrowed from both sides of the gap. We can trace backward, the replication of primitive cells, viruses and the evolution of multicellular creatures on one side of the gap. On the other side of the gap, we can create the building blocks, the amino acids and the nucleic acids that make up a living cell. How they assembled into the first living reproducing cell remains the mystery. Its process lies beyond the cleverness of today's scientists; however clues as to the processes that were involved are abundant.

As we approach the gap we see the enormous build-up of the building blocks, the "organic"molecules that compose every living thing. On the other side of the gap are the most primitive living organisms, the bacteria and viruses, both of which contain the code for life. Stretching between the two sides of the gap are perhaps a billion years of time.

There is no possibility that the familiar organisms that inhabit earth today appeared spontaneously and fully developed. Even the most primitive organisms are too complex to have been assembled from these organic molecules in one step, by chance. The smallest primitive bacteria have a bewilderingly complex inner structure complete with strings of DNA that control their every function.

We do know that many of these new organic molecules form long chains that tend to link up with and form other and more durable structures. Other molecules can link together and form into sheets that will float on the surface of water. Still other molecules utilize helper molecules to replicate themselves from a supply of less complex and more abundant molecules. In the language of organic chemistry, these helper molecules are called enzymes. Enzymes perform nearly all of the chemical transformation in living cells and organisms. The cell manufac-tures these enzymes so that they in turn can perform all of the necessary chemical transformations and molecular assembly necessary for the operation and the reproduction of that living cell.

The relationship whereby one molecule assists another to transform itself into a new and more complex molecule, is an example of one of the fundamental emerging characteristics of an organism; interdependence for survival and growth. In the cell, DNA orchestrates the manufacture of enzymes, and enzymes facilitate the manufacture of a replica of the DNA.

We cannot know how these mutual associations developed, but what we do know is that the conditions for the endless experimentation of chemical interaction and the growth of more complex molecules increased and increased over the aeons. More and more chemicals evolved in the increasingly thick chemical soup of the oceans and seas. There is nothing to" eat" these molecules except more complex molecules that latch on to the less complex ones.

In most chemical interactions the new molecules are more stable and durable than the predecessors. Some energy is given off as these atoms unite. An input of energy is necessary to break the new assembly apart. This makes the new molecules durable. If these new chemicals are broken apart, new and different molecules are created. These in turn start a new generation of re-organization of the surrounding chemicals, and a new round of creation starts.

A living and reproducing organism, even the simplest, requires many parts, the first of which is a controlled environment that shields it from the outside environment, and at the same time allows food to enter through this barrier. In a living cell, the basis of everything that we call life, this is the cell membrane. Inside this envelope, there are a myriad of different domains that perform the necessary interrelated functions that allow the cell to live, grow, reproduce and protect itself. No one part acts in isolation, but they are all integrated into an interdependent system that works.

But let us go back more than three thousand million years ago to accompany this part of grand adventure. For hundreds of millions of years, the lifeless soup of chemicals becomes more and more concentrated. It fills all sorts of niches from the hot to the cold, from the highly salt to the nearly mineral free, from the depth of the ocean to the shallow stagnant ponds.

The immense range of conditions produced by the energy input from the sun and radioactive decay of the elements of the earth is producing an infinitude of different chemicals of increasing complexity. You can envision one chemical mediating the formation of another, and that one mediating the formation of still another and the process "loop" finally closing when the last one formed, facilitates the formation of the initial chemical. Then, a "living" system is created. If this system links with another system that has a similar circular system, an even more complex system is set up. Finally, we can envisioned several such systems finding themselves enclosed in a bubble formed by a sheet of linked up chains of identical molecules. Here they find the environment more protected and conducive to their continued existence. This precursor of a living cell could survive. Perhaps it fuses with a companionable system of similar construction in such a way that they assist one another in growth and exploitation of the "food" molecules in the surrounding liquid.

It would be hopeless to try to duplicate the multitudinous conditions that existed in the lifeless waters of the planet earth in an attempt to recreate the first living and reproducing cell. No one would have the time or the patience to await the endless experimentation of chemical association that could be explored and hope to see the creation of the first identifiable organic cell. That exact process will probably remain the great mystery of life. Possibly, it occurred only once here on earth. The evidence: all living creatures, all living cells utilize the same type of DNA chain with the same four letter code to specify its nature and control its existence and guarantee its immortality. The DNA in each living thing differs from others only in the message that is carried in its codes. If a different system did develop, it probably became extinct when it was eaten as food by this first cell species that evolved some three and a half billion years ago.

All unique and highly improbable? The recent flurry of discussion of the finding what may be the fossil traces of minute organisms in meteorites traced back to Mars, reminds us that previous explorations of Mars produced good evidence that Mars at one time had copious amounts of water and a richer atmosphere than it now does. If this record of life developing on Mars is substantiated, it will show that organic life can and will arise anywhere when the conditions are ripe and right.

With an almost unlimited food supply, and no predators, the initial cell here on planet earth, eventually learns to divide. This leads to a rapid multiplication of cells that begin to sweep the waters of nutrients. Depletion of the food supply reduces the density and the diversity of chemicals in the seas and ponds. With many fewer chemicals available, the probability of completely different forms of life based upon different genetic coding systems being formed, is greatly reduced. DNA won the race and all living things now have their heredity and systems of life preserved and transmitted through their simple four letter codes.

Though the creation of life may have been a one-time occurrence, life itself is not a one time phenomenon. The ability to replicate itself is life's one pervasive and defining characteristic. Any number of fantastically complex organizations of atoms and molecules could be assembled in the primordial soup of the early seas. Unless they had a built-in method of replicating themselves, they would eventually disappear.

No matter how difficult or tortured the path, to the point of the first reproducing organism, there is plenty of time. Nearly a billion years elapse between the time when the first rain begins to fall, and that first living cell begins to forage the seas. Then, about 3.5 billion years ago this first bacteria-like cell demonstrates its survivability. A few traces of its structure are left in one of the few rock strata that are were not remelted and reworked beyond recognition during the subsequent billions of years of upheaval and churning of surface plates.

It took a long time of trying and not getting things quite right. Then a small success, but again not quite right, and another try. The new change never seems to work out exactly right. There is some little defect, some vulnerability. Then there is some promiscuous adventuring, and some-thing new appears. If any of these new creatures got it just right, if it happened upon a rigid, stable, and flawless method of surviving, there would be no ongoing adventure. No whales or mosquitoes, no algae pumping the atmosphere up with oxygen, no humans or music. Actually living things never get things quite right, but they keep on trying with surprising results. Life holds on to its best inventions, like DNA, and plays with its endless possibilities. How many words and how many "sentences can it invent with its four letter alphabet? How many will click and produce something new? How many will be gibberish? Stick around, the invention factory is still going strong.

Although the earth is sometimes called the water planet, a long time observer might call it the algae planet. It takes at least 100 million years from the appearance of the first bacterium, for that first bacteria to change and diversify into this phenomenal successful algae creature. Not only do these single cell blue-green algae inhabit and dominate the life of the planet for a longer time than any other organism, but they do more to transform the planet than any other subsequent creature. Though primitive and prosaic, these creatures change the planet almost beyond description. The blue-green alga is the most successful of the early organisms, because it invented a molecule that can harness the power of sunlight. Before that invention, any energy necessary to promote the chemical interactions, came from molecules such as hydrogen sulfide which can give up energy when torn apart.

The chlorophyll molecules inside algae, absorb light from the sun and extract carbon dioxide from the atmosphere. In the process they belch a deadly gas called oxygen back into the atmosphere. This blue-green algae strings itself along a filament which makes it appear like beads on a necklace. It develops the ability to float on the water. These bead like strings hang together in huge mats, soaking up the sunlight and multiplying voraciously in the nutrient rich water. At first they have no predators, so their propagation is rapid and complete.

The atmosphere in which these algae emerge contains very little free oxygen because oxygen rapidly reacts with most other elements and molecules and became tied up in other compounds. The atmosphere they live in does contain large amounts of carbon dioxide. For about 2.5 billion years, the algae pump carbon dioxide out of the atmosphere and release oxygen into the atmosphere. Some of the carbon from the carbon dioxide is incorporated into the algae. Part of the carbon is incorporated in calcium carbonate and excreted into the water in copious quantities. The calcium carbonate eventually finds its way to the bottom of the seas and ponds, forming limestone deposits many thousands of feet thick. Algae eventually die and sink to the bottom. The dead algae carry carbon within them. Their decaying bodies eventually turn into oil deposits that become trapped deep within the earth under subsequent deposits of salt and silt.

Soon, a large percentage of the carbon dioxide is extracted from the atmosphere. Oxygen is released back into the atmosphere faster than it can react with other elements, and carbon is buried in the bottom of the seas. Those simple single celled creatures are singlehandedly transforming the earth and its atmosphere.

Algae dominates the seas during their 2.5 billion year reign; nearly half of the entire history of the earth! They dominate it partly because they generate oxygen which is a poison for other organisms that might compete with it for food. Gradually other organisms begin to develop a tolerance for oxygen and start to graze on the algae and on one another. They are living off the energy the algae extracts from the sunlight.

Somewhere along the line the single cell organisms invent sex. By invading or fusing with one another they begin to share their own unique genetic codes. They begin to trade their DNA with one another. Sex comes in many forms, but all forms of "sex" involve trading or sharing their DNA. This puts evolution into high gear because each union brings its uniquely different contributions to the possibilities of this new creature. When the new combination results in a compatible novelty that enhances the survivability of a newly configured creature, it becomes a new and different creature, a different species if you like. Of course, many of these adventures are failures, but the few that exhibit superior characteristics, inch the diversity and complexity of life a step forward.

The development of oxygen tolerant or oxygen breathing organisms begins a frenzy of proliferation of different species. Not only do they tolerate oxygen, but they "burn their food with this oxygen to obtain the energy that propels their growth, replication and motion. What do they eat? These new creatures eat the bodies and waste products of the sun seeker, living on the energy stored in their waste products and the bodies.

No longer must these new creature inhabit only the surface of the seas. They can make their home in more protected regions. It no longer is required to wait patiently in open areas for the sun to provide its energy and the carbon dioxide in the air to provide its nourishment They now have the freedom to seek new habitations. They use the ingested chemicals from the sun seekers to form new and different and useful exotic forms of the chemicals of life.

Now multicellular organisms begin to experiment with the usefulness of living in a symbiotic relationship with other different organisms, each different cell providing an important factor. One produces a protective shield, while the other provides a useful waste product for its companion. Dividing cells no longer go off on their own, but attach to one another if this helps the colony to prosper. Meanwhile, the adjacent cells often merge and share their DNA and its useful information. Then the cell begins to perform a variety of functions that may make it even more useful to the colony.

Some multicellular creatures find ways of causing some of their cells to change their structure and their function. These different cells become organs, skin, or any of the many specialized cells the organism finds necessary to flourish and function. DNA instructs the cell how and when to make those important chemicals that cause the cells to alter their form and function. It sends chemical messengers that escape through the cell membrane. These messengers go out to other cells in the assembly of cells to tell them how they are doing and instruct the specialized cells or organs to stop or speed up their specialized operations.

Those successful organisms find unlimited grazing in the sea and they have few if any predators. This living realm now enters a new era, the age of rapidly spreading diversity. It is impelled by the necessity of survival in a realm where food can only come from hunting and eating other species or scavenging on their remains.

Multi-celled organisms now begin to experiment. Specialized organisms develop that adapt themselves to life in every conceivable viable niche of their environment, from the coldest lakes to the hot volcanic vents at the bottom of the seas. Some even adapt to the varying temperatures and moisture of the tide lands of the seas, and then venture onto land.

It is tempting to view this gradual evolution and diversification as a journey to produce higher and more complex organisms with the goal of producing humankind as its crowning achievement. Instead, it has the characteristics of a multi-fingered adventure to produce whatever can adapt and survive in every conceivable environment. It fans out and branches in literally millions of different directions. Some are dead ends that cannot survive the competition of new invaders. Many others change and adapt to changing circumstances, while still others are obliterated by catastrophes. Many survive by being small and unobtrusive, while others thrive by being large, complex and mobile.

The record of the creatures inhabiting earth in these early days will eventually be found imbedded in rocks. Bones, shells and tracks and fossilized bodies will be the most prominent clues. The soft bodied creatures that inhabit the seas and land in this early stages of proliferation of life-forms will leave precious few clues about their identity. Most of these creatures will decay before they can be transformed into fossils; those intriguing relics in which waterborne minerals replace, one by one, the atoms in the fragile molecules of the dead organism. Without these fossil relics, future seekers of their identity will find no clues as to their form, function or even their existence.

One fortunate record of the immense diversity of these soft creatures living more than half a billion years ago will be in the Burgess Shale deposits in British Columbia. As might be expected here are the fossils of trilobite that dominated the fossil record of that geological age. Trilobite are readily preserved as fossils because of their hard shells.

But, to the surprise of present day paleontologists, over one hundred other distinct "families" of creatures seem to be revealed in this Burgess shale. Most of these families were previously unknown and undiscovered. Weird creatures with five eyes, some with mouths like bellows, creatures with forms that you could not imagine in your wildest nightmares were discovered. Only one of those families has a design with its nervous system conveyed through a spinal cord. This is now a characteristic of all animals, including fishes and humans. All of this great diversity recorded in the Burgess shale, explodes in the relative short span of less than a hundred million years as the oxygen content of the planet is rising.

Great and cataclysmic events are continuing to assault the surface of the earth. Only ten of these families of creatures discovered in the Burgess Shale will survive. The other hundred or more will completely disappear. The fossil record will reveal massive extinctions of living creatures occurring periodically through the long history of this planet. In these extinction events, a majority of the families of species of and a majority of the individual species that have evolved of both plant and animal life just abruptly disappear. Their complete demise and rapid disappearance can only be caused by some event with world-wide effects. You only need take a look at the full moon with its tremendous size craters caused by the impact of meteors and asteroids to get a clue to the most probable cause of these extinctions. These gigantic projectiles are also impacting the earth at a tremendous speed during this era. Some of the asteroids that are still orbiting the solar system will undoubtedly collide with the earth in the future, producing similar extinction episodes.

Even small changes caused by unusual events will have serious effects on life on the planet. Today we worry about a few percent change in the carbon dioxide level of the atmosphere or the disappearance of a thin ozone layer in the stratosphere. These small changes have the potential of making earth uninhabitable for humans. The consequences of a meteor, asteroid or comet the size of a large mountain hitting the earth could produce far worse consequences. Such an impact could inject dust clouds into the atmosphere that would block the sunlight for years, ignite fires that would consume all growing plants, produce a prolonged winter that would freeze warm blooded creatures, and pollute the seas lakes and coastal waters where nearly all ocean life lives. Landing in the seas, it could produce steam clouds that would blot out the sun and send tsunami waves across continents and islands.

Large volcanic eruptions and explosions periodically belch hundreds of cubic miles of rock and dust into the atmosphere, along with comparable large amounts of hydrogen sulphide and carbon dioxide. The creatures and organisms that survive these catastrophic events live on to define the biosphere of the future. Such are the forces changing the course of evolution. With the majority of species wiped out by these cataclysmic events, the whole web of life has to be readjusted. Many more cannot cope with life because their symbiotic partners in this web of life are missing, and they too die off. The survivors adapt to the new environment and resume their adventure of re-inhabiting the planet.

The Cosmic Deity

Before going forward on our travels with the adventure of creation of the earth and its biosphere, let us stop and review the basic characteristics of creation discussed in previous chapters. These are the affinities, the organizational relationships that determine the realities, the stability that preserved the new creations, the instabilities that forced change, the replication processes, and the emerging characteristics of the creation.

Without the affinities, atoms of different types would not link with one another to form the tenacious bonds that are necessary to provide the strength and form of any of the parts of these new creatures. The assembly of the four simple bases of DNA into a long spiral chain was the key to the development of life. This development illustrates three of the basic characteristics of creation; organization defining the reality, stability resulting from remembering and preserving the new creation, and instability that promotes change.

The ability of DNA to take on additional information and be altered and "edited" is an example of the function of instability that it possesses which facilitates change. The DNA of even the simplest single cell is far too complex to have been assembled one "word" at a time in the billion years that it took for the first bacterial cell to develop. This has puzzled scientists ever since DNA and its mechanisms were discovered. Possibly an analogy to the computer industry can shed some light.

Super Computers are used when great and massively complicated mathematical problems have to be solved. These were first developed to process the information one step at a time at higher and higher speeds. Massive memory banks were developed to store and quickly access the data as it was created and manipulated. Recently, it was found that many of these complex jobs could be done just as fast and just as accurately by tying a large number of small desk top computers together in a parallel network. In this network, each of the computers was working on a different part of the problem simultaneously. The data are finally collected from all of the computers. Then the results of their effort is combined to form the answer.

The first replicating living cell line has a long "gestation" period. It lasts for about a billion years. Untold trillions of prototype cells are independently experimenting and adding bits of information to their own DNA. They experiment with merging with one another in different ways, adding the information of their DNA to the newly modified organism, a bit tacked on here, a bit there. Most of these additions are fatal to the cell but a few survive. Now they continue to merge with or trade DNA with their neighbors. Viruses still do this. They pickup a gene or two in a cell that they invade, and take it along to drop it into a new host cell. These newly modified cells with their newly modified genetic code are all working in parallel. They appropriate any "good information," adding it to the library or recipe, discarding or rearranging the rest.

One of the rapidly developing industries today utilizes just this technique, the field of genetic engineering. This industry has developed methods of cutting particular genes out of DNA and inserting them into a primitive bacteria, causing the bacteria to produce a needed or wanted protein such as insulin. It is sort of a messy process. First, DNA is cut into many fragments. Then, the technicians introduce these fragments into bacteria, infecting them with new genes. The individual bacteria are then grown and made to multiply in a special chemical soup. The ones that successfully produce the wanted chemical are selected for further use. Next, they "farm" these newly altered bacteria in large vats of the proper chemical soup, and harvest the wanted chemicals that they produce.

Another realm of genetic engineering is to insert the DNA word of a particular gene into a bacteria and then infect a plant or animal with this bacteria. The bacteria in turn inserts the gene into some of the host's cells and alters their function. If it enters the host reproductive cells, this new trait is added to the host cells DNA and is passed on to future generations.

This addition of DNA knowledge produced in other cells and added on to the DNA of still another species is akin the parallel computer solution to solving massive problems with simple machines. Similar transfers and additions of DNA information is going on during this billion year gestation. It continues after that first reproducing living cell begins its three and a half billion years of explosive diversification that results in the millions of living species in our world today. DNA information is building up, it is being copied untold trillions of times. It is added to and discarded from existing strings, and accumulates the information and knowledge to replicate its successful ventures.

Nature performed similar exercises in gene transplant in the past. Through the wide variety of "sexual" activities, these fragments of DNA are exchanged and appropriated. Natural selection preserved the more vigorous and survivable strains and added complexity to the storehouse of DNA information. In such a way, millions of changes were invented and added bit by bit to the genetic code in one organism and added to the genetic code developed by other organisms. The "parallel processing" of DNA information undoubtedly produced the more complex DNA codes that led to the development and survivability of our ancestors.

Knowledge is the new property of creation that is emerging. DNA remembers the successful ventures and preserves the information as to how a cell can use that information in the future. It undoubtedly remembers many things that are not necessarily useful. It appears that the DNA of humans has many genes that are never expressed in any cell of the body, but are there for "future reference." Possibly some of the knowledge is lodged in the other parts of the cell, and this knowledge prevents the cell from reading that particular gene because its use might be harmful. Cells selectively read the DNA code all of the time. A skin cell doesn't read the same genes that the liver cell does, and consequently each cell behaves differently in the body.

Communication is, another new emergent property of living things. We humans really use this one. Communication, is one of the major inventions of these the first primitive cells. When cells begin to reproduce by dividing, some float free while others find it advantageous to hang together. Communication between more than a few cells becomes a problem if they are to work together. If it were not advantageous for them to work together, the multicellular adventure wouldn't have worked and survived. The solution to cooperative association of multi-cell creatures is the evolution of communication systems, a property that all of these newer and more complex creatures posses.

Chemical messengers are the first means of communication. Even in the higher organisms, they still remain the major means of communication between cells and between organs. One cell manufactures and sends out a messenger that it transcribes from its DNA. It is designed to leave the cell and be taken by various means to another cell where it will leave a distinctive calling card or be taken into the other cell as a messenger and not as food. This messenger triggers the DNA in the receiving cell to produce a new chemical that alters its growth or function. Thousands of different types of messenger cells that we call hormones are continually circulating through our bodies to keep us functioning properly. Some go directly from cell to cell, while others travel through the blood or lymph or other similar circulatory systems that the organisms devise.

In our own bodies, the chemical messenger process starts out when the fertilized egg cell divides and our embryo begins to develop. Chemical messengers preside at each step in the division of cells and at each change of the structure of the dividing cells. Other messengers are dispatched to instruct the DNA of new cells to develop into the specialized cells and organs of the body. These messengers convey instructions to turn on the proper genes in the new cells to start the changes and to time the occurrences of these changes that produce the cells of new organs. The entire process of body building, maintenance and repair is accomplished by using these chemical messengers. They instruct the cells how to change in order to form our extremities, and determine how the cells in the brain organize themselves so that we can become a functioning human being. This is why it is so important that pregnant women be careful of what they eat. If unnatural chemicals manage to get to the developing embryo, they can mimic the messenger hormones and send the development of the child off on a distorted path. The chemical messenger system is so complete and so comprehensive in maintaining body growth, repair, immunity from invaders and the processing of food, that a person can be "brain dead" and still continue living on without benefit of most of the nervous system of the brain.

The chemical messenger system has its limitations. When organisms become larger and more complex, those that can move often survive better than stationary creatures. If they move, they can find more food or escape predators intent on eating them. Single cells find that by flexing or squeezing themselves they can control their motion. Multi-celled creatures find that they can move by waving their appendage cells. They achieve this motion by sending chemical messengers to their appropriate cells.

Eventually, the creatures get so big that the chemical messengers are too slow or the messages become ambiguous. They overcome this problem by developing nerve cells. These cells create a chemical reaction that generates an electrical impulses that travels rapidly to other parts of the organism through chains of these nerve cells. Now electrical messengers are rapidly transmitting messages to specific targeted areas within the organism. This new messenger system is more rapid and precise than chemical messengers.

Cells develop an ability early on to react either favorably or unfavorably to chemicals with which they come in contact. Originally these reactions with foreign chemicals, result in chemical messengers that are sent throughout the organism, but later some of these reactions were transferred to the nerve chains and the reaction could be made more rapidly. These were the beginnings of the sensory system of nerves as contrasted with communication systems that produce control or motion.

All of this information about how to react to stimulus, is stored in the DNA modifications. Eventually the nerve cells develop an interacting structure and a central nerve structure, that could not only store information received, but could react through a different set of nerve channels that promoted rapid motion of parts of the organism. We call this central nervous system a brain. The DNA remembers how it formed this brain, and forms similar or more sophisticated networks in the next generations. If we or any other type of organism had to learn the proper reaction to every sensory input every time it happened, our life would be more chaotic and less stable. Therefore, the memory of the brain is one of the new emerging characteristics that increases the stability and durability of an organism and contributes a lot to its survivability. The changes in the DNA recipe that created the system of the brain, are in turn being remembered, stored and passed on to succeeding generations in its DNA.

A new and different system of memory is also emerging. This is a temporary memory that remembers incidents and experiences. This memory is temporalty and is unique to that brain and survives only as long as the brain survives. It remembers the experiences of that particular creature and enhances its survivability. This new type of memory increases the stability and the versatility of the individual, since its experiences are unique to that individual and relate to its specific environment and experiences.

Sight is one of the next significant developments in the evolutionary process. Sight is unique to animals. It evolves as a result of the prey-predator relationship of animals. For those who can not detect a predator till the predator is touching it, life is short. For those who can not efficiently detect prey or food at a distance, life is meager. Plants that forage the air and the ground are fixed in position. They have no need or use for sight. They can neither move to escape their predators nor move about to find a source of food. In a way that is a shame, since flowers and trees cannot appreciate their own beauty, grace and color, or appreciate it in their kin and their surroundings.

Sight is a unique process. It consists of catching photons of light and organizing them in a manner that represents the shape and position of objects from which the photons were reflected. The next step is to detect and utilize the energy in each photon and generate a nerve impulse. This stimulation is next sent to the brain where it is interpreted as an image. To see, first requires some sort of a lens. Without a lens, there is no seeing of objects, just shadows or reflected glints of light can be detected. Many primitive organisms develop simple light sensor cells that alert them to the shadow of an approaching predator or detect the shadow of an object under which they can hide, but they cannot "see" objects. A lens is necessary to create a useful image of the surrounding area.

Photons of light are arrowing through all of space from every direction. They contain information about where they are coming from and how much energy they posses. The process of sight is to select only those photons of light that are coming from objects that we wish to see and to make sense of the information that they convey.

If you hold up a photographic film, it will record light that is landing all over it, but it will not record an image of any object. Place a lens in front of it, and it can record an image of all objects that the lens focuses on the plane of the film. Turn off the light and the film will record nothing.

A lens can be something as unsophisticated as a pinhole spaced some distance from a light receptor. It can be an assembly of small lenses such as some insects possess, or it can be a variable focus lens like the one in the human eye. The part of the eye that detects the photons of light must have a large array of detectors which can separately detect the amount of light landing on each part its sensitive area. The tiny separate grains of silver chloride on a film, perform this function. In the eye of a creature, an array of light-detecting nerve cells develop nerve impulses that are transmitted to an array of cells in the brain where they are interpreted by the brain as an image of objects in front of the lens.

Seeing is so fundamental and important to the life of mobile creatures, that it rapidly evolves to an incredible degree of sensitivity. The energy of a single photon of light is slight, and it would not produce a usable nerve pulse. The eye has an amplifier in each tiny detector cell in the retina. When a photon of light is absorbed in that detector cell, the energy of that photon causes a molecule in the cell wall to contract and close up a hole in the cell wall for a short period of time. During this brief interval, thousands of ionized molecules that normally flow out of the cell through this hole, accumulate in the cell and build up an electrical charge sufficient to generate a usable nerve pulse. Nature pre-dated the electronic amplifier by at least a billion years!

Sight is a very specific operation. It involves detecting light energy, it requires a lens to focus the light and it requires a brain that is conditioned to store and analyze the nerve impulses from the detectors in the eye. Stories of out-of-body experiences where a person has claimed to have left his or her body and seen either his own body or other objects on a journey away from the body are patently absurd. Those elements necessary for sight (the detection of reflected light rays that must be oriented in a two dimensional image by a lens) must be in place at the proper vantage place for actual seeing to take place. You might ask if the lens of the eye accompanies the out of body traveler.

By the time that common fossil animal, the trilobite, develops - nearly 600 million years ago - evolution has covered an amazing amount of ground. Eyes and brains, digestive systems and legs, nerves and a circulating system are already developed. There is more evolutionary distance between a trilobite and the basic chemicals of life, than there is between a human and a trilobite. Human development was an embellishment on the theme that was developing over the billions of years since organized life began to organize the chemicals of life into enduring organisms.

But enough of these details of creation's adventure. Let's back off and take a look on a larger scale. Lets speed up the time. As soon as the first self replicating organism establishes itself and begins to use up the nutrients around it, its progeny sweep out across the waters of the globe in successive waves, changing and adapting as they encounter new and strange environments. These newer and more vigorous adaptations, sweep back across the seas like a wave rebounding from a cliff and devour their prototypes, merge with some of them to make a new and more adaptable creature, form a cooperative living arrangement with others and share their genetic information with others by sexual union. Powered and warmed by the sun, they multiply and divide as they explore all of the niches of the surface of the globe. They feed on the organic molecules fused together by the aeons of lightning laced storms that accompany the condensations of the steam laden atmosphere, which was in turn boiled off by the hot core of the earth. They extract the atoms and molecules eroded from the land.

All this action occurs to the accompanying ferment of the mantle and crust of the earth. There is scarcely a remnant of the original continents discernable on the surface of the earth. The mountains of today consist of fourth and fifth generation rocks that have gone through erosion, remelting, subduction and uplifting, been spewed out of volcanoes and packed together in the bottoms of the seas.

All through the greater part of this titanic upheaval and metamorphosis of the land, the living creatures adapt, survive, multiply and increase in complexity. Their complexity increase is not only in their structure but in their interdependence, creating an ecosystem that adapts and changes with the changes in its members as well as the changes on the surface of the earth and its waters. For long periods of time, a particular species dominates, like the blue-green algae. Later it is the trilobite. It was trilobite everywhere, big and small, primitive and sophisticated, because nothing significant challenges their rule for untold millions of years.

In spite of the upheavals and the transformation of the land, the sea remains relatively stable. It hosts a blizzard of proliferation of new creatures, an explosion of creativity. Apparently every avenue is explored during these billions of years, and is tested for its viability in the developing ecosystems of the deep and shallow seas.

When the blue-green algae releases enough oxygen into the atmosphere to block most of the ultraviolet light from the sun, the dry surface of the land becomes habitable by plants. They gradually colonize the tide lands and later the dryer areas, sending tentacles down through the soil to find the mineral nutrients they require and the water trapped under the dryer surface. The plants proliferate with the abundance of carbon dioxide in the air. By simple division and growth, by pores and seeds, they rapidly invade the hospitable and sometimes not so hospitable land, and continue the job of carbon dioxide removal. Plants permanently remove some of the carbon from the atmosphere by burying it in undecayed form in swamps and lakes. These deposits are later covered over and sealed by sediments to become earth's coal and oil deposits. The success of plants is aided by the lack of predators. Only later, after the amphibians which could inhabit either the land or the seas evolve into dinosaur like creatures, are there any significant number of grazers of the plants on land.

Millions of different distinct species exist. In the water, plankton has the most diversity. Today, on the land it is the insects. Each of these two families outweighs, in total weight, the aggregate weight of its predators by several hundred times. The plant species are often neglected when surveying the majesty and diversity of the creation. After all they just sit there and don't engage in all of the fascinating activities that animal-like creatures do, such as swim, run, and fly, or build nests, homes, airplanes, space probes and television systems.

Plant diversity is equal to the diversity of any of the other realms of life. From grasses to algae, from giant redwoods to mosses, they form an ecological system all their own. They are the base of supply of the food chain for all of the creatures and plants that don't have chlorophyll in their cells. They are the larder of the earth. If they die, so do all the other creatures; those that rely on the energy the plants extract from sunlight and store in their molecules that in turn nourish the other creatures right up the food chain. Not only that, they are less fragile than most creatures. They survive and sometimes thrive by losing parts of themselves to their foragers. Indeed, they often encourage these depredations by enticing the theft of their seeds or leaves as a means of propagating themselves.

The first living thing any visitor will see approaching planet earth is the green canopy of forests and then the great expanses of grassland. Only upon very close examination would any creatures be seen. Other planets may have water and seas, but probably very few have green carpets covering the undulating land. The diversity, the color, the extreme range in size and the durability of the plant life would impress the visitor. The unabashed sexual displays of the flowers, enticing their pollinators with their wonderful colors and intricate forms, would thrill any visitor with a poetic heart. Their incessant production of sugars, starches and cellulose from water from the ground and carbon dioxide from the air would seem a miracle to those not privy to the internal working of its cells and the agility of the chlorophyll molecule as it extracts the energy of a photon and ties it up in a molecule of sugar.

The single cell algae and the largest living thing, the giant sequoia, bracket the ranges in size. The diversity from cactus to water lily illustrate the adaptability to the planet's climes.

Under the seas, the proliferation of life goes on, fed by the sun loving plants and algae living in the upper levels of the water. Dive down along a coral reef and see the diversity of creatures. Observe the shellfish, the myriads of coral animals living in colonies, and the endless streams of colorful and seemingly fancifully designed fish gliding by. Dig in the mud and find the rich life and unexpected diversity of worms, shrimp and shellfish. Then you will get an idea of the tremendous diversity and beauty throbbing in this undersea laboratory of evolution. But momentous things are also happening upon the land after the plants establish their dominion.

Animal life has moved from the sea to the land. As we look about, we might be tempted to characterize the world by its animal inhabitants. Then ours would be called the Dinosaur planet. The dinosaurs are the most prominent and enduring animal group to ever inhabit earth. For more than 160 million years, the various dinosaurs range the waters, swamps and land on all of the continents. They vary in size from a chicken to lumbering giants of a hundred tons. They are everywhere and dominate the ecology of the land. They evolve from lizards. Eventually some of them become warm blooded and develop feathers, the precursors of birds.

About 65 million years ago, all dinosaurs disappear completely from all of the continents of the earth, along with nearly half of the other species that co-inhabited the land and lesser numbers that inhabited the seas. Today, there is good and compelling evidence that this extinction is caused by the impact of a large meteor or by a tremendous series of unprecedented volcano eruptions. But life is tenacious, and small mammals, marsupials and birds reclaimed the land and seas and evolve into the tremendous diversity that we can catalogue today.

Look at all of these realms, the underseas realm, the plants, the animals. Nowhere can you see a direction or a goal, no channeling of effort to produce a single final crowning achievement. All that is evident is the multi-pronged adventure into every niche and climate. Every course is explored. Every avenue is tested, every beneficial association with other species is tried and capitalized upon. Like the succeeding cascades of sparklers thrown out by a firework display in the skies, producing streamers that in turn produce bursts of streamers, the path of life on earth explodes across the landscape and beneath the sea.

Like a real-life laboratory, most experiments are unfruitful, and die out, to be remembered if at all, only in the fossil record. Others run into dead ends like the horseshoe crab, which survives unchanged for over 200 million years. But there are always the new and the more complex creatures coming along, testing their viability, fitting into the organization of the other living things on which they must depend and interact, and adding their fruitful results to the libraries of information sequestered in the strands of DNA.

These newer and more complex creatures are the most fragile species. Like a complicated piece of machinery, they can perform seemingly miraculous functions, but they are more prone to break-down. They are vulnerable in many places and require a more diverse environment than smaller and less complicated species. Being new, they must "learn" to survive in a new environment that their presence modifies.

Viewed from the past, the course is divergent. Branches take off and re-branch and then re-branch again. Sometimes converging and sometimes dying, but ever expanding ever exploring as they adventure off on a new path. The backward path can be followed with a good deal of diligence, but there is no prediction, looking forward from the origins, as to where any new branch will go.

Something else is going on here besides the independent development of species. Something different from just the bigger creatures gobbling up the littler ones. An interdependency is developing. This interdependency we call an ecosystem. An ecosystem is a system of life in which each species not only benefits from the association with other forms of life, but may often actually require other species for its survival. There are no tangible ties or links between these creatures or plants. No chemical bonds or inherited DNA. No electrical or gravitational forces. This ecosystem depends entirely upon the relationships and the interactions between the various members and the environment in which they exist. The ecosystem is the organization within which they function. This organization is not imposed upon it but arises from the individual relationships that develop between the individual members. It is a system that requires each member as a crucial part. If any part or any relationship is altered, the ecosystem must adapt to the change or be diminished as a result.

Each species of organism is usually considered complete within itself. It is not just a bag of cells that seem to get along well living with one another, but there is a complete mutual dependence of each part on every other part. Its identity, its function and its survival depend upon each part doing its job in concert with each other part. No one part can exist on its own. We call it a living organism when the system works, when the atoms and molecules flow into it and out of it as it grows. It operates its internal systems, repairs its damage and replaces worn-out parts. When one part or system operating within the organism fails, and the organism isn't able to re-establish or repair the structure, or it hasn't developed a backup system that allows the system to continue to operate, the organism dies.

An ecosystem is similar to an organism, but it has no means of replicating itself. It has no internal formula or recipe to guide its organization and shape its interrelated activities. The individual species develop within the ecosystem and are in turn dependent upon it. If they cannot adapt to changes in the ecosystem, they die and others more adaptable take their place, and the ecosystem lives on. If the ecosystem is too severely disrupted, there is a good possibility that the entire system will collapse and in effect die, as it has in isolated areas of the world. When a lake becomes contaminated by acid rain, this change in the chemical balance eventually produces a sterile lake devoid of most plant and animal life. When one or more of the critical parts in the ecosystem dies because it cannot tolerate the increased acid, the entire ecosystem of the lake is disrupted. Even the species that can tolerate the acid die off because an important part of their circle of life is now missing.

Interrelationships are not just one way or even two way streets. Each part acts upon many other diverse parts, which in turn react and interact with even different parts. Eventually the results of these interactions ricochet through most of the entire system. The reverberations come back in the forms of ties and dependency that link the organisms more closely together in their interdependence. The paths may be circular elliptical or spider web in form, but they effectively bind each piece into the function of the ecosystem. Pull on one thing and you find that it is tied to all of the rest.

Ecosystems are powerful things. They transformed the atmosphere of the earth, changed its climate by absorbing sunlight, changed rainfall patterns and established a nursery for the development and nurture of new life forms. Yet they are merely an organization of the patterns of life that exist within them. They accomplish more than individual creatures could accomplish, and establish the environment for all of its inhabitants to exist. The reality of the ecosystem is its organization, its dynamic interrelationships that are ever changing and ever adapting, even adapting to changes wrought by its own activity.

We now reach a subject, near and dear to our own hearts, the human adventure.

Chapter 12 Bibliography

Alvarez, Walter, and Frank Asaro, *What Caused The Mass Extinction?*, Scientific American, 263:76-77, October 1990. The most probable cause of the extinction of the Dinosaurs.

Childress, James J., Horst Felbeck and George N. Somero, *Symbiosis in the Deep Sea*, Scientific American, 256:115-120, May 1987. Merging of organisms and trading of genomes lead to major changes in the course of evolution.

Felsenfeld, Gary, *DNA:* Scientific American, 253:58-67, October 1985. The genetic material's double helix, the fundamental molecule of life, is variable and also flexible. It interacts with regulatory proteins and other molecules to transfer its hereditary message.

Gould, Stephen Jay, ed., *The Book Of Life*, New York, W. W. Norton & Company, 1993. An overview of life bewildering variety of forms and the probable events that created new opportunities for new life forms.

_____, *The Evolution Of Life On The Earth*, Scientific American, 271:84-91, October, 1994. Evolution of life didn't progress at an even pace. Difference in the equilibrium of life created opportunities for new explosions of variety of organisms.

Herbert, Sandra, *Darwin As A Geologist*, Scientific American, 254:116-123, May, 1986. Darwin's first interest in the changes in the creation centered on changes in the geological record, which spurred his investigations into the possible evolution of life.

Hillis, W. Daniel, *The Connection Machine*, Scientific American, 256:108-115, June, 1987.

Levinton, Jeffrey S., *The Big Bang Of Animal Evolution*, Scientific American, 267:84-91, November, 1992. The events that led to the explosion of multicellular organisms and animals.

Lovelock, J. E., *Gaia:* Oxford, U.K., Oxford University Press, 1979. A New Look At Life On Earth. Looking at the web of life as an organism.

Margulis, Lynn and Sagan, Dorion, *Acquiring Genomes* ,New York, Basic Books, 2002. Trading or acquiring genomes from other organisms seem to be the main origin of new species.

Margulis, Lynn and Fester, Rene Margulis, *Symbiosis as a Source of Evolutionary Innovation,* Massachusetts Institute of Technology, 1991. Species living in a close symbiotic relationship can trade genes and genomes leading to new species and evolutionary change.

Mullins, Kary B., *The Unusual Origin Of The Polymerase Chain Reaction*, Scientific American, 262:56-65, April, 1990. A simple system that shows how DNA replicates itself. This system is now used in all DNA analysis work.

Orgel, Leslie E., *The Origin Of Life On The Earth*, Scientific American, 271:76-83, October, 1994.

Rebek, Julius Jr., *Synthetic Self-Replicating Molecules*, Scientific American, 271:48-55, July, 1994.

Stryer, Lubert, *The Molecules of Visual Excitation*, Scientific American, 257:42-50, July 1987. Three articles illustrate the processes that enabled the evolution of humans and other creatures.

Chapter 13

The Human Adventure

As we near the end of our exploration of the adventures of that organic film on planet earth, we see something near and dear to our hearts; the human species. Fossils record the bones of creatures akin to humans living about a million years ago. Humans are an incredibly successful species. In a short span of time, humans have dominated the planet not only in numbers but in their ability to master and alter the planet to suit their needs and desires.

We see that humans have several characteristics that are slightly different from some of the earlier members of their family tree. Our bones are shaped so we can walk upright. Our thumbs are more agile, enabling them to better manipulate the tools which we invent. Our larger brain cavity holds a larger and more complex brain that can make better use of their other physical characteristics.

Somewhere along the line a more striking characteristic developed. This is the ability to articulate sounds and ability to move from ambiguous grunts to sounds that convey a more specific meaning. The miraculous appearing emergent property is the development of language. Language not only provides a relatively unambiguous means of communication, but it allows the development of abstract thought.

But do we see anything fundamentally different? Don't we use the same DNA code to orchestrate our bodies as the other members of their family tree? Aren't our bones and teeth made of the same type cells and mineral deposits as their cousins? Is this ability to manipulate sounds into languages one of our major advantages? When we developed the ability to mutually agree on the meaning of these sounds and how they can be organized to have meanings beyond just signs of danger and the presence of food, didn't it give us the ability to survive in an environment populated with more agile and strong predators?

We were quite adaptable as early humans. We slowly migrated to new parts of the world, inhabiting new and unusual environments, ranging from dense jungles to desert oasis. We endured ice ages that wipe out other less adaptable species. We survived on isolated islands and adapted to extracting food from the seas. We followed the herds of migrating animals on which we lived, and found ourselves living in the harsh arctic, the grassy plains and the high mountain meadows.

We seemed to be clearly more adaptable than our nearest relatives, the chimpanzees with whom we share 98 % of our DNA code. This small difference in DNA and its different orchestration in the human body leads to a different throat, tongue, and vocal passages in we humans that makes us more versatile in forming sounds. But more importantly, the human brain seems to be uniquely oriented to forming and understanding language, articulating it in speech and participating in abstract thought.

All of these factors seem to be crucial to the adaptability and the survivability of early humans. They survived and adapted because they developed a new type of ecology, the ability to form cohesive societies which in turn developed the strategies for survival and adaptability. All of this depended upon the increasing ability to form languages, communicate thought and plan the future based upon past experiences and memories.

Language is adding a new dimension to the creation. Language permits the communication of knowledge and the ability to preserve knowledge, but more importantly, it allows the brain to have a mechanism for organizing this knowledge, reflecting upon it, developing scenarios of past and future action and communicating then this to others in an understandable manner.

Language allows knowledge to be transported across the gap between individuals instead of being conveyed only through successive generations. The accumulation of knowledge, preserved in chants, songs, legends and eventually written words gave humans a tremendous advantage over creatures who had to learn individually by trial and error. Think for a minute how you have obtained knowledge, and how it was passed on to you. Remember how you pass knowledge to others. Contrast that to the way that you perceive animals acquire knowledge and pass it along to their fellow creatures.

A significant difference between the early humans and their predecessors, which can be discerned in fossils, lies in the size of the brain. What cannot be divined from fossils is the difference in brain cell organization. This makes a tremendous difference in how the brain functions and in its capacity for versatility. The increased brain size permits more storage of memories that contribute to the range of thought that can be processed. The inventiveness and the unique internal hookups in the brain of the human has produced speech, languages, and developed the techniques and the will to build the pyramids and space ships that travel to the moon. It has invented mathematics to order and quantify the processes of life and the mechanisms of the universe. It invents machines to do its work, powered by the energy stored in the earth and in the atom, and orders its societies and communities according to laws and customs.

For good and bad, it has changed the face of the world and altered the ecology in far reaching ways, putting its imprint on the face of the earth more rapidly than any other species or family of life. Part of the success of the human species has been its survivability. Humans now number over six billion. This weight of humanity has an **enormous** influence on both the micro-environment of individuals as well as the whole exosphere. It might be well to pause here and realize that the ecosystem of the world can survive very well without humans. Humans cannot survive without the exosphere of the world.

We might indulge in some self congratulation here and claim that humans are a cut above the other creatures, that early humans represent a major discontinuity between themselves and previous creatures. People who live with and study chimpanzees and gorillas chip away at these preconceived notions. They are discovering the ability of these creatures to express feelings, desires and emotions, and the ability to comprehend and use simple languages employing other representations rather than alphabets and spelled-out words. Aren't humans then an extension of that continuum extending back some hundreds of millions of years?

But humans are different. Now, instead of just reacting to one another, humans can communicate. They can share their observations, exchange information, plan to act in concert with one another and establish working relationships between members of the community that share this common language. In short, they can establish a human society that in turn can accomplish far more than individuals acting in isolation.

When a working solution to a problem or to the survival of the group is established, the solution is remembered and passed on through oral traditions, taboos, and customs. Often, imagery has been used to created a reminder of the important discoveries of human relationships.

These legends, art and song are part of the heritage created. Those traditions have become the "DNA" of human societies - traditions that can be passed on to others, ideas that can be changed and enlarged upon as society becomes more complex.

If we could observe the human adventure as it unfolds, we would see inventiveness flourishing. Writing might seem to be a minor invention, but it established a new degree of stability. Writing is more accurate than the oral tradition and it outlasts the memory of a human. Mathematics was invented to keep track of numbers and to quantify concepts. Rather than convey an observation of a lot of deer in the meadow, it allowed one to specify that there were seven deer in the meadow. Later, mathematics were used to show the validity of something, a proof. It took abstract ideas (a new form of thought) and put them into a form that could be examined and confirmed or denied, showing whether something was false or true.

Now our focus shifts to a new phenomena involving humans. We see all of these new characteristics of humans; self-awareness, memory, language, speech, writing, and mathematics beginning to be utilized in concert to develop more complex societies and to manipulate the world and its ecology. Systems of agriculture and animal husbandry, shelter building, the manufacture of materials from the earth's resources, channeling of water for irrigation, the development of schools for passing on knowledge and the skills of thinking and analyzing information are being created. These in turn stimulate new thinking and the creation of new social structures and new vocations.

As societies enlarge and grow, the structure of society protects and nurtures the new arrivals. Cultures grow through the hurly-burly of conquest and assimilation, changing dramatically as the new components of the merged societies add their "cultural DNA" to the storehouse of knowledge. The reality of the new patterns of organization of the society begins to affect the society itself and its environment. Societies modify and adapt to the problems created by their growth and increasing complexity and by the furious build-up of interactions between its members. But they work, they endure and prosper in direct relationship to their adaptability. Flexibility and the ability to change are just as important to their vigor as was the durability of the rules, laws, and customs that they had codified into the language of written laws and traditions.

Another dimension of life arose from the expanded capacity of the human brain. This is the life of the intellect, the ability to speculate and to create. Along with this comes the ability to study oneself and to understand how the human body and mind operate. It includes the ability to create music, art, philosophy, literature, abstract mathematics and theoretical physics. The propensity to develop religions which explain and relate the human to its society and to the adventure of creation seems to be an universal trend.

Being able to envision a future, to imagine scenarios about future actions and their results is a relatively new characteristics that humans exploit. This is undoubtedly aided by the language facility that puts words to the images and the action scenarios.

These activities are in a class by themselves. They more cleanly delineate humans from their predecessors than do their physical characteristics and mechanical abilities. They create an entire new realm of reality. In themselves they have no tangible form, Our distant ancestors didn't leave fossils records of these activity imbedded in the fossil record. Only in the last thousands of these millions of years do we find paintings on the walls and carvings, signifying this type of mental activity in our ancestors.

Up to this point in the adventure, the activity has been primarily between things, objects and the forces of nature. Now we can discern abstract concepts operating on one another, using the human brain as its communicating and organizing mechanism. Ideas *together with life situations* stimulate other ideas. One idea tests and evaluates another, and modifies it and creates yet another.

These are the adventures of the mind. There is no plan, no goal, no objective but to explore new territory, to understand what is discerned and to see what can be created and used in human society or to please and satisfy the mind.

Looking forward based on the experience of the past does not dictate a single avenue in the future. The experience of the past points in many directions. Looking forward is an open-ended adventure, an attempt to project or plan the future. What it will bring, and how it will change the face of the earth and the surrounding planets can only be revealed by time.

Clearly we humans lodge in mid-adventure, occupying only a few seconds of the "year" of the cosmic adventure. Where the adventure will go in the future is indeterminate. We are probably a unique part of that adventure but an insignificantly small portion. Yet we are of it, participating in it and privileged to have begun to develop an understanding of it. Our ability to see it probably gives us a view and perception that may not be available to other creatures that may inhabit its vast reaches.

Of this we are certain; in several billion more years, the planet on which we live, will be recycled back into the sun, as the sun, in its death throes, expands beyond the orbit of our planet. The adventure of the Creator will continue on, either with or without humans or their evolving successors.

This adventure of humankind swept over all of the surface of the earth and established its imprint while drastically altering the ecology and topography of the land to suit its needs. The saga is punctuated with the collapse of segments of the society that became too rigid to cope with the problems created by their depredations upon the landscape or one another. Or they were too fluid to maintain the functioning integrity of the system that brought them to their present state of development. Having expanded in numbers and occupying virtually every livable environment, humans have made significant changes in the ecology of their environment. These changes threaten its sustainability. Population numbers threaten the ability of the planet to support such a large and ravenous horde. Humankind faces wrenching changes in the organization of its society if it is to survive. Either it does it by its powers of reason, or the inexorable forces of the experimental process of the creation that spawned the development of humans, will find a different solution.

Chapter 13 Bibliography

Bronowski, Jacob, *The ascent of Man* Little Brown and Company, 1973. The assent of man traces our rise-both as a species and as a molder of our environment and our future. It covers the history of science in its broadest sense, and illustrates how arts helped us to explore our thoughts and give rise to inventions, and in the course of these events developed our various civilizations.

Eiseley, Loren, *The Immense Journey:*, Vintage Books, 1946. An imaginative naturalist explores the mysteries of man and nature.

Tattersall, Ian, *How We Came To Be Human*, Scientific American, 285:56-63, December, 2001. Language development seems to define and spur on human evolution.

Chapter 14

Emerging Properties

"The Universe is Change;"
-Marcus Aurelius Antonious

The creation has not always exhibited the diversity of properties that it now possesses. New properties emerged as the creation increased in complexity and diversity.

I will not attempt to catalog all of the emerged properties but will illustrate some of the more profound and noticeable ones that appeared as the creation has evolved. The first properties appeared when the power or energy of the Creator transformed itself into the matter of the universe. The newly created matter had *mass*, the ability to resist being pushed around. It also exhibited the force called *gravity*. This force attracts every other particle having mass.

Early on, there was a splitting of symmetry as the physicists describe it, when the creation split into positively and negatively electrically charged particles. The charged particles exhibited a new and fundamental property, the *attraction* of oppositely charged particles (and the repulsion of similar ones). At a slightly later stage this property allowed the particles to assemble themselves into atoms.

Atoms represented a gigantic leap in the scale of structures. Atoms are billions of times bigger in volume than their constituent parts.

Here is the key to recognizing an emergent property. An emerging property is both a property of this new arrival and it also defines an entire new level of the creation. By the principle of affinity, each new level of organization tries to associate itself with parallel organizations. When the next level of association is made, it is possible that it too demonstrates an emergent property. Accordingly, the reality of a phenomenon always remains inherent in the organization of its parts.

As we have seen, *magnetism* is not a property of fundamental particles, but any time electrically charged particles move, they create magnetic fields. Any time that electrons are given extra energy, they eventually give up that energy. They give it up abruptly in the form of electromagnetic radiation which travels at the speed of light.

Now the creation has developed a method of communicating within itself and a means for transferring energy through the void of space. Gamma rays, x-rays, light, heat and radio waves are all examples of this electromagnetic radiation.

Gravity pulled together such huge masses of hydrogen and helium that the pressure forced the bared nuclei to engage in nuclear *fusion*. Incandescent suns now appeared in the dark void - an especially dramatic emergence. In the heart of the new suns, entirely new breeds of atoms appeared, up to about 100 in number, each one with unique properties not found in the starting materials of hydrogen and helium.

The emergence of these different species of atoms allowed the entire world of chemistry; the bonding of different type atoms to form entirely new *molecules*. Each of the new molecules had *its* own emerging properties. Chlorine, a corrosive gas, and sodium, an inflammable metal combine to form common table salt, far different in nature to its constituents. Reality, and its corresponding organizations, was becoming complex.

Add a whiff of instability to the constancy of various affinities and we find some types of atoms and molecules trying to pack closely together into solid materials. But not just any old way. Their propensity is to link up in highly regular three-dimensional forms like *crystals*. As more molecules add themselves to the group stick to it in the same pattern of arrangement. These new familiar materials are metals, rocks, soil, bone, teeth and etcetera. They have hardness, stability, and even a tendency to extend or *reproduce this new structure*. This property was not evident in the atoms that made up the new molecule.

A little further ahead, in that organic world which so intrigues us, we find that organic molecules tend to link together in long chains. Among their many fascinating new properties, one property that deserves special mention is the ability to *carry information*. Often a pattern or subunit is repeated over and over again along a chain. If these subunits vary slightly, they can be thought of as a kind of informative code, waiting only for an appropriate apparatus to "read" them. In the evolution of life, of course, this is exactly what happened. DNA and certain enzymes began to recognize each other's strings of subunits as information, and the rest, as they say, is evolutionary history. An entirely new, unexpected, and amazing property was born.

Another far-reaching property to emerge in chain-like organic molecules is that of *self-replication*. This is not quite as obvious as it looks, since relatively few molecules can copy themselves on their own. But when different kinds of molecules work together in a *cooperative association*, they make replication much easier for themselves. The decisive example is that of the association among enzymes, DNA, and energy-harnessing molecules. Working together, the replication of all three is very rapid; working separately as they did early on, we can see why the pre-cooperation period lasted a billion years!

Let's gather up these three new properties of chain molecules - association, replication, and information. We can see we're closing in on something. Sure enough, as these associations group themselves together into larger and larger clumps with greater and greater internal diversity, an exquisite immaculate conception takes place. Somewhere, someday, one of these new organizations gels into a discreet cell enclosed by sheet-like molecules, a *self replicating living* cell.

We scarcely need to emphasize the importance of this event or list all the new properties that appear when life appears. From now on we'll touch just the highlights. In particular we'll look at life's properties as the affinities go to work - as cells associate with cells and organisms with organisms.

As soon as there were two cells, the activities of the first had an impact upon the second. It was just so highly favorable to coordinate and not get in each other's way. These primitive creatures experimented with and invented *chemical messengers* to communicate among themselves and better survive. Later, the phenomenon of chemical messenger communication aided the formation of multi-cellular organisms.

The cooperative association of cells may seen as a self-reinforcing impulse: the various affinities bring cells into proximity, they try out communication and cooperation, this causes both to survive better, the next generation carries it a step further, and the adventure continues. After billions of generations the planet has both simple organisms and highly complex ones, and both kinds still make abundant use of communication and cooperation.

Another important invention was *sexual reproduction*, the mixing of DNA from one organism with that of another. This mixing of DNA puts the diversification of organisms into high gear. So many different combinations can result when two slightly different versions of a similar DNA code are combined, that the gradual evolution of one species into another is enormously speeded up. A truly wonderful new property!

Early along the line, living cells began to detect light, temperature, and harmful chemicals. They registered these by changing their mix of chemical products and messengers. From *sensory ability* it was a short step to *response* and *mobility*, using the sensory information to protect itself or to forage for food. This sensory ability soon became a preeminent property of successful organisms.

Chemical messengers that performed so steadily in the early stages proved to be too slow to drive creatures that had to move in order to mate, eat and avoid being eaten. Specialized cells appeared that made use of electrical impulses to carry the message - forerunners of today's nerve cells. Mobility and reaction to sensations became many times faster.

When organisms developed sufficient numbers of nerve cells, very powerful new properties emerged. These animals could *learn* from past experience and store their *memories* of them. The rudiments of a *mind* appeared. In one notable species, *consciousness* and *language* followed on not far behind.

This brings us to the properties and capabilities that seem to be specifically human, including economic relationships, love, creative ability, analysis of our environment, ethics and religious thought, music, contemplation of the creation and the Creator, and the appreciation of the combinations of colors reflected from clouds in a sunset.

The Principle of Interdependence

All through this long history of the amazing development of life, the principle and custom of *symbiosis* - the interdependence of different organisms - has been developing. It seems to be an integral part of and a necessity for successful life.

Too often we look at life and see it as a combative struggle of prey and predator, hunter and hunted. The reality is that there are more cooperative relationships shaping the existence of living communities than there are destructive or competitive ones. The flower adapts its shape and scent to attract insects. The insects pollinate the flower and are rewarded by the nectar that sustains its colony. The Portuguese

Man-o'-War is simply a colony of different species that cooperate in its life cycle. The algae and fungi living together in lichens create a tight community serving each other's needs. Many of the multi-cellular creatures we know today began as assemblies of different cells working in symbiotic relationships developed over many generations. These relationships are usually as important to their survival and success as are their internal activities.

On a different organizational level, humans form families, tribes, towns, societies, governments, and all sorts of associations that further their aspirations and well-being. These higher-level organizations show capabilities that we could not have expected from observing a single human: social and cultural behavior, laws, rites, traditions, and a body of understanding about the Creator and the creation. These capabilities were not previously found on our planet; nor have they been perceived so far in our examination of the cosmos.

This list of emergent properties is by no means exhaustive, but it represents the genius - the very essence of the ongoing creative process. The creation evolves, the creation changes, and new properties emerge from its endless organization and reorganization.

Chapter 14 Bibliography

Clayton , Philips. *Emerging God,* Christian Century, January 13, 2004 vol 121 No. 1 Theologians are beginning to wrestle with the consequences of understanding the new creation story, and speculate how the Creator is involved in the evolution of the cosmos.

Lewin, Roger *Complexity, Life at the edge of chaos.* J M Dent (London) 1993. A rather detailed study of how complex structures and new realities might evolve. The insights revealed rely mightily on computer simulations and their comparisons to real life processes.

Chapter 15

I'm Thankful for Little Things

"The Universe looks like it was a put-up job"
-Fred Hoyle

Very small things about our universe have a tremendous influence on the outcome of the larger events and on the very character of the universe. Just consider water and ice. When water freezes into a solid, it expands and becomes less dense. It then floats on top of the water. Most other liquids become more dense when they freeze into a solid form.

Consider what would happen in our world, if ice was more dense than water. It would sink to the bottom of the lakes, the rivers, and the seas and gradually fill them up with ice. This would drastically alter the habitability of the seas and lakes and have far-reaching consequences on climate and the ecology of the entire planet. The sun's heat would be shielded from the winter's accumulation of ice and the ice would build up in the depths of lakes and seas. Some of it would begin to melt on the bottom. The heat escaping from the core of the earth would do the job. Then the melting would produce liquid water which would try to rise. When this warmer water broke through the ice layers, it would probably produce titanic upheavals in the body of water, making the seas a very hazardous environment.

I'm thankful that earth contains at least a bare trace (possibly less than a thousandth of a percent) of long-lived radioactive isotopes of some of its atoms. I'm thankful for isotopes with such exotic names as rubidium 87, neodymium 144, uranium 235, tellurium 130.

When an isotope of an atom has a half-life of say three billion years, half those isotopes will radioactively decay into a stable element or a more stable isotope within three billion years. In the next three billion years, half the remainder will decay and so on. The heat generated by the decay of these isotopes remains in the depths of the earth. It powers the upheaval of mountains, the drift and collision of continents, and the eruption of volcanoes. We would have evolved as fish or dolphins if these isotopes had not been present, releasing their energy to the molten core and the mantle of the earth. The mountains would have long ago been washed and eroded down into the seas, and water would cover the entire planet.

Without the power and energy these decaying isotopes inject into the earth, the earth would have cooled and ceased its boiling and churning and would have hardened into a solid sphere long ago. Short half-life isotopes would not have done the trick. They decay much too rapidly to provide the energy needed to keep those upheavals going for the billions of years since the earth began.

I'm thankful for the evolution of the blue-green algae that transformed the atmosphere of our globe from a carbon dioxide to an oxygen-rich atmosphere. Their contribution resulted in an atmosphere that screened out the deadly ultraviolet rays of the sun. Then this climate and atmosphere nurtured the development of trees and flowers, grasses, and vegetables. Eventually it allowed the development of oxygen-breathing creatures that make use of this free oxygen.

I'm thankful that the waste products of the blue-green algae tied up excess carbon in an insoluble form. Thankful that it sank to the bottom of the seas and was permanently removed from the atmosphere. Otherwise, the algae would have been fighting a losing battle in its endeavor to extract carbon dioxide. If all of the carbon it inhaled was incorporated in its cell tissue when the cell died and decayed, most of the carbon in it would have oxidized and returned to the atmosphere as carbon dioxide. This is at the heart of the present controversy over using renewable versus fossil fuel. Using fossil fuel which was buried hundreds of millions of years ago reintroduces sequestered carbon to the atmosphere. Burning renewable fuels such as wood merely does what nature would do anyway, because dead wood decays and releases carbon dioxide to the atmosphere in a relatively short time.

We can be thankful for the evolving of the chlorophyll molecule. It enabled the blue-green alga to intercept the energy of sunlight and to use the energy to break apart the carbon dioxide so that it could assemble the carbon into its own body chemicals. And I'm thankful that it could pass on the genetic information on how to manufacture this molecule to all of the plant life that evolved subsequently.

We should be thankful that in the scheme of things, just by substituting the lone atom of magnesium in the chlorophyll molecule for one of iron, nature produced the hemoglobin molecule that our body uses to transport the life-giving oxygen to each of our cells. The chlorophyll molecule appeared hundreds of millions of years after the first living and reproducing cell appeared. If the evolution of hemoglobin had to start independently from more primitive origins, the evolution of oxygen-breathing and warm-blooded creatures would have been set back hundreds of millions of years, or perhaps it would not have occurred at all.

We can thank the design of molecules that make up the spiral strands of DNA and the four protruding bases that make up the code of DNA. Thankful, because they hook up to one another in a long twisting spiral with their active base ends pointing inward. Otherwise, they would have great difficulty in replicating themselves.

I'm grateful that just a simple four-letter code can spell out the entire recipe for the formation and the replication of any of the living organisms of the world, past or present.

The entire universe can be thankful that only one billionth of the protons, electrons, and neutrons that precipitated out of the Big Bang survived, while the remainder rapidly annihilated themselves as they collided with their anti-matter counterparts. Actually we should be more thankful that there was that minuscule imbalance in the creation process that apparently produced one billionth more matter than anti-matter. The energy that was re-released in the annihilation process powered the expansion of the universe. This expansion gave it time to organize itself into the infinitude of diversity that it now possesses. If the residual matter had been just a tiny bit greater, the gravitational pull would have formed giant stars that lived out a more furious and violent life, burning their fuel at a more rapid pace. This would have left too little time for the patient assembly of life on the cooler planets.

Far more important, the increased gravitational pull of a denser universe would have reversed the expansion, and the universe would have collapsed back on itself long ago. Just a tiny bit less matter surviving after the annihilation process, and there would not have been

The Cosmic Deity

enough density to form and ignite stars. Then the universe would have continued expanding on a cold, dark, and uneventful course instead of coalescing into stars and galaxies.

I'm thankful that gravity is such a pitifully weak force compared to even the electromagnetic force, being only $1/10^{38}$th as strong. Although we would not feel small differences in our daily lives, just having gravity increase by a factor of 10, being only $1/10^{37}$ as strong as the electromagnetic force, would have the same effect as a tiny increase in the amount of matter in the universe. It would drastically jack up the size and burning rate of the stars and ensure the early collapse and implosion of the universe.

There are other "constants" of nature discovered by the physicists, which if they had been only slightly different, would have drastically changed the very nature of the universe. The odds on chance of life as we know developing in such a universe would be negligible.

I'm thankful that the earth is 93 million miles away from the sun and not 97 million miles. That 3% difference might today bring the average temperature of the earth below the freezing point of water rather than a comfortable 60°F. I'm even more grateful that the earth circles the sun in a nearly perfectly circular orbit. If the orbit were only slightly more elliptical, the summer season would be unbearably hot and the winters would bring frost down to the equator.

I'm eternally thankful that when the Great Extinction occurred near the beginning of the Cambrian era, hundreds of millions of years ago, the chordates survived. Chordates are the ancestors of all vertebrate species, including ourselves. Their nervous system is channeled through the body via a central spinal cord. Of the estimated 100 different large phyla of creatures that existed prior to the Great Extinction, only 10 exist on earth today. What incredible luck, that aside from the many biological groups that permanently disappeared from the face of the earth, about 10 did survive, and ours is one of them. If this extinction had occurred in some different manner, it might have been other groups that survived, and the course of the adventure would have been entirely changed.

I'm also thankful for a big thing: thankful that the asteroid that slammed into the earth 65 million years ago wiped out the dinosaurs. Maybe this is a little selfish, but if the dinosaurs hadn't been wiped out, the probability that humans could have evolved by this time approaches zero, and our furry little ancestors would never have been able to evolve to the point where we can contemplate the very nature of the creation. Somewhere up the evolutionary ladder we would have become big enough to be the prime prey for the smaller dinosaurs and they in turn would have been prey for the likes of *Tyrannosaurus Rex*. Those dinosaurs had already lasted for about 100 million years and might have been good for a 100 million years more if that asteroid had not wiped them out completely.

I'm thankful, because if even one of these little things did not exist as they do, I wouldn't be around to rejoice in their existence or to complain of their absence. These observations of course raise a host of other questions. Is the creation purposeful? Is it planned? Does it exhibit what we call intelligence or genius? Is there anything behind it, planning and shaping its form prior to its appearance?

Instead of postulating the genius that seems to be inherent within our universe, some philosophers/scientists have hypothesized an infinite number of universes, each with completely different characteristics. Only universes that can evolve and sustain life would have humans or similar creatures that could be aware of the creation and speculate upon its nature. By inference, then, we are inhabiting one of these fortunate universes.

Whether the creation is the result of astounding luck, whether the genius it exhibits is inherent in the creation, or whether there is a genius "behind" the visible universe will be the subject of a subsequent chapter. In any event, an incredible number of small factors have combined to make the creation the marvel that it is. Its very nature appears to be exquisitely tuned to enable the marvelous adventure that we experience as a result of its unique design.

The Cosmic Deity

Chapter 15 Bibliography

Davies, P.C.W., *The Accidental Universe*, Cambridge University Press, 1982.

Foster, David, *The Philosophical Scientists*, Dorset Press, 1985.

Rees, Martin, *Just Six Numbers*, Basic Books, 2000.

The above three books show how our universe is uniquely configured in its basic characteristics and its "laws and physical constants" which allow life to evolve

Chapter 16

Religion

The Search For Cause And Meaning

"Don't go around hurting each other.
Try to understand things."
-Hopi Spider Grandmother

The search for causes is as fundamental as the search for food and shelter. It is as ancient as the ability to reason and think in terms of the past and of the future. This search was undoubtedly impelled by curiosity as well as by the necessity of sheer survival. Later, when humans had a modicum of security and had developed a more comprehensive view of the surrounding world, they made attempts to make some sense of it all. They expanded the search for causes, to a search for *meaning*, for the underlying or all encompassing explanation of life and the world around them.

Humans' ability to discern causes had an immense effect on survivability. The ability to understand the causes of good and bad events were matters of life and death. Humans were preyed upon by animals. In their view, they were also preyed upon by natural events, catastrophes and illnesses. Their survival depended on finding food and shelter in a world where things were continually changing with the seasons. Their existence depended upon the migration of their prey, the seasonal appearance of forage fruits and their interaction with other human bands.

Some causes and events are rather obvious and others more obscure. The sun became a fixation of many cultures because of its immediate presence and its daily and seasonal activity. The sun was very powerful. It heated up the cold earth after being absent at night. Solar radiation was also sometimes lethal to those caught in the deserts without adequate shelter or water. It soon became obvious that the sun controlled and promoted the growth of plants and trees. Sometimes it wandered away and its effects on the earth waned. When it wandered back again, food plants began to grow as the climate warmed. It is not surprising that the sun was worshiped as a controlling factor in people's lives. It became a revered spirit of awe and power whose good graces were cultivated. It became imbued with human characteristics and was entreated to return when it wandered away with the change of seasons. Its return was celebrated when it appeared more directly overhead. In short it became the Sun God, the maker and sustainer of life.

Of course it became evident to astute observers that the seasons were caused by variations in the path of the sun and that these variations occurred on a regular and predictable cycle. Simple mathematical tools were applied to observations of the shortest shadows of the sun in summer and again in winter, allowing these curious observers to determine what was going on. A simple counting method - such as putting a pebble into a basket every day that the shadow became longer and taking one out every day that it became shorter - could eventually allowed clever observers to predict just when the sun's rays would be at their hottest or coolest.

Before the facts of a predictable and dependable cycle were established, there was undoubtedly sadness and panic as the sun seemed to desert the world, and rejoicing when it started to come back. If our ancestors gave the sun human qualities, the next step in their logic was that maybe the sun could be persuaded to stay or return. Relics from past human societies show that there were offerings, icons, and ceremonies dedicated to enticing the sun to return. They also recorded the celebrations that marked the seasons.

Different people apparently tried their hand at enticing the sun to return. When one of them pronounced the proper incantations or offered the proper prayer at the proper time, his results were apparently successful. These were then repeated over and over again. Of course if the timing wasn't right, they might fail the next time around and that particular seer would be discredited.

If one observer was equipped with the facts, if he knew just how many pebbles in the basket indicated the return of the sun, he would be in a position to time his offerings and apparently be successful. Knowledge became power. This person's ceremonies would always be successful. The power accumulated by this person and his associates was literally pyramided into pyramids. Incas, Aztecs, and Mayans of Central and South America focused on the Sun God and built elaborate and massive pyramids dedicated to the observations of the sun. These became ceremonial sites as well. The custodians of sun knowledge became so powerful that they commanded vast resources and labor for the construction of their temples and pyramids. When they offered the Sun God their choicest foods and animals as an enticement for its return, they were apparently always successful. Sometimes the power that they exerted over others allowed them to offer up humans as an offering to their Sun God, leading to famously gory rituals.

Several important ways of thinking developed here which shaped the course of future civilizations. Observations of physical phenomena were done systematically; tools for these observations were devised. The length of a noonday shadow on the shortest day of the year - a long winter shadow - was recorded by marking a rock. The approaching longest day was then anticipated by watching successive noonday shadows become shorter and shorter. Or, in a specially built wall, a hole was made that allowed a beam of light from the sunrise of the shortest day of the year to fall on an appropriate design on another wall. As this occurred on no other day of the year, it was displayed as a magic omen.

Mathematical language to describe the passing of the solar year was devised later. At first the early reckoners didn't need a system of numbers. They could just add or remove pebbles from a basket to keep track of the sun's migration. They wouldn't have needed to know how to count. Well, not quite. If their pebble reckoning were done for several years, they would slowly find that things were not exactly right, that the sun would reach its lowest or highest point a day late. If this was repeated over several decades, they would have to conclude either that they were counting things wrong or that the cycle of the sun was not as precise as they thought. Perhaps some assistants or apprentices were disgraced for failing to perform proper record keeping, unless several observers had come to the same conclusion. Every four years, there seemed to be a day missing.

Puzzles such as this led to the development of more refined counting methods, then to a system of numbers, and then to methods for accurately manipulating these numbers. The keepers of knowledge became inventors. They created elaborate calendars and the mathematical tools needed to explain and predict the events upon which their success and power depended. Their calendars then included the leap year where a day must be added every four years. Eventually they included predictions of the cycle of full and new moons and the movements of some planets.

Let's stop for a moment and look at these different thought processes and see what they mean. Here is a major force in the lives of people, the sun, that seems to vary, change, and wander about. Just when folks despair of the sun returning, someone performs a ceremony and the sun begins to rise earlier and climb higher. It happens every year.

Several explanations might be offered. The first is that the sun is enticed to return as a result of ceremonies, entreaties, and sacrifices. If the sun begins its return after every ceremony that is a very powerful argument in favor of the ceremonies.

Another conclusion that could be drawn is that certain people cause the sun to return because they are such powerful people or have more powerful ceremonies. If that individual or group of individuals were successful every time, one might be justified in believing that they were indeed imbued with special powers.

Alternatively, if a person was equipped with knowledge and observations to predict when the sun would pass the winter solstice, that person could merely announce the day that the sun would start on its return journey. From this it might be deduced that the person was in communication with the sun or was its special envoy here on earth. Of course this view could be exploited shamelessly by a person having the proper knowledge. Con artists are not a 21st-century invention!

A final explanation might be that a shrewd observer had determined the facts about the earth's revolution around the sun. These facts were then used to predict how the sun would appear to people on earth, taking into account different points in the earth's annual journey around the sun.

All of these explanations are examples of attempts to understand things. Each approach is radically different from the others. The first is that human ceremonies control or change events. Another is that certain priests are empowered to control events. The next explanation is that some persons are the mediators between people and the Gods. The last is that by observation one can understand what is going on and to a certain extent predict the future by using this knowledge.

In early human societies, various versions of the first three explanations won out. Early civilizations, their religions, and their cultures were shaped by these perceptions. Given the knowledge the average person possessed, any one of them was understandably valid. Besides, they were probably more fun! They led to more enjoyable activities than sitting around counting beans or stones and developing mathematical models of the sun's motion. (A poster I once saw in a marketing department proclaimed, "Bullshit beats science any day.")

There is a paradox here. There is good evidence that the priestly caste, who derived their power because they could understand and influence the Sun God, used their advantage to enhance their power and control the lives and thoughts of others. They also became the keepers of knowledge. They were the early scientists, mathematicians, astronomers, and botanists. Collectively, they tried to fit all their observations and knowledge into a better understanding of the world and its people. They also attracted and recruited the brightest and most promising youth of their society to carry on their traditions. They became both charlatans and philosophers.

Different societies developed different patterns of thought as they tried to understand and harmonize the important things in their lives. When you are preyed upon by lions or tigers, or your straying children are carted off by hyenas, your life is likely to be governed by fear and the feeling that things are out to get you. Thunderstorms with their fury and sound, and the fires and floods that ensue, take on great importance.

People become sick and die. A drought kills off the vegetation. Children are stillborn, or a volcano bursts from a nearby mountain. All these important events in life happen with no perceptible cause. But they *do* happen, and the attempts to understand and cope are perceived differently in different societies.

On the other hand when plants that can be eaten spring up from the earth, when trees blossom and bear edible fruits, and when migrating herds of game animals troop by, it may seem as though miracles are taking place with no obvious cause. Miracles or gifts may be the general perception of folks when children are born, when rain comes to cool the land and make the plants grow, and when fires are tamed to produce warmth and protection. Something" makes these miracles happen, and life itself depends upon that something continuing to cause these life-giving events. (On the other hand, if the other "something" that causes bad things to happen can be chased away or appeased, maybe the bad things won't happen).

Since this "something" isn't visible, it takes on the character of an unseen force or spirit. Life is seen to be dominated by unseen spirits, spirits that cause both good things and bad things to happen. The trick is to cultivate the good ones and appease or fend off the bad ones. Sometimes these spirits are thought to inhabit the object itself. In other views they are disembodied spirits that wander about, powerful but unseen.

Although the history of early humans is far from complete, relics tell us a lot about them. A good deal of activity was dedicated to making images and models of the things that concerned them. Quite likely many were designed to appeal to the spirits. Drawings and pictures in clay or stone show the patterns of thought of these early people as they tried to come to grips with their surroundings. The rituals, customs and spiritual images used by pre-scientific peoples have persisted even into modern times.

If you painted a picture of a deer on a cliff and a herd of deer showed up soon after, you could conclude that a deer spirit inhabited the picture and attracted other deer to the vicinity. Or if you dressed up in a deer hide with antlers and paraded around the forest, and deer appeared shortly thereafter, that ritual would seem to be effective. If you dared to climb up to the rim of an active volcano and throw in some choice food or even a young maiden to appease the volcano spirit, perhaps it didn't erupt in your lifetime. If these efforts were apparently successful, they became a part of the culture. The rituals or images were thought to have the power to control events. If they grew ineffective, they were abandoned. At other times they were intensified to make them work more effectively. If the more intensive method happened to "work", it became more firmly embedded in the culture and the more successful practitioners were commissioned to carry on the tradition.

Early on, rituals became an established part of human society and human thought. Not all rituals were based on chance happenings and faulty reasoning. Some rituals worked for good reason. The North American Native ritual of putting a fish into the ground with seed corn produced a robust crop of corn. The corn flourished, not because the spirit of the fish entered the corn, but because the minerals and nitrogen released from the decomposing fish helped produce a healthy plant.

Rituals are an integral and important part of the working of all cultures. Some are intended to change the course of events while others serve as reminders of past events. In the 20th century a child psychologist, Piaget, discovered how human thought patterns change as people reach maturity. In the middle childhood years, a child perceives itself as the center of its little world. The child is not aware of the causes of the things that happen in its life. To the child, things happen in a magical fashion. Children often invent an invisible friend to talk to and that friend helps to make things happen. Rituals become very important to children. They perform them in an attempt to make desirable things happen and to fend off undesirable events. A.A. Milne illustrates this type of thinking in his children's stories. A little child avoids stepping on the lines and walks only on the squares in order to keep away the bears.

Piaget shows that this way of magical thinking and dependence upon rituals is usually supplanted in later life. It changes to thinking that employs logic about cause and effect and introspection into the person's own emotions and reactions. Other researchers have followed up his research and found that about 15% of all adults persist in the magical/ritual mode of thought throughout their lives. Over 50% seem to operate partially in this mode, while 30% seem to think in a purely logical way.

It is not obvious that humans who are not exposed to modern education and thought would necessarily achieve the maturity of thinking that Piaget discovered. There are small societies in Africa today who attribute all illnesses to spells put upon them by others. These people devote much time trying to find out whom they might have offended in their community. Then they take extraordinary steps to amend the wrong so that the spell is withdrawn and the illness goes away. As the modern world has found, this way of thinking may promote domestic tranquility and be good mental therapy, but it is not very effective against infectious diseases!

The next preoccupation of human thought, one that dominates nearly all cultures, is trying to understand the world. Where did it come from? Who or what is responsible for the appearance of the world? Creation myths are rich in imagination and scope. Some of these appear as the result of deep thought and observation. Others come from sheer poetic thinking or whimsy. Still others are explicitly the result of visions or dreams, such as the creation myths of Australian aboriginal's dream times. Others are reported to be the result of revealed truth. Someone is told or shown the creation story, who then reveals it to others in talks around a nighttime fire. Many individuals report hearing voices of unseen people talking to them or voices inside their head. So far, it is not possible to delineate which, if any, of these events are truly the result of communication from some other being. Some are clearly the result of schizophrenia, a type of mental illness that produces unexplained voices in the mind of the sufferer.

Regardless of the source of these myths, there is a major preoccupation with trying to understand how or why the world was created, what lies behind it all. This is important, if for no other reason than to get on the "good side" of the God or the Gods. This ensures that the individual enjoys the continuing benefits that the living world provides for its inhabitants. But beyond the survival aspects of this desire for knowledge, there is also curiosity to know and to understand for its own sake. Thus begins the search for knowledge and for truth.

Religion is the name that we commonly give to such systems of thought and inquiry as well as to the practices and rituals associated with them. The deeply held beliefs and thoughts that motivate the actions of humans also define their culture. They provide a mental framework in which people act and react to one another and to the surrounding world. By providing a secure cultural framework, religions promote the stability and continuity that is necessary for the orderly evolution of thought and ideas. Within this framework they permit constructive change and facilitate adaptation to new circumstances.

If religions are the stable and enduring forms, cults are the one-time phenomena that capture the imagination of a few but do not generally endure. They cannot stand the test of time and experience. Cults are usually centered around a single charismatic leader. This individual often caters to the persistent tendency towards magical thinking which is always present in some of the population.

Enduring religions have three major components. The first is a view or vision of truth which supplies a satisfying creation myth and a world view that accounts for what is going on. The second is an ethic, a proper way for people to act toward one another. The third is the provision of emotional security.

Providing emotional security is the most important factor. Recent studies in psychology show that until a person attains sufficient security in his or her emotional outlook, that person is unable to function to his or her full potential. Individuals are unable to progress and develop other capabilities and talents without this internal sense of security. Failure to find emotional security reduces a person to preoccupations with internal worries, perceived threats, and the inability to concentrate on other factors of life.

Emotional security is secured by many means.
1) It can come about through rituals or ceremonies.
2) It can be the result of certainty provided by a holy writ.
3) It can come through group action, a common purpose and group activity.
4) It can be based on a belief system that copes with the fear of death and illness.

A belief system offering emotional security may be based upon almost anything. Truth or facts have little to do with it, as long as it provides long-term security for its believers. Surrounded and protected by this security, individuals feel free to explore and develop a fuller life. It does not depend upon a rational view of truth or a sustainable ethic; it may rely only on a magical interpretation of events. Such security systems can and do collapse when faced with inescapable facts that conflict with unfounded beliefs on which that security system is based. If the facts persist and are unshakable they result in the death of tradition and faith. Distraught believers lose their "security blanket."

A poignant example of the consequences of this loss occurs in the biographical novel, *The Star Gazer*. Galileo is implored by a friendly Priest to recant his explanation of how the earth revolves about the sun. The friend has been appointed to the board of inquisition to investigate Galileo's heresies. He asks Galileo, "Has it ever occurred to you what a wonderful organization the church is? With what splendid skill she has managed to make use of everything that can bind and uplift the human soul? Think of our churches and their splendor, the very sight of which comforts the poor, since we make them feel that the shimmering gold of holy vestments, the pomp of processions is really theirs. ... Think of the deep and soothing beauty of our music, the lulling harmony of our plain chants of the fumes of incense which chain the believer even through his senses to his religion. Think of the sacraments which sustain human beings from birth to maturity, and assist them until they die in the arms of the Church. ... No movement of the human soul can escape the loving vigilance of the Church in her battle with the weakness of sinful men. And yet the whole miraculous institution, whose wisdom cannot be praised enough, is grounded on the truth of Holy Writ. Every rite, every word of the Mass has its origin there. . . . We priests who by God's mercy have been raised to posts of command and authority have the sacred duty of defending and strengthening this wonderful institution. . . . The whole cosmos relates to humanity, to man's struggle to save his soul. Nothing can be of more significance than the salvation of a single individual, of the poorest beggarly human being. . . . Can I permit the thought to enter his mind that the earth is only a tiny satellite and the sun the real center of the cosmos? Can I let humanity form this terrible thought that the earth, with its men seeking salvation, is not the heart of all created life? Can I allow doubt to invade their minds? . . . This first doubt would be followed by hundreds of others. The whole structure would crumble. Instead of faith, capricious disputation would be supreme: men would lose even their earthly happiness. No, Galileo Galilei: as long as I remain in authority, I will never permit this thing!"

Galileo then asks, "Monsignor, may I ask one question? . . . Is it conceivable that these teachings can be true?"

His inquisitor answers, "I don't know. . . . They may be true for all that. I am not interested, however, in the truth. I am only concerned with teachings. . . . For me the faith of millions of poor people is far more essential."

Galileo stubbornly goes on to say, "The time will come when the faith of hundreds of thousands is strong enough to bear the truth of Copernicus so that in the end even the multitudes will accept him and still believe. Why am I forbidden to reveal this truth to learned men?"

The Priest's reply: "Because there are many priests among them. And a priest must not think with his own mind but with the Pope's. No priest can persuade his hearers with a sermon in which he doesn't believe."

There is a great deal of truth in this exchange. Any upset of the thinking that undergirds cultures and religions may have disastrous emotional consequences. These disasters are anticipated by wise leaders. With good justification they resist ideas that disrupt and undercut the emotional fabric so essential to humans.

The fiery controversy raised by Creationists has nothing to do with scientific method or facts. They do not oppose the discussion of evolution and evolutionary processes because these are inaccurate. The controversy is in fact a protective screen. The Creationists' wish to preserve the emotional security of those who base their whole lives on faith in the literal accuracy of the Bible. For them this God-given book establishes a necessary security in their lives. A rift in their fabric of belief would be disastrous in terms of emotional damage to the faithful.

Karen Armstrong in her book *The Idea of God* stresses that the core emotional value of the great religions is the aim to replicate the great mystical experiences of their founders. These experiences are inter-preted as direct contacts with or as directives from the Creator, and they very profoundly shaped the founders' world view. They try to share these experiences by devising rituals and legends that invoke their great original meanings. The encounters themselves are usually revered above any theological content that they may have. For the adherents of these religions traditions, this component of their religious life provides a great deal of emotional security.

The second factor common to all religions is an ethic. These are the rules and values governing interactions with one another and with the creation. It is not surprising that there are consistent themes in the ethical guidelines that pervade most religions and cultures. At least they are consistent where members of one's own society are concerned.

I submit that similar codes of ethics evolved in various societies because they produced a strong survival value for each of these groups. If there is little mutual respect among individuals in a community, that community and its members have a smaller chance of survival in tough times than do communities where there is cooperation and respect for each individual. It is likely that wise leaders in diverse cultures when observing their communities over a long period of time would arrive at similar conclusions. They would introduce standards that promote a harmonious and orderly community and proscribe practices that weaken its social fabric. Such standards become woven into the religion as absolute values, values ordained by God or gods. They are most effective if backed by the authority of the Deity rather than relying on human teaching.

Human beings have not yet developed a universal ethic, an ethic that applies to persons outside their own society, one that effectively deals with the interaction of diverse cultures and societies and is embraced by all. Eventually human society must evolve such an effective and common "external" ethic. Otherwise it will self-destruct just as small dysfunctional societies do which do not have a shared internal ethic. The Hopi Spider Grandmother simply advised, "Don't go around hurting one another."

The Search for Knowledge and Truth

The third component of religion is a claim to knowledge, to truth, to an understanding of what is going on in the universe and why. This is ofttimes called a "world view", but in fact it means a "universe view", encompassing all of creation.

The idea of the creation, something that we live in and are part of, and a Creator, a power and intelligence that creates and controls the universe, converge in this aspect of religion. Religion's role in truth-telling is to understand and explain the relationship between the creation and the Creator.

Although this does not suddenly appear as a full-blown theological task, it undoubtedly arises from questions about why things happen when their causes are not evident. What is the unseen hand that makes inexplicable things happen? As we have seen, spirits and magic are frequently invoked.

Simultaneously, attempts are made to come to grips with creation. What is it, where does it come from, who or what created it? Is it eternal without a beginning or an end? If there was a beginning, what created it? If there will be an end, how will it come about?

The rich and diverse accounts of the creation are a tribute to the imagination and to the creative thinking of the human species. Most of these represent an honest search for the roots of our existence. They show keen observation and insight about the processes that were going on around them, in their societies and in their environment. It is when they collide with new facts that they sometimes reveal their flaws and contradictions.

The creation myth of the Great Turtle illustrates this. Earth's surface was curved and hard. The image of the earth being supported on the back of a giant turtle seemed to fit the observed facts. The earth was a hard shell that shook at times, and the waters seemed to run off the earth and flow through the seas to the horizon. So far, all of it seemed to make sense. What this view lacked was depth of thought. When an outsider asked a modern adherent of this belief what the turtle was standing on, the reply was, "Young man, you just don't understand, it's turtles all the way down."

Attempts to understand the nature of the earth were expanded to include thoughts about how the earth came to be in its present form.

What created it, or was it simply made out of something else? If so, what created that something else? Most of the early concepts involved human or animal-like beings. Others fell back on an unseen force or spirit as the creator. When the unseen spirit was invoked, that created conceptual problems with all of the other active spirits. Sometimes these were viewed as subordinate spirits, but at other times they were perceived as being part of one great spirit.

Note that this presents some problems with logic. If there is only one great all-powerful spirit, a spirit who created all and controlled all, that spirit must be malevolent as well as good. It has to be responsible for everything: the good, the bad, and the ugly, as well as the beautiful and benevolent. If it has power only for good, and does not control the bad and the ugly, it is less than omnipotent and is not all-powerful. In that case there must be both a good and a bad great spirit that are both powerful but neither all-powerful.

This line of thought leaves the matter of the creation and Creator still unresolved. Eventually the overwhelming magnitude of creation, and of forces it contains and exhibits, pushes the search for its origins to a prominent place in philosophic and religious thought. If there is this creation, there must be a Creator, and the Creator must be all-powerful, all-wise, and by inference, all-knowledgeable. Everything about creation would be known and noted by its Creator. "There's no hiding place down here!" we might sigh.

In many religious traditions the Creator then becomes central, living at the core of the religion. Everything and everyone stems from the Creator. The Creator made it, the Creator "owns" it, and the Creator controls it. The Creator makes the rules and enforces them. The Creator is The Supreme Being.

For the most part, traditions describe the creation of a two-level universe. The Creator creates the universe and then operates it. It is akin to a contractor who builds a hotel and then operates it and sets the rules for the guests. Note that if the Creator is the source of everything, it creates the guests as well as the hotel.

The great religions do not have a consistent view of how the Creator "manages" its creation. Their explanations range from the Creator residing at a distance and operating with agents (priests, prophets, or holy spirits), to the Creator being present within the creation, present but not visible, and controlling every event. Others take a position somewhere in the middle in which the Creator launches the creation, sets the rules by which it and its inhabitants must function, and then sits back to judge the results. Play by the rules and you win; flaunt them and you lose.

All these versions of truth used by the durable religions have a two-level structure; that is, a Creator separate and distinct from the creation. Many religions envision the Creator being present in the universe. None of them fully accept the Creator and the universe as being one and the same.

Note that there are some exceptions to the sweeping summary above. At least one religion, the Christian tradition, allows the two levels to intersect in an earthly person. At just one time and at just one place, the Creator and a part of its creation become one. That is how the Christian Bible describes the man Jesus. Apart from this exception, the Creator is usually pushed off to a separate level in the scheme of things, a higher level, worthy of veneration and awe. Such a Creator is not as interesting as a presence that is in and of everything.

The Creator as the Creation in Religious Terms

Although the concept of Creator and creation as one has been posed by philosophers and other visionaries, this outlook has never embedded itself as the core of any enduring religious tradition. Over the centuries it has been one idea among many, with no substantial evidence to make it compelling to the intellect. Nor did it offer a robust framework of belief and culture that would generate a satisfactory level of emotional security.

Perhaps now the time has come to explore the Creator as creation. A large segment of humanity, the Christian portion, has shown that it believes the Creator and creation are synonymous in at least one historical person, the Nazarene teacher, Jesus. Why not as the whole of creation? The knowledge explosion of the 20th century has moved the earth under our feet. The combination of scientific knowledge with an appreciation of the overwhelming majesty and magnitude of the creation changes things in a very fundamental way. Again the Spider Grandmother advises, "Try to understand things."

Now we are able to make more rational judgments and more factual explanations. We have new insights into human thought and human emotional needs as well as the realization that we may all be a part of the Creator. We should be able to forge a more satisfactory internal ethic as well as for the first time an external (universal) one. This ethic will include our relationship to the creation as well as all the creatures in it. Together, this ethic and these insights should provide the basis for a more satisfactory and a more inclusive life and culture. Through this understanding and this inclusive ethic we could achieve the emotional security we need.

As Bishop Robinson said in the foreword of his book *Honest To God*, "We must not only be honest to God, but also honest *about* God." Any view of the Creator that does not encompass all the vastness and diversity of creation and does not acknowledge the immense time span involved in the creative process - such a view only diminishes the Creator.

Chapter 16 Bibliography

Armstrong, Karen, *History Of God*. Knopf, 1993. The 4000-Year Quest of Judaism, Christianity, and Islam,

Barbour, Ian G., *When Science Meets Religion: Enemies, Strangers, or Partners?*, HarperSanFrancisco, 2000. Compares the approach to the understanding or use of scientific knowledge by the different religious traditions.

deHarsanyi, Zsolt, Paul Tabor translation to English, *The Star-Gazer*, G. P. Putnam Sons, 1939. A novel on the life and work of Galileo Galilei illustrating the climate in which his ideas were received.

Jantzen, Grace, God's World, God's Body, Philadelphia PA, The Westminster Press, 1984. A lucid story of how the Creation can be thought of as the body of God.

McFague, Sallie, *The Body Of God: An Ecological Theology*, Fortress Press, 1993. Another clear analysis of how the creation can be considered as the Body of God which leads to a Theology of Ecology.

_____*Metaphorical Theology: Models of God in Religious Language*, Fortress Press, 1982. An attempt to steer religious thinking toward a cosmic perspective.

Porter, Roy, *The Creation Of The Modern World: The Untold Story Of The British Enlightenment*, New York, W. W. Norton & Company, Inc., 2000. How the English scholars, although totally educated by and in the church institutions, managed to begin to think in new paradigms of religious, political and scientific thought.

Robinson, John A. T., *Honest To God*, Philadelphia PA, The Westminster Press, 1963. Breaking new ground in the mid-20th century in thinking of the idea of God.

Serban, George, *Tyranny of Magical Thinking: The Child's World of Belief and Adult Neurosis*, E P Dutton, November, 1982, A psychiatrist discovers that in early life children believe things happen by "magic." This method of thinking persists in an amazingly high number of adults

Chapter 17

The Creation and the Creator:-

A Search for Truth

> *"You shall learn the truth,*
> *and the truth shall set you free."*
> -Jesus of Nazareth

> *"The fact that a believer is happier*
> *than a skeptic is no more to the point than the fact*
> *that a drunken man is happier than a sober one.*
> *The happiness of credulity is a dangerous quality."*
> - George Bernard Shaw

One of the three pillars of religion is the claim to truth or the way to find the truth. The nature of the Creator - and the relationship of the Creator to the creation - are the ultimate truths sought by most religions of the world. Their versions of truth are offered as a major factor validating that religion.

In spite of Shaw's skepticism expressed above, the perception of truth and knowledge provided by religion plays a major role in maintaining another of the three pillars of religion: the underlying foundation of emotional security for its adherents. This security and happiness, or inner peace, stems from a deep inward confidence in the understanding of the world that religion provides.

The Cosmic Deity

But as Shaw comments, it is a dangerous quality. The bloodiest conflicts and most brutal displays of the worst of human nature have resulted from the fear of the loss of religious heritage. This fear of loss has brought about the religious wars that blot our history.

The underlying cause of these conflicts probably lies in religion's claim that there is another dimension to reality and that through religion one can gain access to that dimension. It is as if there were a wall between our world and this other dimension of reality. Through this wall there is a hole or several holes that are occupied by observers - religious leaders and other "spiritually" oriented individuals. These observers can see both sides and relay observations back and forth between the two realms.

This concept conveys tremendous power and prestige to those perched in the hole. It has been observed in many human societies that "power corrupts and absolute power corrupts absolutely." Many religions have not escaped the corruption engendered by the power that their leaders have derived from their position of perceived privilege.

Jesus of Nazareth lived in an era of sharp conflict in religious claims, conflict that had tremendous consequences for the everyday life in his community. The claims of the Jewish elders to truth, and to a special relationship of the Jews to the Creator, conflicted with the claims of the Roman invaders about the divine nature of their emperor. The Romans claimed that they had divine support and power from their God or gods, as demonstrated by their success in subjugating a good part of the known world.

That claim was hard to refute by those who claimed that God was on the side of his chosen people, the Jews. Doubt and despair permeated the Jewish community. How could their Creator let them down if they had a special relationship and privileged position by virtue of their being the chosen people? How could the Creator have allowed allow the destruction of their Temple, the centerpiece of their religion and culture, unless perhaps the Romans and Babylonians had a better vantage point in the "wall" or had a more privileged relationship to the Creator? They were an enslaved people, looking for answers.

One of the answers was "*Seek the truth, for the truth shall set you free.*" Although that answer sounds easy, the way to the truth is unending. As Paul, one of Jesus's followers remarked much later, "We see through a glass darkly," and expressed the hope that in the future they would see truth face-to-face.

Human thought keeps going back to the creation. What initiated it all? What controlled it, what makes things happen? The immensity and complexity of creation leaves us with a feeling of awe. It encompasses the innumerable stars and galaxies; it contains the incredible complexity of living plants, creatures, and people. Whatever caused the creation to come into existence was worthy of veneration because of its immense power and intelligence. The Creator was the initiator and the inventor, the planner and the controller of everything, everyone, and everywhere. The Creator was the supreme being, the prime mover.

The Nature of the Creator

The nature of the Creator and the Creator's work continue to pose the greatest mystery. Humans tend to think in human terms. However, human emotions often interfere with the process of clear thinking. No matter how hard we try, we usually come around to viewing the Creator in some sort of human framework. The Creator is thought to have human methods and values.

There are many schools of thought on the nature of the Creator. Many seem to rely on the concept of "the old man up there." But that is only the beginning of the question. There is a division of opinion on the function of the Creator. Loosely defined there are two schools of thought, *theism* and *deism.*

Theism conceives of the Creator as actively involved in the ongoing world. Deism envisions the Creator as one who just "wound up the watch" and allows it to run without interference. In his book *A Brief History of Time*, the physicist-philosopher Stephen Hawking conceives of creation appearing from nothing, having an absence of boundaries. At only one point in time, at the inception of the Big Bang, was the earth related to the Creator. From that point on, the universe proceeds on its own path under its own internal control. Hawking's vision is probably the most explicit and succinct explanation of the deist school of thought. It is based primarily on scientific reasoning and mathematical explanation and rather little on philosophical argument and inspiration.

Theism, by contrast, envisions the Creator involved with the creation on an ongoing basis. There is a wide range of speculation on the degree of the Creator's involvement with the creation. This involvement ranges from a passive role in keeping the universe on a preordained course, to making slight mid-term corrections to that course, to the extreme of deciding and causing every event in the universe. In the latter view, nothing happens except those events decided and ordained by the Creator at that moment.

There is also a variant of theism that does not envision the Creator as omnipotent or all-powerful. The Creator is the positive factor in creation. There is also a destructive force that is bent on destruction and disruption. The Creator is continually involved in fighting off this disruptive force and is not always successful.

Other views of the Creator range between these extremes. Some envision a Creator that is subject to manipulation. The Creator can be influenced either by the pleas of the pious or by the behavior of worthy individuals in need. Similarly, the Creator monitors the behavior of the worthy and favors them by causing fortunate events in their lives.

Is the Creator Responsible for Both Evil and Good?

This latter view has often puzzled me, as it has undoubtedly puzzled others. Occasionally it has jarred me. One winter day a friend of mine and I were flying a plane down to Florida for our vacation. We were flying in clear weather but there was threatening weather on each side of our course. My companion commented in all sincerity, "The Lord is being good to us, giving us such good weather for our flight."

Just that morning, while checking the weather forecasts, I had heard reports of sub-zero weather moving into the Ohio valley. The day before, thousands of people had been forced out of their homes by flood waters from a storm front. That storm front had now moved off the east coast, providing us with good flying weather. The frigid air following the storm was settling in over the Ohio valley. I couldn't help feeling dreadfully sorry for those poor flood victims now freezing because of "what the Lord did for us."

On another occasion our farm neighbors remarked, "The Lord has been good to us this year, our crops are far better than usual." It was the year that a big long-lasting drought had firmly settled into the sub-Saharan region of Africa. Millions of its inhabitants were starving and migrating out of the region.

By implication the Creator was rewarding some and punishing others by deliberately manipulating the weather patterns. In another sense these views could be interpreted to mean that the "Lord" was interested in simple acts such as causing a few clouds to evaporate here and there. In another view, the Creator could have been overwhelmed by destructive forces that caused winter floods and freezing winds, or thwarted by evil forces that sucked moisture out of the air before it could rain on Africa.

Still another interpretation of these views of cause and effect could be that people of the Ohio valley and the Sahel were being punished for their errant ways.

Humans, cultures, and sometimes religions gain wisdom as they mature. The human child begins life viewing itself as the center of its world. As the child matures physically, its thought patterns also change. It grows in understanding of its relationship to the world and to its parents. It begins to understand itself better and the causes and effects of events in its life.

Cultures and religions also evolve, mature and change. Religions dominated by a theistic view of the Creator face a particular dilemma. As more and more things are understood as a result of scientific investigation, our understandings change. Such basic things as meteorological events or the radiant energy of the sun become more clear. Mysteries about human form and function are dispelled as we develop an understanding of the role of DNA. These matters were previously ascribed to decisions and actions by the Creator. Now they are seen as things that are inherent to the creation and explainable in recognizable terms of cause and effect.

Most events can be explained this way. They repeat themselves in a predictable way under similar conditions. They do not result from whim or chance.

What about truly random events? Many of the events that still seem to happen by chance can be understood by appreciating their *probability*. Flip a coin. Which side comes up is not a determined event but is random. We cannot predict the outcome. Flip a coin a thousand times. How many heads and how many tails? Now we can predict the outcome of those thousand flips with a good deal of accuracy and reliability. Even where no cause and effect exists, as is true of coin flips and quantum events in subatomic particles, we are nonetheless able to find regularities and make predictions.

When events that were previously attributed to decisions and actions of the Creator are understood as inherent characteristics of the creation, the interventionist role of the Creator gets squeezed down into a narrowing gap. As one thinker said, "God is relegated to the measure of our ignorance of the moment." Under the theistic conception, there is the risk that God will be relegated to the insignificant as our knowledge expands.

It's akin to the "old blanket trick." A parent tries to wean a child from dependence upon an increasingly tattered blanket by cutting off an edge each day. The loss of that little piece each day is not noted, but eventually there is not enough remaining to argue about, and the blanket becomes irrelevant.

Another part of the theistic view is a Grand Plan. The universe and its parts and inhabitants are on a journey to a predetermined destiny. The role of the Creator is to see to it that the course is followed and to make it happen.

As far as humans are concerned, they are charged with discerning the grand plan and helping it to occur. They have choices to make, and if their choices thwart the grand plan, they will be subject to punishment. This of course puts humans in a position of fear, engendering servile behavior and constrained thought.

The religions that emphasize the theistic view developed primarily in feudal societies. They reflect those societies in their outlook and structure. In small feudal societies, the patriarch or father of the clan was the ultimate earthly authority. As well as being the biological procreator, he held authority over the clan's land. His kinsmen owed him allegiance, obedience, and service. In return he provided protection, guidance, and wisdom. He established the rules of his little fiefdom and administered justice. Those who did not follow the rules were punished or cast out. Those who conformed, prospered and received favors.

This pattern held true in larger feudal societies that combined many clans. Now the lord required agents and messengers to be his eyes and ears, to carry out instructions, and to pass out the rewards of fealty. When the kingdom was threatened by outside forces, his subjects were called to do battle in the name of the king or lord. Subjects had to give loyalty and service as directed by the lord or his agents. For their services, he promised protection and perhaps loot or wealth. If they "joined the club" they bound themselves to the system and were assured of security for themselves and their families. If they rebelled, they were banned and sent out of the kingdom.

The lord of the realm became its absolute ruler, creator of society and responsible for it. He held power and didn't have to answer to anyone. If he wished, he could make every decision and direct every change. His proclamations were recorded and became the laws of the land. He could grant pardons for transgressions or he could consign transgressors to death or the dungeon. Almost without exception the lord was a male who transferred his power and position to his son when he died.

Being human, he was susceptible to flattery. To curry his favor or to ward off his anger, his subjects heaped adulation on him. When he wished it, they erected monuments to his achievements, preserved his likeness in statues, and organized festivals to celebrate his rule. He might have been the worst scoundrel imaginable, but the praise and adulation given to him bore no relationship to his character. The image of his grandeur and prowess was regularly inflated beyond recognition.

To administer such a realm, he selected loyal retainers to be his agents. They passed along his instructions and acted in his name. He held himself aloof, and all petitions to him and benefits bestowed by him were channeled through these agents. Outside his realm was the enemy, the forces of darkness and evil.

For an individual to rebel and reject the authority of the lord of the realm and his agents was considered an act of betrayal. His friends and neighbors would think that he had aligned himself with those forces of evil.

All in all it was a life of subservience in both thought and deed. The individual was considered to be definitely a lesser being than the lord or his agents. He could rise in the hierarchy but only by pleasing the lord and receiving a higher position or status from him. Honors and praise were heaped on persons of higher position, but not because of their personal virtues. They were lauded because of their position, authority, and ability to grant favors to those below them.

That was what the world was like for most humans during the feudal period of human societies. It is not surprising that the religions arising during that period mirrored the social reality around them. Their religious beliefs were modeled after the only experience of life they had.

Try re-reading the above description of the feudal lord as if it were written about a theistic God. That is the kind of Creator that people believed in before the results of scientific investigation and social movements brought about great upheavals in religious thinking.

Does the Creator Get Involved?

The idea of a Creator that determines every action of the creation is appealing in one way: the Creator presumably has a clear goal, and thus the universe has a purpose. But this viewpoint breaks down when humans realize that they have freedom of action, freedom of choice, and can change the course of the creation.

Historically, this realization led to the modifications of the theist concept. The Creator withdraws partially from complete control, and humans at least are free to act at they please. The Creator reserves the right to reward them when they do it right and wallop them when they don't. Under this concept the Creator partially determines everything, intervening only when things get too far out of control or too far off course.

Some theists also have the conviction that the Creator is subject to pleas or flattery. The Creator can and will intervene in the creation to order changes for the benefit of worthy petitioners. Since the Creator is omnipotent, any intervention is possible, and nothing can thwart its will or power.

This assumption of omnipotence collides with the reality of evil and the destructive things going on. In the view of some, evil lurks only in the hearts of humans and erupts into the world through their actions. But then there are destructive non-human forces such as disease, floods, volcanoes, earthquakes, and famine that have a decisive and destructive impact on humans. These too are often called evils. Their occurrence in a creation fashioned by an omnipotent Creator is a puzzling problem to the theistic view. If these impersonal forces are a part of creation, then the Creator has created evil and uses evil as a tool.

Rabbi Kushner, in his book *Why Bad Things Happen to Good People* examines the common heritage of the Jewish/ Christian faiths which traditionally ascribes justice, goodness, and omnipotence to the Creator. He shows how these attributes are discordant. Any two may be affirmed, but not all three. Evil things happen to the innocent and to good and just people. If a just and good Creator is omnipotent, justice and goodness would prevail for those people. It obviously does not. So there is a dilemma in deciding which two of the attributes are really in effect.

One way around this dilemma is to redefine evil events. Some have held that evil events are used by the Creator for the ultimate good, that apparent evil has a long-term good purpose. There are inconsistencies in this approach. The same people who argue this way often devote a good bit of effort to battling what they call evil in their lives and in society, and they help others to do the same.

In this view the Creator is the originator of both good and evil events. If the Creator is believed to be good and just, then there is no distinction between good and evil. They are just different actions of a good Creator.

Sometimes evil is defined as only those things that occur as the result of wrong *intentions*. Those that are caused by accident are not evil. If we attribute bad accidents to chance, then we define the Creator as less than omnipotent or at the very least inattentive. The disease AIDS is universally looked upon as a terrible evil, as it is a one-way trip to a painful death. AIDS can be contracted by illicit intercourse with an infected prostitute. It can also be transmitted through contaminated blood used in a medical transfusion.

If the disease is thought to be the Creator's punishment of the prostitute's client, it would have to be defined as good and not evil. As for the hemophiliac who receives contaminated blood, it is hard to see how it could be considered good and not evil. His disease is not the result of wrong human action or evil intent by any human actor in the drama.

Another problem with the theistic view lies simply in *methods*. How does the Creator intervene in the creation? Is there a big unseen hand that pushes things about? Does the Creator intervene at the atomic level, or at the subatomic level? Does the Creator, as Saint Francis claimed, act only through humans?

At the beginning of this examination of creation and Creator, it was shown that all matter is energy that has "condensed" into the subatomic particles. The actions of these subatomic particles, and those of the larger structures to follow, are determined solely by the four forces of the universe. The key aspect of these forces is that they reside in or are generated within matter. None of these forces resides anywhere else.

The question regarding the primacy of human action is problematic for another reason. If the Creator acts only through humans, what was the Creator doing for the several billions of years before humans appeared on this earth?

Primitive societies viewed the natural disasters of life such as earthquakes, volcanoes, lightning, and thunder as acts of the gods (the Big Hand). Of course they are now understood as resulting from the local and regional forces at work between different parts of the material universe.

The sex of an offspring or defects in a newborn child were once believed to be gifts or punishments from the gods. Knowledge of genetics and congenital abnormalities has taken the mystery out of that part of life. Birth defects are caused by damage to genes and chromosomes or by toxic influences reaching the embryo early in its life in the womb. That is to say, by specific causes and events operating at the molecular level of creation. What were once seemingly arbitrary acts of the Creator are now well understood, even if they are not yet easy to predict.

Is Uncertainty a Sign of the Creator?

As noted before, in the early history of the USSR it was forbidden to teach certain aspects of the new physics relating to quantum mechanics. These theories described the behavior of subatomic particles and demonstrated the uncertainty and unpredictability of their actions. The Soviet authorities feared this might open the door for students to imagine that a Creator might possibly be at work changing or controlling the universe by intervening at this level.

This, of course, is a distortion of quantum mechanics. Although it is true that individual electrons cannot be predicted to follow any particular path, the collective motion of a large group of electrons can be predicted very well. They are like coin flips in this regard.

What about the one-at-a-time little actions? Couldn't they add up by following one other, each one pushing just a little further from the main path? It is true that every action of every thing, big or little, animal or human, electron or photon, changes the course of the universe in some tiny fashion. The changed situation that each small action produces could be immediately changed again by another unpredictable action. Such chains of events and their short and long-range effects are unpredictable and unknowable.

The weather illustrates what is being discussed here. When a cold front approaches, the likelihood of rain is high. When the dark cloud and high winds come over the hill, the prospects for rain are almost certain. Part of the moisture in the air falls as rain. But there is absolutely no certainty about *which* water molecules fall and which ones stay in the atmosphere.

The thunderstorm could have been anticipated several days before from clues in the atmospheric patterns. Predictions of a thunderstorm a week or more in advance at any particular location are virtually impossible. The predictions of specific weather events a year away are little better than chance. Overall, random events intervene all the time at all levels, but generally they can be explained quite well by existing knowledge. It is hardly necessary to invoke an intervening Creator.

In the one-at-a-time case above, it is known that small or even microscopic events can "cause" large effects if they are followed by many other such events. It has been speculated that the fluttering of a butterfly wing in Argentina could be the initiating event of a tornado in Kansas! Looking backwards one, event/one cause at a time, may show us that such an improbable idea is in fact true. To observe the wings of butterfly first and then predict what the air motion might build up to -

that would require observing the outcomes of trillions of similar events. Looking forwards is often like watching molecular soup and trying to predict the appearance of life!

Returning to the problem namely if the unpredictability of subatomic particles is indeed where the Creator operates, we have huge problems of logic. In this case the Creator must have instantaneous knowledge of the actions of each particle of the universe at every moment. This extends from the center of the black holes to individual hydrogen atoms anywhere in space. It also implies advance knowledge of the planned actions of humans, who have some degree of free will in their actions.

Such a complex scheme flies in the face of the elegant simplicity of the observed universe, a universe composed of organized energy and a recognized ability to organize itself. Such a universe enjoys both stability that preserves new creations and instability that forces change, with no further push at all from the Creator.

Does the Creator Communicate?

The concept of an interventionist Creator poses two more problems, that of communicating with the universe and that of effecting control. If the Creator is located at a point, it implies instantaneous communication from that point to every point in the universe. This, in turn, implies a terrific amount of communication to and from each particle of the universe. If the Creator is thought of as permeating every part of the universe, then the theistic Creator is in fact a parallel universe. It is superimposed on the existing universe, but with a vast communication and action network extending throughout all parts of the Creator. Is this what is really going on?

A fervent wish of humans is to communicate and become acquainted with the Creator and to divine the Creator's intent. Some persons have not been content to confine the Creator's role to mentor and guide for humans. They believe, or wish to believe, that there is some method for communicating between humans and the Creator, a two-way system.

Setting aside the problem of the medium of communication for the moment, there is a major problem of language and understanding. For humans, language developed as a way of reducing the ambiguity of communicating facts and ideas. Sign language and body language can communicate some thoughts and facts, but these lack the precision and versatility of a verbal or a written language. If communication between the Creator and humans is so important, and if this communication is the only contact of the Creator with creation, it certainly would not be carried out in an ambiguous and unreliable manner!

If this communication is to be the only contact of the Creator with its creation, a communication ability should be inherent in the creation. We would expect it to be firmly established as a basic characteristic of human capability and to be a preeminent part of the human experience. This is not so.

The problem of how this communication would be transmitted *between* humans is another obstacle to taking this view seriously. The communication medium would have to be capable of stirring or exciting the neurons of our brains and sensory organs so that we could process the communications as thoughts and memories. The brain, in turn, would need to have the capability of coupling with this medium in order to transmit thoughts to the Creator or other humans on the "party line." If such communication does take place, it is undetectable or at the very least intermittent.

To substantiate the concept of communication with the Creator, some persons point to the claims that humans can communicate with one another by mental telepathy or extrasensory perception. Much effort has been expended trying to find and develop this facility. Some people have claimed that it is a developing or emerging characteristic of humans as they further evolve. Others claim that it is a common trait that has been submerged but can be reawakened in humans.

The claim that it is a recent evolving and expanding capability of humans ignores the fact that human evolution occurs first on an individual level. Then the changes spread out through succeeding generations as that altered characteristic is genetically passed on to future generations. It would take hundreds of thousands of years for this capability to spread to the majority of the population through genetic pathways. It would not simultaneously evolve and appear in a whole species at the same time.

As to the claim that telepathic communication is a submerged characteristic of humans which can be redeveloped, it is not impossible that humans communicated in this way early in their history. That now seems unlikely. If so, telepathy has long ago been superseded by the more precise communication afforded by language.

Unfortunately for careful investigation, this claimed ability of extrasensory perception has above all been taken over by charlatans who prey on the gullible and promise communication with past ancestors and departed loved ones. Attempts to verify their claims by any reasonable test have been unsuccessful, and any such means of communication does not meet with consistent results when evaluated by an unbiased observer.

An unbiased observer is an important ingredient. In one case where a series of serious evaluation took place, two sets of observers were asked to record the results of the tests. One set of observers were "believers" and the other set were disinterested. When the results of the test were compared, the data taken by the believers showed that extrasensory perception did occur with a statistically significant regularity. The data recorded by the disinterested observers showed the opposite.

It is far easier to accept a version of the theistic concept if the Creator were permeating every part of creation yet being apart from it. Such a view of a diffused Creator avoids the problems of communication at a distance. It also avoids the conceptual problem of locating the Creator at a point somewhere within or outside the universe.

Is the Creator Everywhere?

There is an undeniable urge in humans to communicate with parents, relatives, or friends who have died. We wish that we could get the advice or guidance that our parents had given in the past, or question them on things that happened that we do not remember. Our parents were the ultimate authority and the judge of all events. They settled disputes and established the rules that made the family function. They made the home and provided food and shelter. We realize later in life that they gave us life itself.

Many religious yearnings transfer these parental images to the Creator. The Creator is given these attributes and satisfies those comforting images of our childhood, thus becoming the parent of our adult life. We yearn to communicate with this parental image and experience the warmth and love of our childhood. We want to have our needs and yearnings fulfilled. We would like once again to have rules and guidance to solve our problems and order our societies.

But what of those who have a different parental image? Suppose one of us had an abusive or tyrannical father, an unloving mother, parents who had to be placated by obsequious behavior? The parental image transferred to this Creator might be of someone to be feared or from whom you had to hide. It would be a Creator who would require appeals and favors in order to give a hearing or grant a wish. It would be an image of someone who made arbitrary and harsh rules, someone whose love and approval were given only when the rules were precisely obeyed, and perhaps not even then.

Unfortunately, these are the images of the Creator in the minds of some people. They too become embedded in religious traditions, reinforcing the sensibility of a harsh and unyielding father.

Just because humans have an urge or tendency for certain beliefs does not validate these beliefs. Unfortunately, many people hang on to childhood's magical image of the way that the world works. They fail to mature into thinking and reasoning people. They remain tied down by the mental tyranny of the "magical" mode of thinking that is characteristic of childhood thought.

Humans have many experiences that they cannot explain, so they may attribute them to communication with the Creator, or at least communication from the Creator. It is not at all clear whether these experiences always stem from the same phenomenon. Nor is it clear how one could be distinguished from the other. The experiences of those who have used mind-altering drugs demonstrate similar effects. Certainly the question of unexpected and unexplained "communication" remains open, but it does not seem necessary to invoke a Creator to account for them.

Humans also have feelings or urges which are sometimes attributed to communication from the Creator. Among these are urges or "instructions" to become involved in a different course of life, feelings of warmth and acceptance, compulsions to do things against their wishes or judgment, ambiguous messages or urges, feelings of awe and wonder, and feelings of unity with all of creation.

Did the Creator Wind the Clock and Walk Away?

As we have seen, if communication with humans is believed to be the only contact of the Creator with creation, we immediately encounter many logical difficulties. If indeed, as Saint Francis claimed, we are the only hands, feet, and mouth that the Creator has to do his work and spread his thoughts, then the Creator has been quiescent for most of the life of the creation.

What if the Creator *has* been quiescent? This view takes you very close to the deist view of the Creator, a Creator who was present and initiated the Creation and has been absent from involvement with it ever since. Considering our present knowledge of the universe, certainly the deist view seems more sensible than the theist view. The Franciscan view is a deist view if humans are removed from the scene or if they have not yet appeared.

Both the theist and deist views embody a bi-level universe. The first level is the cosmos as we experience it in its physical form. The second is the Creator, which stands apart from it. Either the Creator is intimately involved in each part and at each point, or it is a distant observer observing its handiwork as the creation evolves and changes.

A bi-level universe has an attraction in human thought, since it promises supernatural help or guidance and a Creator not sullied with the vulgarities of existence. It also offers the possibility of escape to a more perfect realm. This other realm is not clearly defined in most religious traditions. In some it is a union with the Creator, in others it involves transportation to yet another level of the universe, this one better managed than the one in which we now exist.

The link between these levels of the universe is not defined in theology, nor is it self-evident. Its mechanism of contact is said to be in the realm of the miraculous or beyond comprehension.

The deist view - of a universe created once and then detached from the Creator - is usually associated with a universe that has all its parts in place and works smoothly. Deism is not a completely defined view, but its general philosophy implies a universe set on a predetermined course to a final objective. Some have viewed this objective as a final union with the Creator. Others have singled out humans for that final union, and then only if they have satisfactorily completed the obstacle courses of life. These include the tests of worthiness as set out by the Creator.

Because the deist's creation is detached from the Creator, either every part of its course of action is determined at its creation, or, it is completely off on its own, its course determined by its inhabitants or by chance.

Taking the first view, nothing in our understanding of the creation supports the view that every motion, every change, every turn of the evolution of the creation is preordained. On the other hand, the course of the creation does seem to be an adventure, in which each turn is determined by chance and is influenced by internal forces. But a completely detached creation would be a discard, a toy created for the amusement of the Creator, a cast-off, an apparent waste of tremendous power and energy.

An "accidental" universe is another view that has recently been put forward. The universe simply exists or happens without cause or plan or effort. Steven Hawking's universe, for example, is one that appears out of nothing, balancing the "positive" energy necessary to produce the material world with the "negative" energy of some of the forces holding things together. In this view, the universe appeared from a gigantic quantum fluctuation of the vacuum energy, seemingly out of nothing. But that vacuum energy is something, a something that transforms itself into the creation.

(In this view, there could be an infinitude of universes, each one created out of nothing. Only some universes would be observed - those that were ordered in such a way that they could produce conscious and observant beings. One aim of modern physics is to try to determine if the laws and forces that control the universe are the unavoidable consequences of the creation process. Could the transformation of energy into matter have occurred in an infinitude of sets of laws and forces? Or in just the ones that we know?)

A Creator Intimate in Every Part of the Universe

Let's leave the idea of a detached creation. If instead we view the Creator as manifesting itself as the creation, this eliminates the many inconsistencies embedded in other theologies and Ideologies. First, it eliminates the difficulties involved in bi-level or multi-level views of the universe. When the Creator transforms itself into the creation, this creative force - power that exhibits what we call wisdom or genius - becomes the physical universe itself.

The Creator is then intimate in every part of the universe, not controlling it but actually being the universe. By being every part of the universe, it eliminates the problem of levels and of communication between them. It also avoids the conceptual problems of communicating from a single point in its own location to every part of the universe.

The universe that we know communicates with itself. The forces that mold it and transfer energy between its parts know no boundaries. They travel and extend to the infinite in all directions. Each part acts upon every other part and feels no forces other than those generated within these parts and pieces. With its built-in affinities that shape and stabilize the elements of creation and the instabilities that force exploration and change, the creation is surely alive in the sense of growth, change, and inter-relatedness.

Its course is an adventure. Its realities are determined by its dynamic patterns of organization which are forever and relentlessly changing, exploring every possible avenue. Each new successful entity in turn provides a new and different platform for the adventure to explore further.

What of the genius evident in the creation? Does this genius remain behind and aloof from the creation after the creation event, as it does in the deist view? Does it hover over and parallel the creation as envisioned by the theist view, or does it reside intimately within the creation as articulated by this new view of the Creator as the creation? The role of genius in the creation is a heavy question, and we will address it in the chapter called "The Mind of God."

So far in this book I've capitalized the C in Creator and not creation. This may seem puzzling, but it refers to what might be my prejudice or perhaps my limited view of time, cause, and effect. To the Creator I ascribe the inherent genius evident in the creation and the immense power that it represents - a first cause, if you will. This manifestation of the Creator when it transforms itself into the creation (not capitalized) continues to contain and exhibit the Creator's genius and power. My distinction is an acknowledgment that the Creator remains primary over the form that it has now assumed. That is my prejudice, and if it offends or distracts you, please ignore the distinction.

If this view of the Creation contains an image of the truth, what are its implications for our view of ourselves as part of this creation? You, I, and everything else **are** an integral part of this creation. We do not exist as separate entities. We cannot escape our interrelatedness with the past, the future, and our contemporaries. We breathe in air exhaled by other people and creatures, incorporating some of its molecules into transient materials in our bodies. We reuse the same atoms and minerals that once roamed the earth as the building blocks of dinosaurs, and those same atoms were present when blue-green algae transformed our planet's atmosphere. Each part of us was with the Creator in the Big Bang, and we have been with the Creator ever since.

Each particle of us has been molded in the heart of the stars, forged in the explosion of a supernova, drifted in the cool void of space, pounded together in the dust of the planetary cloud, and melted in the interior of the earth. We've been spewed out of a volcano, buried in the depths of the sea, thrust up in the mountains, and washed down to the seas. We've inhabited the oceans, crawled out on the mud, and colonized the land. We've been part of the drama of all living creatures, been annihilated in the cataclysms that caused the great extinctions, and were part of the survivors that re-inhabited the planet.

The codes in our genes link us with every living creature in the earth's past. They link us to all other living creatures with us now, and they will permeate and determine the characteristics of our progeny in the future.

Each of our actions changes the creation and shapes a part of its evolution. Having a role in this adventure is our immortality. Our essence, our reality persists by imprinting in the creation the changes that we make. Advances in organization are not erased. Our shared immortality with the creation/Creator is the common ground of all society, all life. In our present form we exist as a part of what we call humanity. All too soon we will merge our identity with the Creator and continue on the grand adventure, our imprint forever changing its course in its own unique way.

In our own little human bit of the adventure, we've participated in the emergence of consciousness, memory, knowledge, language and culture as emerging properties of the creation. As we participate in the search for truth, as we use the gifts of memory and knowledge that inform our consciousness, we have been privileged to begin to discern the nature of the Creator. Our task is, as always, to be "honest to God as well as be honest about God."

Chapter 17 Bibliography

Barbour, Ian G., *When Science Meets Religion: Enemies, Strangers, or Partners?*, HarperSanFrancisco, 2000. The author examines patterns of though in different religious traditions.

Spong, John Shelby, *Why Christianity Must Change Or Die*. San Francisco: HarperSanFrancisco, 1998. A Bishop speaks to believers "in exile" who maintain a religious faith and connection while being skeptical of traditional thinking about God.

De Chardin, Pierre Teilhard Chardin, *The Phenomenon of Man,* Harper& Row, 1959. This Jesuit Father/ Paleontologists traces the course of evolution through the evolution and continuing evolution of "Man." He is scrupulous in acknowledging the reality of the scientific knowledge we possess and comes very close to declaring that the creator to be the "stuff of the universe, but veers off. Although he acknowledges the adventure and the role of organization in creation, he envisions life merging toward and "Omega Point where human lives at last will merge with the creator.

Chapter 18

The Mind Of God

"I only want to know the mind of God.
All else is details."
-Albert Einstein

The concept of the Creator as the creation implies a genius that determines the form that the creation takes. In this study of the Creator, I claim that the power of the Creator transforms itself into matter and the genius of the Creator determines the form of that matter. We have seen that the newly created matter possesses internal forces which compel and allow the grand adventure of creation to take place. Darwin's "dangerous idea" explains how the universe evolves following its explosive birth: it simply applies its own internal forces again and again. There is no additional motor. Thus the genius of the Creator is continually exhibited in the initial design of the creation: one that enables repeated self-transformations without an external guiding hand.

We will explore the concept of the "mind" of the Creator as part and parcel of the creation. Then we will explore the genius that is evident in the form that the creation has taken. In the process, we will discover a mind that learns, a mind that remembers, a mind that creates, and a mind that communicates. All of these properties have their counterparts in what we call a human or an animal mind. But, crucially, we will show that a mind need not be centrally located nor function as an individual control center. This greatest Mind is a collective and comprehensive work, one that is present in each and every bit and piece of the creation.

Does a Mind Imply a Brain?

If we see and observe a genius within or behind the creation, that genius is, as Einstein described it, "The mind of God." But what is a mind? The mind is not a physical thing with a size and shape. In human terms, *the mind is what the brain does.* The mind is the functioning of a physical brain and body, not something that is endowed upon it or separate from it. A simple brain, a "bird brain", does simple things. A more complex brain functions more profoundly and exhibits a more imponderable or unpredictable mind.

A mind *learns* and *remembers* its new knowledge. The human mind also *creates.* It takes memories and new information from the body's sensors to create ideas. It then directs the body to create physical inventions, music, art, poetry, literature, war, and politics. The mind also communicates with its surroundings and fellow creatures, using the brain and body to send and receive signals, and most potently, to intervene in the external world.

Let us contemplate the mind of the Creator. In a parallel fashion does it physically control or intervene in the ongoing creation? What about communications? Does the mind of the Creator consciously communicate with the individual "creatures" that it creates? Does it communicate with all of the bits and pieces of the creation or does it communicate only with those creatures which have developed brains? Does it only communicate with those creatures which have developed language? Does it remember? These seem to be unanswerable questions. But let us not be daunted. Rather, how can we ponder the imponderable?

Thought Experiments to Expand the Imagination

Albert Einstein conducted what he called thought experiments. These were inquiries or experiments that he couldn't possibly perform physically. His thought experiments together with rigorous mathematics and previous scientific discoveries led him to profound new insights. Hopefully our generation will do the same.

Einstein started out his major thought experiment by imagining what the world would look like to him if he were traveling along on a beam of light like a passenger riding on an extremely fast train. Of course he couldn't actually ride on a beam of light and no passenger train could approach the speed of light, but he could do this in his imagination and apply the things he knew from the world around him. Einstein gained all sorts of profound insights when he did this. He found that time was not a constant. He found that space and time were interrelated. He found that matter and energy are interchangeable, thus forever changing our understanding of the universe.

Now let's try a thought experiment of our own. Suppose you are the Creator. How would you comport yourself? How would you establish your relationship to the creation? What would that relationship be? Would you have a purpose for everything in the Creation? Would everything be planned out ahead of time and carried out faithfully? How would you communicate with your Creation? How would you manipulate it? Would you manipulate it? How would you make thing happen?

Let's first think about purpose, relationships, and communication, which are some of the major concerns of philosophy and religion. Would you have a purpose for everything in the creation - the black holes, the galaxies careening into one another, the vast supernovas and their titanic explosions? Would your purpose extend to the minuscule, for instance the uncounted quadrillions of neutrinos which pass through us without so much as a greeting? Or would your purpose extend only to creatures that move about on their own under their own internal direction?

Would you concern yourself with creatures anywhere in the vastness of the creation? Or would you worry about only those on one small insignificant planet in one of the rather commonplace small galaxies of stars among untold billions of other galaxies? Would you want to have communication with, and a purpose for, all creatures: slugs and bacteria, insects and beetles? Or would you restrict it to large complex creatures that have mastered the skies, dominated the land, and learned to survive on and under the sea such as Pterodactyls, Tyrannosaurs Rex, and Whales? Instead would you wait to communicate for an extra hundred million years and then begin to communicate with big primates such as chimpanzees and their close relatives?

If you as the Creator had not built in a purpose, had not instilled this purpose into the very nature of these creatures, and had not included in their very nature a means for them to faithfully carry out that purpose, would you then devise a method for communicating their purpose to them? If you did, would it be delayed until they had developed a spoken or written language? Would you communicate it to them in a written language? If so, would it be in every language or would you start out in a small way and hope to have it spread and be translated to other languages in the future? Would you write it out in the form of history, the form of allegory, or in flat-out instructions?

Perhaps you would instead hope to communicate it to every individual? How would you do that? Would you speak to individuals in private? Would you speak to them inside their heads, in their own language? Would you give them urges that they could distinguish from their own desires, from the effects of the hormones and adrenaline that course through their bodies? Would these be distinguishable from the effects of drugs and alcohol? Would such creatures be able to distinguish a voice in their head from the symptoms of paranoid-delusional mental aberrations?

When you have delved into these thought experiments and thought them through from every aspect, you will probably find that you have posed more questions than answers and that many of your previous assumptions appear to be absurd. But if you follow these questions and trends of thought to their logical conclusions, you, like Einstein, may make amazing discoveries that transform your understanding of the Creator.

Because this matter of communication is a major aspect of human minds and human interaction, it tends to dominate the historical concepts of the Creator. It cannot be lightly dismissed. We shall see later how it fits into the wider aspects of this inquiry into The Mind Of God.

Recognizing an Inherent Genius

The creation undoubtedly exhibits a genius, either within it or "behind" it. Speculative scientists and philosophers who do not like the idea that there is something behind or within the universe - a mind if you wish - have come up with an alternative explanation for the genius that they think they observe in the form and substance of the universe. Their explanation is that there has been almost an infinite number of universes with wildly varying physical characteristics. Our universe is only one among the infinitude of possibilities that have existed or will exist.

This theory of an infinitude of different universes is an extension of Darwin's theory of the evolution of living species. In that theory there are an infinitude of biological mutations and combinations, with the best-adapted ones surviving the longest. Similarly, it is possible that there have been and will be other universes, presumably with particles and forces different from ours. At this time, of course, there is no evidence for such an infinity of universes, so this theory remains pure speculation.

In the chapter entitled "Thankful For Little Things", we explored the exquisite fine-tuning of the physical constants of the creation. We found that if these characteristics were only slightly different, our universe would have evolved in a much different mode and time scale. If the universe had not always existed in this apparently fine-tuned form, there is a very small likelihood that creatures such as humans would have evolved, i.e. creatures which can observe and study the creation.

Some speculative scientists or philosophers have called this phenomenon - of a unique assembly of finely tuned inherent characteristics that favor the evolution of consciousness - the *anthropic principle*. The full-strength version of the anthropic principle states that these favorable conditions are the result of an *intent*; the universe was created in such a way so that observant creatures like ourselves would inevitably come about.

The Genius in the Universe Is Not Human Genius

Before we go more deeply into "the Mind of God", we will have to let go of our anthropomorphic concepts, concepts that organize everything in terms of human minds and bodies. The Creator/creation may well have a "mind", but we should not expect it to function in the same way that a human mind does. We should not expect it to have emotions and thoughts similar to those of animals and humans. Human and animal minds have developed to cope with the necessities of human and animal lives. Thus our minds are uniquely adapted to functioning in our particular niches within the creation.

We have already seen that the processes of the human and animal mind are not confined to the brain but involve the interaction of the entire body. Similarly, we should not expect that the Mind of God will necessarily reside in an isolated, discrete, well-demarcated brain.

Terrestrial Minds and Brains Have Defined Tasks

What does a mind/brain do? The most simple brain reacts only to external stimuli such as light, heat, and chemicals. It is aware of the factors to which it reacts. A more complex brain/mind remembers and learns to be aware of these various inputs. In the case of mobile creatures which have a specialized brain structure, the brain/mind also controls locomotion, movement, and their associated vital functions.

Far beyond that, the human mind also creates thoughts and impressions. It combines and associates its memories. When a new situation occurs, it combines prior memories with new inputs and it reacts, sometimes well, sometimes poorly. Comparing and combining memories leads to learning and to new memories, a function that takes place entirely within the mind/brain.

The mind then is a creative thing. In humans it contains an ability to imagine; to create poetry, literature, science, and music from memories and stimuli held within itself. And the memories it holds! More than in other creatures, the human mind is an apparatus for learning. Our brains seem especially well designed to learn and remember, and they have to be. We come into the world with precious few instinctive behaviors. We must learn nearly all of our functions, from eating solid food to locomotion to speech.

A bird's mind/brain, on the other hand, shows the opposite characteristics. It comes with a great deal of genetic memory. A newly hatched duck knows how to walk, swim, eat, and dry its down. It quickly learns to identify its mother, but will slip up and identify a human being as its mother if the human is the first creature that it sees.

Many newly hatched birds come with a lot of built-in knowledge but lack the ability to learn more than standard bird behavior. I remember when a particularly learning-challenged robin took up residence in our maple tree and one day landed on the picnic table. Several feet away was our patio door. His image was clearly reflected in the glass. I suppose his genetic knowledge told him that it was a male intruder that must be repelled from his nesting territory. So, into the window he flew, crashed to the deck, shook himself, and flew up to the table. As he turned around, there was that intruder again. Another crash into the window. Again and again, hour after hour and day after day, the performance was repeated. His bird brain was very slow to allow trial-and-error learning to replace his instincts.

What Is the Organic Basis of a Brain?

But let's think about the brain itself for a moment; this brain whose functioning we call mind. First of all, it is composed of highly specialized cells called nerve cells or neurons. Although nerve cells are found in connected nets throughout the body, they are concentrated in unimaginably large numbers in the cranium. Here each neuron has complex interconnections with its neighbors, allowing cooperation and above all memory.

Not all inputs to the brain come via the body's neural network. Some inputs are chemical messages. Testosterone, estrogen, adrenaline, alcohol, and opiates are all very strong messages to the human brain, and it reacts strongly to these inputs. Indeed, these mind-altering substances can seemingly overwhelm the normal rational functioning of the brain for a while.

Interestingly, the brain also makes chemical outputs. It sends out small amounts of key chemical messages to other parts of the body. These brain hormones are often the "master" regulators of other bodily functions such as growth and fertility.

The mind, then, is the functioning of the brain. It extends throughout the entire body, reacting to and in turn acting on all parts of the organism. Although most of the complicated processing of inputs and memories occurs in the cranial cavity among the interconnecting brain cells, there is no center of the brain as such, and no center of the mind. Although we do tend to think of the mind as the center of a person and that a mind resides at a particular place, we also have to acknowledge that there is no physical center within the brain/mind. Our mind functions as a part of the whole.

Further, no brain/mind exists or is able to exist on its own. It is dependent upon other organs of the living creature for its nourishment, waste disposal, and protection. It is not and cannot be an entity separate from the creature itself.

Brains/minds as we know them, including a central nervous system, are only apparent in mobile creatures. Locomotion requires a sensory and control apparatus because the creature must forage for food, look for a mate, and avoid predators. Only mobile living things have what we normally call a brain. Brains/ minds developed only where they were necessary. Contrast the needs of a mobile creature with that of a tree anchored in the ground which cannot move. It extracts its food from the air and soil and sun and broadcasts its pollen to other trees. It has no need to develop or evolve a central nervous system. It has no need to move about to find a mate, or seek food.

Centrally Organized Versus Diffuse Minds

A central brain is a necessity for some organisms but superfluous for others. One little creature, commonly called the sea squirt, starts out life with a rudimentary brain and nervous system. In its juvenile stage it propels itself about seeking an appropriate living space. When it finds one, it permanently attaches itself and remains there for the rest of its life. Once attached, it proceeds to "eat" its brain, because it doesn't need it any more.

All living things develop the "minds" that are required for them to function. A caterpillar has a brain that controls its functions as a crawling and chewing creature. When it makes a cocoon, it dissolves all of its body except its digestive tract and eats the discarded material. A butterfly develops around the digestive tract. It becomes a new creature complete with a new brain -capable of operating a butterfly.

Lesser organisms, like colonies of slime molds, get along very well by utilizing only chemical messengers to communicate between cells. These organisms have neither a center nor a brain. Yet these colonies can move about, change their collective shape, enable some of their cells to become stalks or flowers, and cause some cells to form spores that are broadcast to assure the survival of the species. This knowledge resides in the DNA of every one of its cells. The DNA interacts with the other structures in the cell to specify the messengers to be sent to nearby cells. Collectively the mass of cells behaves in a coordinated and purposeful way by using a "brain" that is distributed equally throughout its body.

At the other end of the size scale is the world's most massive living thing - and one of its longest-living creatures - the Giant Sequoia tree. It has no brain, no center of control, indeed no "center" at all. Yet it knows how to grow to unprecedented heights, how to survive winds, storms, drought, and freezing climates, how to defend itself from predators, and how to reproduce itself.

The ecosystem of planet earth is a living, growing, interdependent organism in its own right, yet it has no center, no brain as such, no all-encompassing nervous system. This ecosystem has survived the catastrophes of collisions with asteroids and massive volcanic eruptions. It has adapted to momentous change in the atmosphere wrought by its own workings of extracting carbon from carbon dioxide and converting the atmosphere into one highly charged with oxygen. It continuously adapted to the changing environment caused by the aging and ferment of the earth beneath and has coped with variations of the energy input from an evolving sun.

This ecosystem has nurtured and played an intimate part in the development of hundreds of millions of different life forms. It has birthed and nurtured huge creatures such as blue whales and clever bipeds such as humans, doing it all without a brain or a center.

The concept of diffused genius should not be too hard for modern day humans to comprehend. Just contemplate how our own bodies undergo embryonic development. The single fertilized cell divides and divides again, then differentiates into a host of different kinds of cells and tissues. The body is built without guidance from a central mind. Rather each cell is using the experience of our species patiently gained over the aeons by trial and error and stored as DNA information. These DNA codes or memories have been passed on from generation to generation and from species to species in an unbroken chain, for billions of years of creative evolution.

Cell-to-cell communication is carried out by chemical messengers also specified by their individual DNA. Newly developing cells are told to switch on those genes which will turn them into this or that specialized organ. Each organ replicates its own cells and grows, following the embedded DNA plan. Indeed fetal growth and differentiation involves mainly DNA coordination and orchestration. The central nervous system and brain, which are also present and growing, do not direct our bodies until relatively late in development, first through hormonal messages and then through thought and behavior. The most important part of our early development occurs via the distributed knowledge shared by every cell in its DNA - a classic example of a *diffuse mind.*

An ecosystem is coordinated in a similar manner. Instead of cells, tissues, and organs, we find organisms, clusters of organisms, and cooperative communities of different kinds of creatures. Each is able to replicate itself or its parts when necessary. Some have specialized functions: communication, waste recycling, healing, and food transport. None are under the control of a central mind of that ecosystem. It isn't necessary. The genius of that ecosystem is distributed throughout every one of its parts.

Did Man Create God in His Own Image?

I suspect that most humans have an idealized image of the human mind and expect the Creator to possess a similar mind. It's as if bats were to examine humans and then be astounded that humans can't locate a mosquito at 20 feet in the dark and know which direction it is flying. For bats, that is their nature. We humans don't hunt food in this fashion and our brains did not evolve to perform this seemingly impossible task. Similarly, humans might want to ponder just what type of mind a creator of universes would possess.

This inquiry may allow us to better understand the genius and wisdom inherent in the creation. Remember, the reality of a thing lies in its organization. The genius of the Creator is inherent in how it has organized its immense energy or power to "condense" itself into the physical universe. The creation requires no central nervous system and no brain to keep it functioning. It experiences or senses its activity at each point and at all times. It communicates with each part of itself through its forces and messengers and through the continuous transfers of energy from place to place.

In the organic realm, it remembers its advances by writing down successful experiments in DNA code, allowing this knowledge to be handed down from generation to generation. It perpetually combines and recombines previous experiences, concepts, and experiments to make new ones, and it remembers the survivable results. Through its internal forces, it ensures that there is unceasing change, yet always within rule-determined limits. We may think of the rules and patterns as the "mind," acting on the "body," the creation.

A Distributed Mind Present in All Things

The defining characteristics of a human mind are its ability to sense and communicate with its surroundings, to learn, to remember, and to manipulate its knowledge. These distinguish us from machines that function smoothly but have no creativity. Those human minds that create and manipulate knowledge in novel and unique ways, we call "geniuses." When we look at the creation, we see each of its parts in communication with other parts. We see how learning takes place, we see the preservation of that learning, and we observe how the knowledge gained is put to use in the continuing creative process. In this sense the creation possesses a mind. When we stand in awe at the infinity and diversity of unique and beautiful entities in the universe, we realize the creation surely possesses and displays a genius that transformed itself into a universe capable of evolving these wonders.

Creative self-organizing - genius - is not confined to living creatures. As we have seen, each proton and each electron "knows" how to make an atom. The wisdom, power, and creativity of the Creator is infused through each and every part of the creation. The new elements created in the "fires" of the stars know how to make new crystals and new molecules. Each new and useful DNA sequence is remembered by being replicated and passed on to new organisms. In this sense the entire creation functions as a mind.

It was pointed out earlier that the essential essence of our individual minds, minds that die with us, is in the memories and knowledge that we accumulate. Yet a creative and activist mind does not have to reside in a single place or body, nor does it have to plot and plan and reason as does a human being whose survival depends upon these skills. It needs only to ensure that its successful organizations of matter and energy can be duplicated and used again. The creation itself demonstrates and performs these functions of memory and knowledge - the Mind of the Creator.

The Traditional View of God

If we would wish to seek the Mind of God/Creator in a single place somewhere outside of the creation, it would behoove us to conceive of that place. If we seek a Mind that controls the universe, its body, to accomplish its conscious goals, it would behoove us to try to determine its method of nurturing and influencing the universe.

This of course brings us up against the conundrum of the vastness of the universe. We would have to postulate instantaneous forces and communication methods to guide the stuff of the universe and the other minds found within the creation.

Perhaps we imagine instead that the Mind of God operates parallel to and intimately coupled to the universe but as a diffuse mind, i.e. not residing in any single place. Then we would expect some evidence of external control of the creation that shapes and guides the universe as we know it, evidence that science has nowhere found.

A third alternative is that the creation and the Creator are but one entity and that the universe itself is the location of the Mind of God/Creator. This is the alternative that we have explored in the Great Adventure.

We have see how the four inherent forces keep the creation in dynamic stability while providing rules and limits for its process of change. We have seen that the universe communicates with itself and through itself by a myriad of different means. In the living world here on planet earth we have seen how knowledge can reside in the code called DNA. Among humans a vast range of additional knowledge is held and communicated in culture and language.

What survives is what replicates to appear again. Everywhere the common principle of organization and memory reasserts itself. Each bit and piece of the universe "knows" what it can do. That is knowledge in its purest form.

This concept of the Mind of the Creator - that it exists within the creation, learning and remembering and guiding the creation inherently - is in conflict with the traditional concepts of the Creator. The traditional concept sees God as an omnipotent being, all-knowing, all-powerful, and all-seeing. But let us make another thought experiment here. If the Creator is all-knowing, it implies that the Creator does not operate by learning or remembering what is learned, since nothing unforeseen can occur to be learned and remembered. This concept seems to put the Creator into a straitjacket; an inability to create new knowledge, new creations, and new manifestations not already part of the creation.

To say that the Creator's mind knows and foretells every maneuver of every electron and molecule, every thought and motion of every creature that ever lived or will live, seems an improbable line of reasoning. It implies that every aspect of creation is pre-planned and ordained, and that we individuals are nothing more than automatons in a museum of creation.

Affinities as Love Within the Mind of God

Fine, you might say we can acknowledge a diffuse mind inherent in the creation. But its forces are just the mechanics. Where is the personality, the imagination, the verve, the "humanity" if you will?

Remember that the human mind evolved to enable a frail and defenseless creature to survive and flourish. Language and culture are the most wildly successful inventions of its evolution, allowing humans to communicate and develop strategies for survival as a group. The seemingly limitless memory of these minds and their ability to create images and form associations has led to literature, poetry, music, science, and religion. When we anthropomorphize the Creator, we tend to cast the "mind" of the Creator in these same terms. But our minds evolved to enable the success of our one species on one planet. If humans were marooned on a asteroid or a neutron star, these characteristics would prove useless and none would survive.

We can see, then, that the mind of the Creator *must* function in a manner entirely different from human minds in order to be the organizing force inhering in the whole of creation.

However, again the question comes up, where is the "humanity" in that vision? Where is the warmth in the breath that animates the clay?

To answer that question we must return to the principle of affinities, those propensities that pull each part of the creation together in its loving embrace, its creative embrace. It is an embrace that creates, nurtures, promotes and preserves new creations of the creation. These affinities weld everything into a creative whole. Is that not love in its purest form? A loving embrace that provides a support for the new entity to exist and to participate in the ongoing creation? Isn't 'love" the essence of the "Mind of God"?

Chapter 18 Bibliography

Calvin, William H., *The Emergence Of Intelligence*, Scientific American, 271:100-107, October, 1994. Thinking about how a brain/mind functions are evolved.

Losick, Richard, and Dale Kaiser, *Why And How Bacteria Communicate*, Scientific American, 276:68-73, February, 1997. Some early forms of communication and reaction in primitive organisms.

Weiss, Joseph, *Unconscious Mental Functioning*, Scientific American, 262:103-109, March, 1990. How much of our creative thinking and our reaction to our environment is done at an unconscious level.

Chapter 19

Of Good And Evil

*"Who Knows what Evil lurks
in the minds of men?"*

-From the radio show, *"The Shadow"*

I'm the god of the trampoline. It's our backyard exerciser. I built it and I control its destiny. I've found that both good and evil enter the picture when humans try to use the trampoline.

I didn't get the trampoline right the first time or even the second time. The beams of the frame supporting the springs rotted in the ground, the pit filled with water, and then weeds grew. The sides of the pit washed down and the nails holding the spring attachments pulled out. I kept trying, though, and finally the whole thing held together fairly well.

Then I was faced with the matter of its use. Clearly a trampoline has some good nourishing values. You can bounce and soar in the air. You get good exercise and acquire dexterity and balance. Evils, however lurk in its shadows. Injuries to the jumpers and destruction of the trampoline are distinct possibilities. How could I avoid those evils and assure the good that can come from exercising on it?

I could call it mine, refuse to share it, and avoid the problem. Or I could decree many elaborate rules and stand by to enforce them as the neighborhood children came by to try out the trampoline. I could adjudicate all the fights and arguments and punish all the wrongdoers.

It was impossible for me to predict all of the outcomes in advance. We had to experience them first. Some of the root problems were only discerned following astute observation. All of the users participated in this task, knowingly or unknowingly. We found out what worked and what didn't. We found out how to do amazing things that were good and enjoyable. We identified those activities that caused injury and destruction.

What follows is the system that was evolved. Again, it is the result of things not working out right the first or the second or even the third time.

First, we had to find out what contributed to the survival of the trampoline itself. The sun's rays disintegrate nylon. The first mat disintegrated in a short time. So, the trampoline had to be covered from the sun when the jumping was finished. The kids did not learn this until the thing fell apart several times. In fact, neither did I. It is not obvious to a child that shoes can scuff and tear the pad apart. We discovered this from the damage we eventually saw on the mat. Shoes were not welcome.

These early observations also allowed us to predict evil events that were not obvious to any of the kids seeing a trampoline for the first time. We correctly predicted that two or more jumping at the same time would lead to three, four, and more. That leads to stretched springs and bumped noses and heads. When one kid successfully dares to do a flip, a beginner is sure to try it too. That kid wants to show the bravado and skill he doesn't possess. This can lead to landing on the head and possibly a broken neck. Children don't anticipate these things. An accident with a fortunate outcome warned us of the tragedy which otherwise could have resulted from flipping.

Then there was the issue of behavior while using the trampoline. It soon became evident that I might have to be present all the time to run the thing. Instead, we began to establish a neighborhood culture. Here's how it went. Again, as with the mechanical problems, it was the result of things not working out right the first or the second or even the third time. The word was passed around concerning what would and would not be allowed on the trampoline. When children came to the door and asked for permission to jump, they were asked whether they know the rules. If they could enumerate them, they could jump. The word got around fast. They learned the culture of the trampoline.

What were we to do about fighting and arguing? Our door bell was continually ringing. "Pete is hogging the trampoline." "How long can each of us be on?" "Can I be first?" "Will you come out and tell Susie what the rules are?" "Juan and Ben won't let the little kids on 'till they're tired out."

A new part of the culture had to be added. Again, it was the result of things not working out right the first or the second or even the third time. This next bit was: Any fighting or squabbles, then everyone goes home. The results of the new rule were absolutely amazing. Those kids taught themselves to negotiate a workable system. Sometimes it was fifty jumps each. Others used a watch. Disputes were discussed, not shouted, because they found that when the argument decibel level reached a certain level, the trampoline was shut down and they were all sent home. When one of them felt put upon and knocked on the door, asking for a referee to come out and settle it for them, they found that they were all soon heading for home. Either they found a way to solve their problem or the game was over for all of them. They found a way.

When we found out that some kids had jumped without permission during our absence, we closed the trampoline for several weeks and told the kids to spread the word. The cultural communication channels worked. The children stayed away for several weeks until they found the welcome sign out again. The big board saying NO had been put away. The word got around that good behavior was everyone's responsibility. Bad or dangerous behavior died out.

We'll return to this modern-day parable when we point out some parallels to the creation process and the nature of the Creator/creation. But first, we'll think a little further about the nature of good and evil.

Good and Evil Have a Context

In our society, evil has many faces and meanings. Violence is called evil. An action, accident, or attitude is dubbed evil if it results in harm or destruction. Evil produces terrible misfortunes, pain, and sorrow. Evil is sin, an affront to the Creator. Evil diseases cause suffering and death. Discomfiture of the mind is produced by evil events or evil forces. People feel revulsion against them.

People sometimes do terribly evil things to one another. Oppression and exploitation are evil ways of conducting human affairs. Lies and deception are evil. But these examples don't answer several key questions: Are all bad things evil? Are there any "natural" events that can be called evil? Or does evil lurk only "in the minds of men," stem only from human actions? We'll take up that issue later in the chapter.

We call actions and events "good" when they result in favorable outcomes. For example, health and freedom from want are good. Favorable happenings are good. Behavior that conforms to the moral order is good behavior. Praiseworthy endeavors are good. Truth and kindness are good. Freedom from injury or disease is good. Anything with a good outcome seems to be good.

Are good and evil just two moral extremes of actions and events? Is everything in between simply neutral - or un-valued altogether - in the scale between good and evil? Are there degrees of good and evil measured off each way from some neutral point, so that everything must be valued as having some degree of either good or evil? Maybe so and maybe not. Is it possible that there is no clear distinction at all between many of the things we call good and evil.

Good and Evil in Previous Eras of the Creation

Let's look at the adventure of the Creator in three phases and then explore each phase for signs of good and evil. The first interval covers most of the adventure, that is the time before living creatures appeared on the planet earth. The second deals with the interval between the appearance of living creatures and the appearance of humans. Human experience fills the third and shortest interval.

Ten billion years from the Big Bang to living things is a lot of time. The most amazing transformations occurred during this period. Temperatures exceeded anything existing in the universe today. Basic building blocks of matter frothed up to make atoms. Unimaginable violence flung the parts away from each other. Vast amounts of matter and energy disintegrated and re-formed. Galaxies lit up as the nuclear fires in the hearts of their suns destroyed atoms and created new ones. Death, destruction, and resurrection of the different forms of creation reigned. Galaxies smashed into one another, throwing their pyrotechnics across the cosmos. Black holes grasped suns and their daughter planets into their selfish embrace and retreated from view. There was every manner of invention and complexity. The creation process constantly experimented, discarding those entities that could not survive and nurturing those that did.

Violence, extinction, and calamity on an unprecedented scale were the hallmarks of this period. Evil processes they were, as we would normally classify or view them. But they were all part of the creation process. Without them there would be no cosmos, no suns, no water-drenched planet, no us. Because entwined with the destructive events were those factors that we call good: creativity, growth, harmonious outcomes, and entirely new realms of creation. "Evil" processes complemented "good" ones to produce good outcomes. In the vernacular of our time, if you want to make an omelet, you have to break some eggs.

As we have already seen, if all "good" outcomes survived unchanged and unchanging, creation would come to a halt. The process would stop if we banished the "evil" of violence and annihilation. If the creation as a whole is good, it was at least half born from processes we commonly brand as evil. If one defines the perpetual survival of the good as being good, then in another view the results become evil. Un-changeability thwarts the discovery of new realms of goodness.

Clearly, our everyday definitions of good and evil do not apply to the creation of the cosmos. Otherwise evils would create good things, and the good things themselves could be interpreted as evil. We are on firmer ground if we consider them all as parts of the process. Stability is the preserver of previous changes. Instability is the maker of new changes, disrupting every established equilibrium. Both are creation processes; the Creator at work on its adventure. Just like the creation of my trampoline, there were mistakes. Some things didn't work out or survive, but they eventually led to arrangements that were more enduring. Learning took place in the process. I regarded some of my trampoline mistakes as calamities at the time. I remembered them, and gained valuable lessons from the experience.

Life Itself Is Good - and Bad

New processes kicked in when organic life appeared on our planet in the second act of creation. Remember that when the first cell organized itself some 3.5 billion years ago, it merely scooped up the chemicals awash in the seas. Clever little rascal. That was a good idea. No harm done here. Well, maybe a little. When it and its progeny soaked up most of the food, the concentration of nutrients was diluted and the opportunities for other life forms to appear was diminished. The cells just took over, taking everything for themselves. Selfish we'd call it, hardly virtuous. Is it possible that evil was beginning to appear?

A good thing was also going on. At first all of the cells were the same, doing the same thing, grazing on the same chemicals, each minding its own business. But then a few of them began to branch out. Some grew bigger while others learned to squirm and wiggle, getting to the food first, cutting out their brothers. Nasty little fellows. One day, a bigger one swallowed up its smaller neighbor. It didn't even have the decency to cook it first. It swallowed it alive! Tranquility was violated, and the world order disintegrated fast. Clearly, we might think, evil was rearing its nasty head. Things were going downhill now, no question about it.

But wait. One inventive cell, floating on the surface, discovered how to capture and harness energy from the sun. P-h-o-t-o-s-y-n-t-h-e-s-i-s! It no longer had to graze the sea for energy-giving molecules. It could just lie there, enjoying its expanding family, sucking in water and minerals, soaking up carbon dioxide from the air, doing its photosynthesis thing. Surely this was the good life.

There was only one minor problem. This cell exuded a noxious poisonous gas, oxygen, that was harmful to anaerobic creatures, meaning almost everybody else at the time. The cell didn't worry about it. That little bit of oxygen would get lost in the rest of the air - for a while. But the photosynthesizes multiplied like mad, and lo, after enough time the oxygen built up to dangerous levels. It began to poison the neighbors. Many gagged and died. Some sneaked into the mud or sank to the deepest seas to get away from it. A corrosive plague spread over the planet.

Certain lucky cells began to adapt and tolerate the oxygen. Tough little rascals. Some began to team up to help one another to survive. They ganged up into multicellular creatures, showing remarkable teamwork in their common endeavors. Of course, this also made it much easier to gobble up the neighbors. They got good at it. Eventually they wiped out whole families of less successful organisms. We might say how cruel!

If that wasn't bad enough, some of them engaged in sex. Without benefit of clergy! Groveling down there in the mud and the dark, they tried all sorts of perverted things, invading each other, sticking little bits of their DNA into one another's cells. Most likely some of them killed each other in the process. Sometimes they produced grotesque offspring that looked funny and behaved very differently from their parents. Now the world had to look out for these new creatures and learn to cope with their strange ways and ferocious appetites. The bigger the newfangled predators became, the more dangerous they were to their neighbors.

Soon, some of the emerging multi-celled organisms began to get their revenge. They started to gobble up the green and blue-green algae, those poisoners of the atmosphere. They probably gagged on them at first but eventually relished grazing on them wholesale. Now the little green things that had it so good, lying there floating on the surface of the water, got their just reward. Some fled to the beach and discovered how to survive in the damp places on land. Having escaped their predators, they too learned how to adapt. They extended themselves down below the soil's surface to find the moisture and the minerals they needed. Here they were safe, until the neighbors began to crowd in. The lucky ones who happened to exude noxious garbage discovered that it kept the neighbors away. Good or evil? It was, and is, hard to tell.

You know the rest of the story, how species diversified, how one species preyed on the other, how each made a living, generally at the expense of the smaller and less agile creatures. All the while the whole community was at the mercy of floods, earthquakes and exploding volcanoes. Some species were able to endure when the occasional asteroid smashed into the earth. Others were wiped out. Glaciers forced mobile species to move south and froze the others. Seas and oceans dried up, wiping out entire populations. To us, watching a speeded-up version of history, it might appear as though evil dominated the land.

On the other hand, the growth, the diversity, and the increasing complexity and interrelatedness of all of the living realm, appeared to be good. It better have been. If it hadn't happened, we would not be here.

Let's look a little closer at the good side. Other properties of the living changing planet became evident long before humans evolved. They include symbiotic relationships, interdependency, and acceptance of one another. Bees and flowers are a beautiful example. The bees need the flowers, and the flowers need the bees. Squirrels need the nut trees, and the nut trees need the squirrels in order to prosper. Grasses need the grazing animals to spread their seed, and the animals need the grass for their food.

To Eat and Be Eaten

There are other aspects of this interdependency which often make us uncomfortable. Almost always, the death of one organism is the life-giving sustenance of another. We readily espouse the idea of the lion becoming a friend to the lamb - without asking what we expect the lion to have for lunch. When I hear a rabbit scream at night in the woods, my reaction is to set out fox traps. If I were a rabbit and knew there was a fox next door, I'd head out for the next county. But this is not the way of the rabbit. Instead, the rabbit trusts to its fast reactions and convenient groundhog holes and goes about its life.

Ducklings being pulled under the water on our creek urge me to set out baited lines for the snapping turtles. I want to reach for a gun when I see a crow picking a young robin out of the nest in our maple tree. My reaction is to wipe out these evils, clean up the neighborhood. I don't get quite as excited when I see the parent robin gobbling up a live worm. I'm even pleased when I see a wren taking a beak full of insects into the wren-house hole. I suppose I identify more with big cute and cuddly things. But really, is there a difference? Are the wiggly, crawling, biting creatures lesser breeds, deserving of destruction? Can we call the actions of any creature evil? If they are not evil, are they good?

As I've often said there are times when I'd like to make and enforce a law in my neighborhood; no more eating of one another, no more killing. Would I be doing good? Would the starvation of all of the predatory creatures be a good outcome? In any event when fast-breeding insects began to cover everything, when my household routine bogged down under the weight of too many little living things I'd probably change the law.

I cannot find a way to put any label of good or evil on this period of the creation. Before the arrival of humans, the words good and evil simply do not apply. Each creature and each plant does what it has to do. It lives as part of the intertwined process of life and death, change and decay. Each species, each individual, finds a way to exist. There is no door to knock on to complain of mistreatment or misconduct, no referee to settle the arguments. The different creatures either learn how to live in a contentious environment or the game's over, just as it is for the children jumping on the trampoline.

On another level, these activities that we may wish to label as good or evil are all necessary to the creation and its process. If this process is evil, so is the Creator. If the creation is good, so is the Creator. Intuitively we don't like to look too closely at the process. It is likely to offend us in some way. We prefer to follow the old adage: If you like to eat sausage don't watch it being made.

The Vicissitudes of Human Life

The era of humans is the final period to examine for evidence of good and evil. There is no sharp dividing line between this era and the preceding one. You wouldn't expect a human being to appear full-blown on the planet any more than you would expect to see the first dinosaur simply wade out of the sea.

For millions of years, the human species and its immediate predecessors made an imperceptibly small impact on the rest of the biosphere. Let's go back and see it as it was then. We find a fragile species, these humans. They have no fierce teeth or claws. They're not nearly as swift as the other large animals. No camouflage blends them into the scenery. They depend upon their brains instead of their instincts. They form bands to hunt and protect one another. They think, remember, plan, and scheme. Language and culture are becoming their distinctive features.

Early humans are subject to the same vicissitudes of life that plagued their pre-human ancestors. Earthquakes, floods, drought, disease, and famine periodically wiped out large numbers of their kind. They undoubtedly looked upon these things as evils, especially as they begin to recognize cause and effect in the events surrounding their lives. Judging from their spiritual imagery, they looked for unseen hands that inflict these evils or for beneficent spirits that help fortunate events to occur.

The question we need to ask here is: If natural calamities are not evils when they descend upon non-human creatures, do they become evils when they afflict humans?

We know that humans have developed a great fear of early death. It's quite terrifying, so final and so unfair, an evil to be avoided. But would we want it otherwise? Would we prefer life to be so ordered that everyone would die at the same age? That would be the fair way. Now imagine the terror and apprehension a person would have as that age approached. On the other hand, we might be maimed and crippled while we were still very young. Then we would have to live a life of pain, suffering, and dependency 'till our appointed day arrived. We can't have it both ways. If we prefer the uncertainty that allows us to die at any time, fine. In this case we accept as good that part of life which we may have previously defined as evil.

Disease also brings much suffering. Many diseases are caused by viruses that worm their way into our cells and use our own cellular machinery to replicate. A virus disrupts a cell, hijacks its DNA apparatus, makes copies of itself, and heads out to another cell. It leaves behind some of its DNA, and it also steals bits and pieces from its host, often changing or mutating in the process. When it invades the next person, it repeats the process, this time bringing along some new or altered genes. The new genes carry with them the potential for change: sometimes good, more often bad. Should we be thankful for infectious diseases? Should we rejoice that we remain a part of the continuing experimentation of the creation, that Great Adventure?

It seems clear we cannot call all the physically harmful things that happen to us "evil." They are just the price we are called upon to pay for the privilege of being a part of the creation.

Good and Evil in Human Choice

We should investigate several other matters as we consider this era of human dominance. Possibly we should confine our concept of good and evil to what we *choose* to do to one another and how we *choose* to relate to the rest of the creation. These ideas deserve a closer look.

Ethics and *morals* are terms that are broadly used describe aspects of human life governed by conscious choice. Ethics are systems of idealized behavior devised to regulate human activity. They are traditionally confined to the realm of human-to-human relationships. However, if the Creator is indeed the whole creation, we need to broaden our ethical system. We need to extend ethics to include all of creation.

Our fragile human species finds its survival in group action. Survival depends upon social relationships that promote the well-being of the group. Consequently in every society rules are established which then become part of the very fabric of life. Deviations are not and cannot be tolerated.

This fabric of society - the expected behavior of its members - becomes its ethic, its defining nature, its culture. Ethics defines good and evil in terms of human behavior. Some actions are good while others are evil. Some rules tell you what to do; others tell you what not to do. Good actions promote the well-being of the society; evil actions tend to tear at its fabric.

Morals are a measure of how an individual conforms to these societal expectations. Morals measure an individual's internal and external conformity to society's externally imposed expectations.

Early human societies lived in intimate connection with the rest of the creation. Although we don't know the thoughts of our hunter-gatherer ancestors, some of their art and artifacts have survived. These, together with the attitudes of hunter-gatherer societies living today, show that they had a strong ethic in relationship to their fellow creatures. They also revered the wind, rain, water, fire, plants, and earth.

The same set of ethics may not work well for all societies. The circumstances and harsh realities of life determine the perspectives of any particular group. Different societies in different circumstances are likely to develop different ethical standards. In a small isolated society beset by cycles of climatic disturbance, it may be necessary to preserve the elders of the tribe at all cost. It is they who have the accumulated wisdom to know how to respond to these changes.

Contrast this to the nomads who follow the herds on which they depend for food. Stopping to care for an infirm elder or injured family member who cannot continue with the chase might mean the death of the entire tribe. The ethic of such groups requires that they abandon very elderly or disabled members.

Thus we see that two different societies, enduring under different circumstances, have developed and live by quite different codes of ethics. Can we say that one ethic is good and the other one is evil?

Ethical Complexities and Dilemmas

Similarly, what works in a small society may not work well in a large society, where the variety of human interactions is multiplied and life is much more complex. A simple ethic may work in the smaller society. A more complex one is needed in a larger society encompassing a number of subgroups, each with a somewhat different set of ethics generated by their distinct circumstances.

What happens when ethical values differ? A clash of ethical views is the cause of many of humanities conflicts and problems. Moreover, there is an almost unbridgeable gap between the ethic imposed by nature and the preference of individuals. The nomad elder left behind to die may fervently wish to have an exception made!

There are long and short-term perspectives. Frequently, actions that are obviously good are good mostly in the short run. In the longer term they may appear to be evil. Here is one example from recent history. Is it good or evil to take up residence in a different society and create conditions that eventually resulted in widespread starvation and poverty? Most of us would call it evil. Now, think about the well-meaning persons who introduced themselves into stable aboriginal populations. The newcomers brought modern medical marvels that cut down the death rate. They cured and prevented infectious diseases and made life more enjoyable for the inhabitants. Improvements were made to water supplies, halting the spread of disease and parasites. Wasn't this unadulterated good? What could have been more charitable and compassionate?

Because the modernizers drastically reduced the death rate and did nothing comparable to cut down the birth rate, we need to come back and take a look one or two generations later. We find starvation, poverty, and strife caused by competition for scarce resources and land. Historically it actually happened this way in Central America and Africa. Now we should ask ourselves again, what is good and what is evil?

Before recent advances in medical science, persons born with certain severe genetic abnormalities had a short life. They didn't marry or have children. Now, by the grace of medical science and technology, they often lead productive and reproductive lives. When they have children, they may pass their genetic disability on to unsuspecting future generations. Is the act of preserving the reproductive life of a genetically abnormal child an act of good or of evil? For the individual concerned it seems to be good. For future generations it might be considered evil.

These issues raise fundamental problems about whether there can be, or whether there really is, any absolute distinction between good and evil. We have already seen that our categories of good and evil apply only in the realm of human behavior. Even catastrophes in the context of the nonhuman universe cannot be considered as intrinsically evil.

If good and evil are solely confined to the realm of human behavior, what is the definition of good and what is the definition of evil? Suppose that good is what promotes the survival of the human species and evil consists of practices that will result in its extinction. Then we have to decide what we mean by the survival of the human species. Is it the survival of every person that is born? Is it the proliferation of the human species to the point where it occupies every square foot of land and then begins to build floating houses on the seas or artificial, habitable satellites orbiting the planet? Does the ethic guiding such survival tactics apply only to humans? Does it extend to relations with other creatures and to other parts of the creation?

Good and Evil in Group Behavior

While we think about these broader questions, let us look at what presently goes on in human relationships and in the social systems that prevail among human beings today. Each unit of human society has its own culture, its own way of living, that seems to work for that unit. Often this culture is not spelled out in any detailed way. Children learn by observing their parents and neighbors, experiencing how life is ordered in their small part of the world. Sometimes they do receive explicit sets of rules. Other times, it is just tacitly assumed that certain things are not done, that they are just not proper.

Each small family, extended family, tribe, village, and town is unique. Each has its own standards that they find to be desirable. These standards work reasonably well for the group and are tacitly agreed upon by most of its members. Often they are formulated by the elders, who have a wide perspective and much experience to draw upon. They reach conclusions about the results of human interactions which are not obvious to younger members. The tests of time and experience are probably the major factors that shape these traditional codes.

Systems of rules and standards have to account not only for different perspectives held by different societies but also for different types of individual persons as well. Some people are inclined to favor the democratic process. They want to be involved in all decisions and deliberations about rules and standards. Others, like some of my relatives, prefer the authoritarian model in which a strong leader decides how things should be done. My nephew who is making the military his career says he likes the regimented life. Still other people, like a former colleague of mine, are happy to rely on specialists. This co-worker always declines to discuss matters of religion or ethics. He claims that if he wanted to get answers on such matters, he would consult his priest because the priest is trained to deal with them. Finally some folks, like some of my grandchildren, don't want anyone telling them to do anything.

Generally, friction within a segment or subgroup of society is minuscule compared to the conflicts that arise when different cultures collide. On a global level, the very worst crimes are done in the name of country, God, and clan. The rules that are acceptable to guide behavior within small groups are not considered to apply between groups with a different cultural or genetic heritage. It is entirely possible that there is a genetic carry-over in human makeup that predisposes us to be hostile toward people of a different clan. Small bands of nonhuman primates - such as gorillas and chimpanzees in their native habitat - settle their personal differences with noise, fury, and intimidation. They rarely resort to violence. When different clans collide, or an unknown individual wanders into an established family group, the results are shockingly different. The intruder often gets torn limb from limb.

Setting a Global Standard?

If this clannish tendency is indeed a part of our genetic makeup, we must acknowledge it. It has to be considered when attempting to establish a wider social order to sustain human life. If the record of the past is any guide, such a framework cannot be rigid or all-encompassing. It must be fluid and evolving as human society changes, evolves, and clash.

Historically, most religious bodies and their ethical prescriptions assume a universality. Their standards are promoted as absolutes. This is understandable, since absolutes are enforceable. It is hard to adjudicate a general principle or to enforce a relative ethic. Religious systems are generally intended to be universally applicable to all individuals and to all societies. They aim to mold all people into one viewpoint and one way of living.

Such a prescriptive system flies in the face of the history of the creation. Diversity of action and diversity of form are the hallmarks of creation. Although universal conformity to a single set of ethical standards might promote temporary tranquility, a single standard would probably not be flexible enough to adapt to all different societies or malleable enough to change along with the evolution of society. The history of imposed standards is also the history of repression. Self-imposed tyrants have often used religion as a means of controlling their societies. They wrap themselves in a claim that their authority is given by divine mandate or they proclaim themselves to be defenders of the faith.

Revealed ethics are those which are supposedly given by a higher power for the benefit of humankind. They are presented as timeless and infallible codes of law. In fact they endure because they are reinterpreted by different generations and different societies. The same religious and legal code that defended slavery for centuries was later invoked to condemn it. In our time the patriarchal domination of women by society, once enforced by many religious traditions, is being reinterpreted as a lapse in semantics by previous translators or scribes. The definition of "murder" undergoes a continuous transformation from generation to generation and from society to society as broader and broader groups attempt to live by the same ethical standard. A successful standard endures because it is flexible enough to be reinterpreted and allow changes in emphasis. One Catholic priest famously commented that the church never changes its ethical rules, it just stops talking about certain things.

Standards that are invented to serve our hopes and expectations but are not developed from the experience of life seem to fail. The constitutional prohibition of alcohol in the United States lasted a mere

13 years. Twentieth-century communism was invented by intellectuals who devoutly wished to overcome the ills of their society. However, instead of inspiring the population to experiment with their vision of a better society, communist parties imposed it by force. Its ethic was not tested, modified, and confirmed by real economic and social life, and it eventually failed. Today's "war on drugs" may be another misguided campaign doomed to failure.

The means for enforcing individual conformity to the ethic of a group are varied. They range from the threat of punishment or banishment and the withholding of one's livelihood to the threat of eternal damnation. One very effective method has been to control people's sex lives. If religious and governmental authorities are able to control a person's access to sexual activity, they have a very powerful handle on their behavior. Bishop Pike of the Episcopal church observed, "When most ministers talk about morality in their stained-glass-window tones, they are usually talking about sex." Indeed, in recent years, the most fervent debates among many religious groups in the U.S. have centered on abortion, teenage pregnancies, and homosexuality.

During the VietnamWar those sexual moral values of American society were being debated against the background of napalm, indiscriminate village bombing, and the planned murder of civilians. The presumed civic responsibility of citizens to their government's rules stood in contrast to battlefield torture, killing of prisoners, imprisonment in tiger cages, and choking off the aspirations of a colonized people. It is not surprising that many U.S. citizens rejected the "American Way" including its social and sexual norms.

The Role of Individual Leaders

It is tempting to use individual human lives drawn from history as examples of good and evil. That would be a cheap shot. The societies to which these individuals belonged almost always took part in the good or the evil that the historical figures represent. Hitler did not appear out of a vacuum. He was the product of the active anti-Semitism of the Christian church and the culture that permeated German society and government during his age. He was heir to the militaristic traditions of Europe and the concept that might makes right, that "God is with us."

The New Poland created after World War I foreshadowed Hitler's policies toward Jews. The Polish government ghettoized the Jewish population with the ultimate objective of ridding the country of all of its Jews, one way or another. Hitler arose to power in an impoverished country where anti-Semitism was an established majority point of view. It would be a mistake to see only his personal evil and not the evil of his society.

It might be a parallel mistake to canonize Mother Theresa as the embodiment of all good for her unstinting work for the poorest of the poor. It may be, due to her faithful support of the ban on birth control espoused by her church, that additional poor people around the world will outstrip their food supply and starve. Actions, as we have seen, cannot be judged only in the short term.

The Good and Evil That Lie Within

Are humans endowed with tendencies to both good and evil? What is the evil dimension of human activity? How is it defined? How is it recognized? Is the evil absolute? Is there any activity that is always defined as evil? The same questions must be asked of good. If something is not evil, is it good? Or are good and evil just the extremes of human activity, with the middle ground being neutral in the value system? If good and evil apply only to human activity, are they restricted to relationships between humans? Or do they also apply to human activity involving the rest of the Creator/creation?

Humans seem to come with some built-in characteristics that are usually labeled as good. The nurture of children and love of family appear to be universal. Altruism and generosity are regarded as good, as is respect for elders. A more curious characteristic is a tendency to tell the truth, to avoid lying. Our bodies betray our inner aversion to lying in lie detector tests.

As we know well, humans are also endowed with selfish and power-seeking characteristics. Are these tendencies evil or are they good? In the business world, the characteristic of getting the most for oneself is frequently considered a virtue. In children, the selfish tendency leads to fighting and is more often considered to be evil.

Sex, in its unique way, also appears in both "good" and "evil" packages. Sex and sexual attraction have distinct evolutionary advantages. Sex permits favorable genetic changes to spread quickly, while sexual bonding encourages prolonged care of the young by both parents, from birth to young adulthood. A female who has to care for her offspring alone and forage for food may lose a vulnerable child. The presence of a protective male greatly improves the chances of survival.

If sex seems to be good in this light, let us note that the human mind has been able to invent all sorts of perversions of sex and sexual attraction. These have led, among other things, to the evils of the subjugation and degradation of women.

Religious traditions have been especially aware of the evil forms of sexuality gone astray and have made heavy-handed attempts to control them, including sanctions and taboos. A few religions have imposed the principle of the obedience of a woman to a man. Others have gone further, prescribing mutilations in the form of female circumcision to dampen the fires of sexual attraction. Still others separate love and affection from sexual activity, overriding their essential nature. Some have banned the subject from discussion or have even declared sex to be evil, forcing people to deny and submerge their sexual urges. In this case internal violence against the self soon matches the external enforcement of the taboo.

Uninhibited sex, on the other hand, leads to its own problems and evils. It spreads disease. It may allow the physically powerful to dominate the weak. Children are particularly vulnerable to forced sex and other abuse, and they may develop long-term scars. Yes, sex has a destructive side. We haven't yet learned how to avoid its excesses or how to always to these built-in characteristics and urges in a non-destructive manner. In sum, sexuality can cause us all types of trouble unless we learn how to use wisely this powerful affinity that we find at the very core of our natures.

The Impulse to Violence

Then there is violence. The flow of adrenaline into a person's bloodstream often primes it for violence or flight. No doubt it was a good and necessary survival characteristic for early humans when they roamed the savannah full of predators. A human being on its own has a limited capacity for violence, as do small groups with few weapons. However, in modern times we have invented technologies that multiply our capacity for violence until we have become a major threat to ourselves and to the rest of the creation.

Unlocking the secret of atomic fission was one of the supreme examples of human ingenuity. The production of nearly unlimited power in explosions or nuclear reactors multiplied human power immensely. Unfortunately, humans hadn't yet developed an ethic for its use or non-use. We didn't know how to handle this power and keep it from getting away from rational control. Nuclear power was and is an exercise in human curiosity and creativity that could lead to the annihilation of a good portion of all life on this planet.

We don't let children play with matches. However fascinating and spectacular they might appear, children must first learn the proper and appropriate use of fire. They get the privilege of using matches when they have attained the maturity and self-control that warrants their handling of a potentially destructive force. If only whole societies behaved so well!

Unfortunately we turn over the most destructive weapons that humankind has invented - "weapons of mass destruction" - to the more violent personalities in our societies. These are people who have been recruited and trained by military forces to use aggressiveness to solve problems. Are they really likely to handle nuclear power for the betterment of humankind and all of creation?

An Instinct for "Me First"

Humans are distinguished from other animals by one curious and potent characteristic which seems only loosely connected to survival. Humans want to accumulate things, to own them, to store them up for themselves, far beyond their actual needs. This tendency is at the root of many things that we call evil. One day it may well lead to the demise of our whole species. It is hard to find this characteristic elsewhere in nature. The squirrel gathers nuts and stores them for winter, but it doesn't keep gathering down to the last nut, leaving none for others, and then defending its store against all comers. The little mountain pika cuts grass, dries it on a rock, and then stores it underground as food for the winter. It doesn't store it up for years and years in advance, far beyond its ability to consume.

Many animals are territorial. They stake out a claim to an area and fend off others of their species. This territory provides them with their livelihood and assures their survival. They do not claim or defend a territory larger than necessary to ensure their food supply.

Humans, on the other hand, have a drive to acquire as much territory as they can. They want to accumulate land and possessions far beyond their ability to consume them. Perhaps this tendency derives from humans' great memory and reasoning power. They remember hard times and famines, and they fear the specter of old age when they cannot provide for themselves. They try to ward off these disasters. They store up assets for the bad times ahead.

Wandering bands of hunter-gatherers did not accumulate much, because they had to carry everything they possessed. They did not stake out personal territories because they were always on the move. The tendency to accumulate seems to have grown as a consequence of non-nomadic civilization. When people settled down to an agricultural and then urban life, they indulged in this propensity to accumulate more and more.

One result was a major clash of cultures and civilizations. When Europeans first made contact with Native American cultures, the Native Americans could not understand the Europeans' actions. They viewed with horror the white men's tendency to take all the fur-bearing animals that they could kill and to cut down all the trees. They could not understand the motive for digging up so many minerals from the earth and simply accumulating them. Even the idea of "owning" the land was alien to Native Americans, who had a quite different concept of their place in the creation.

Lewis Thomas has characterized modern humans as "world-eaters." Instead of giving and taking as part of the natural world, they own it and consume it, building up temporary riches far beyond their actual needs. In accumulating these assets, they deny their use to others. Left unchecked, humans are capable of denuding the earth of its forests and flora, stripping it of its minerals and fuels, depleting the oceans of its fish and coral, and paving over its fertile soils. As a species, we humans may be the only one destined to "die rich."

A Whole Pandora's Box of Evils

Is this the full range of evil that flows from the tendency to acquire things? Are there other dimensions and other connections?

Wars, slavery, subjugation of women, fear or hatred of foreigners, cruelty, murder, emotional and sexual abuse, jealousy, theft, and lying are among the usual litanies of evils. Clearly these all "lurk in the minds of men"; certainly they are well embedded in our species. Most of them have their roots in that curious and unique human characteristic, our tendency to accumulate possessions. Perhaps such behavior had survival value earlier in our long adventure, but now it carries within itself the seeds of destruction.

The institution of war exemplifies this litany of evils. The causes of war lie in the just-described innate and archaic characteristics of humans. Their exceptional brainpower and memory have allowed people to advance these tendencies toward destruction and self-destruction. The urges to define and protect a living space necessary for physical survival are carried to extremes in modern warfare. Witness the reasons invoked by Nazi Germany for "living room" for the Aryan race. Witness the "strategic interests" invoked by the American government whenever it intervenes in a poor and distant third-world country.

Behind every war of aggression is the prospect of spoils and the vision of accumulating extra possessions and wealth, always catering to the human's characteristic greed. In the countless wars of history, the outcome is always the same no matter who wins. Prime territory is annexed by the victor, assuring the continued accumulation of possessions. Treasuries are looted and tributes levied on the loser. Women are taken by the victors as a spoil of war, satisfying the drives of the male warriors for both dominance and sexual conquest.

Wars encourage us to dehumanize our opponents. "Enemies" are labeled evil and animal-like, deserving of destruction in battle and subservience after defeat. These views promote slavery and the oppression of one human group by another. Slavery is an ancient institution, having its roots in warfare which in turn goes back to the drive to accumulate land and wealth. Forcing dehumanized slaves to perform economic and personal services greatly enhances the slave-holder's ability to accumulate wealth and power.

The instigators of modern wars are not usually so blatant in their justification of warfare. Their conquests are usually cloaked in virtue and noble purpose, such as righting ancient wrongs, defending religious and national heritage, or upholding the honor of national leaders. It is fair to say that wars have been the national "sport" of many countries both ancient and modern. All too often the cheerleaders for the sport have been religious institutions, claiming to represent the will of the Creator and bestowing their blessings upon the killing.

Tour the great churches of Europe and the civic centers of its cities, and one finds countless monuments to the leaders of war. The evidence of their ascent to national leadership and domination is everywhere on display. Follow their trail to the palaces. One is amazed by the opulence of their spoils of war and conquest and by the accumulation of wealth by those holding governmental power. Note that a triumphant military leader often claims or seizes a right to governmental leadership, even today. After the Vietnam war, General Westmoreland, the commander of the U.S. forces, reportedly bitterly lamented his failure to ascend to the presidency, an honor he felt that he deserved.

Relearning to Be Part of the Creation

This clever brain we humans inherited has undoubtedly gotten us out of many scrapes and has helped our species immensely in its saga of survival. Along with this brain, though, comes baggage from the past. Although territoriality and aggressiveness served their purpose in the savannah, they are poor characteristics for survival in today's global village. Our clever brain continues to succumb to the temptations of power and accumulation. Our curiosity has led us inside the atom, inside the genetic code, and into outer space. When these new abilities get mixed up with the old ghosts we carry from the past, we don't cope very well.

Our innate drive to accumulate food and goods to tide us over lean times has now been carried to extremes. We have invented money to make the accumulation easier. With money we don't have to build big barns to store up food and goods for our old age or spend time preserving our assets. We store up money that is redeemable for these things later on. Now we are free to accumulate without the burden of carrying everything along with us. Since it's easier, it's also easier to indulge in excess. As a result we plunder the planet, trying to "own" an ever-larger hunk of the creation. Perhaps we should wonder, Who belongs to Whom?

Even if we contain our tendency to own and consume the planet, we retain that tendency for a possessiveness that excludes others. It is one matter to assume the stewardship of a part of the creation for its own protection and for its nurture. It is a quite different thing to deny its use and enjoyment by others. The first attitude seems to be good, while the latter appears to be evil. If the Creator is the creation, an attempt to usurp it for oneself is clearly an evil, while the desire to protect and nurture its evolution is good. In our present culture we have trouble sorting out the difference.

I'd like to conclude by going back to the parable of the trampoline. Its development beside my house showed the same processes at work as in the creation itself. The trampoline came into existence by trial and error. The right combination of fabric and springs, children and adults, rules and rewards finally produced a workable device. Its good and evil were only determined by long-term thoughtful observation of what worked and led to good results. The outcome of these observations was then embedded in the culture of the trampoline. If the participants couldn't find a way of enjoying it in harmony, if they couldn't negotiate a modus operandi that worked, the game was over.

So will it be with humans as part of the creation. Either we learn how to live symbiotically with all of the creation and to make changes in harmony with the rest, or the game is over. We will disappear like all the other species of plants and animals that have failed to survive in a changing environment.

We have seen that evil lurks "in the minds of men." This mind of ours must learn to cope with the demons that dwell within. Every enduring species has had to learn to survive in the big world outside, the ecological culture in which it lived. We have the added task of controlling the selfish forces that push up from within our very nature, characteristics from our earlier evolution that now carry the seeds of our extinction. We will not survive at the expense of the creation. We will only survive by living as a viable, integral and creative *part* of the Creator.

Chapter 19 Bibliography

Thomas, Lewis, *The Fragile Species,* Macmillan Publishing Company, 1993. The Author broaches the observation that Humans are the only species that seem to have the propensity to continually accumulate and appropriate land and resources. He sees this tendency as an evolutionary and cultural characteristic that could spell the demise of human culture and civilization.

Chapter 20

The Theology of Ecology

"We are not here alone
nor for ourselves alone,
but . . . we are an integral part
of higher mysterious entities
against whom it is not
advisable to blaspheme."
-Vaclav Havel

"For all of eternity,
God lies on a maternity bed giving birth."
-Meister Eckhart
circa 1200 A.D.

Ecology is viewed as the totality of relationships between living things and between them and their environment. We think of human ecology as the relationship of our own species to the world around us, as well as our relationship to the biosphere of which we are a part. Our concern for ecology is to maintain a healthy relationship among ourselves and the biosphere.

The biosphere, the total interrelated network of all living and growing things, does not exist apart from the physical world. It is inextricably tied to and integrated with this watery planet and its atmosphere. It is completely dependent upon the sun for its radiant energy. The sun in turn is an intimate part of the cosmos, that seemingly infinite burst of solar fires loosely constrained by gravity. The concern for the ecological health of our biosphere is in a sense, a concern for the well-being of all creation.

An international environmental conference held in Rio de Janeiro in 1992 attempted to hammer out a "constitution" for the earth and its biosphere. The participants hoped to establish some rules and guidelines for the future that would harmonize human activity with the rest of the biosphere. What was the motivation for this conference? Nothing more nor less than self-interest - ensuring human survival.

Human ecology, however, is situated in a context larger than concern for our own well-being and survival. The widest view tells us where we are in the biosphere, and the deepest view wrestles with what we should do. What is the "theological" dimension? Is there "A Will of God" for this part of creation or for all of creation? If so, what are the rules, where are the guideposts? Is there a Theology of Ecology? If so, what imperatives should we seek? Why should we be concerned at all with the well-being of creation?

If, as we suppose, the Creator *is* the creation and every part of the universe is a part of the Creator, then you, me, every atom, every star, every creature, every ray of light, every raindrop, every aurora borealis, every black hole, every supernova, every grain of pollen, every strand of DNA is a part of the Creator and of all creation. If this be so, then what would be your theology, the guiding light for your life, your view of your relationship to the creation and the Creator?

Those of us who come from the Judeo-Christian theological heritage realize that there is already a general willingness to believe in a Creator coming among us here on earth as a Messiah. There is God present among us as a person as well as being a transcendent God that is involved everywhere and with everything.

Let's go one step beyond and solidify those uncertain concepts based on faith alone into something more understandable in our daily lives. Everything around us is, literally, the Creator manifested as the creation. Likewise we ourselves have been assembled out of the Creator's initial force. One hundred years ago this could not have been conceived and articulated with any kind of believability. Today this concept is based on stubborn facts or knowledge about the universe that have been slowly and reluctantly revealed, one by one, over several centuries of scientific inquiry.

When the creation is seen as the Creator itself, as the immense power that transformed and manifested itself as the creation, then everything changes in our field of view. The awareness that every part and parcel of the universe is continuing the creation process without pause comes as a revelation. The universe ceases to be static like an "is" type of thing. It reappears as a "being and becoming" type of thing. Every part of it is vibrant and active, changing and experimenting, pushed and pulled by its built-in affinities, stabilities, and instabilities. The creation creates and holds, modifies, changes, complicates, simplifies, and always endlessly experiments. In the end it is this sweeping realization of a universe unfolding that causes us to break out and come to grips with a new "theology."

Some elements of a man-within-Creator theology have been articulated before. The ancient Hebrews postulated that humans descended from a common ancestor. Jesus of Nazareth envisioned all people as brothers and sisters. His disciples envisioned Jesus as part of the Creator. Muslims declare that Allah is all. Mystics of many kinds have felt the force of the Creator within. Meister Eckhart was branded a heretic in the 1200s for imagining God giving birth to the earth, a female deity in labor. George Fox based his 17th-century teachings on the conviction that there is a bit of the Creator in every person. Coming to our own time, we can at last make this visualization in full, with no contradiction from the observations of science. We ourselves, and all creation, are a part of the Creator.

A Shared Creation Story

Some forty years ago, when I first dared to air these ideas in public, there was little support for them. Few thinkers ventured to combine the revelations of relativity, the cracking of the DNA code, the whisper of the Big Bang, and the indeterminacy of quantum physics into one simple theme. Telliard de Chardin Came within sight of it but had veered off as if seeing visions of inquisitions past.

In the past 20 years all this has changed. Numerous theologians, philosophers, mathematicians, and physicists have elaborated a version of what they call the common creation story. Significantly, and quite recently, Vaclav Havel, the playwright called to the presidency of the Czech Republic, stated in his ringing "Declaration of Interdependence", "We are not here alone nor for ourselves alone, but we are an integral part of higher mysterious entities against whom it is not advisable to blaspheme." By blaspheme I think he meant destructive words and actions directed against the sacred creation. To walk in arrogance, to deny knowledge of the creation is a denial of the Creator.

Planting the New Ethic

If this is a Theology of Creation, what is the *ethic* of this theology? If every part of the creation is part of the Creator, how do we decide what is the right decision for each of our actions?

Guidelines of this sort are rare. Some insights from the Native American tradition seem close to the mark. Observing that all things ultimately come from the earth and return to the earth, Some Native Americans called the earth the Mother of every creature and plant. They couldn't understand the European concept of owning and selling the land any better than they could countenance owning or selling their mother. They regarded other creatures as their spirit brothers. They thanked the animals whom they killed for food and rendered them high respect, for all had to live together in harmony. They couldn't understand the European compulsion to kill more animals than they needed for food. "Walk lightly on the earth," they reminded one another.

In our daily lives, we are concerned with the well-being of humans. We often hear that life is a struggle for survival in which the law of the jungle dominates. It is eat or be eaten. This, however, is not the main characteristic of the biosphere that emerges from a close study of its ecology. Rather, the dominant themes of life and evolution are mutual dependence and symbiotic relationships.

This pattern guides the simplest life forms as well as the most complex. For example, we harbor many microscopic creatures in our bodies. We cannot live without them and they cannot survive outside of us. A bacterium that kills its host is a failure, because it deprives its daughters of a place to live. A carnivorous animal that indiscriminately kills all its prey shortly thereafter starves to death. Predator and prey live close together, in balance. Predators eat the weak and the ill of the other species, leaving a healthy population to grow and reproduce. Similarly, many grasses thrive when they are grazed. Grazing spreads their seeds, while the animal droppings they receive provide nourishment for future growth. If humans consider themselves superior to and outside of such relationships, they make a serious error. We are inextricably embedded in this web of life. We tamper with it at our peril.

As a Guide to Action

The ethics of this life-based Theology of Ecology bring us to some innovative theological perspectives. Part of it is exemplified in the bumper sticker that asks, "Have you thanked a green plant today?" Such thanks can be extended beyond plants. It can extend to the soil and its hard-working bacteria and to the fruit-pollinating insects. We should thank the hydrogen undergoing nuclear metamorphosis in the center of the sun. It yields the heat that keeps this green planet at a temperature where life-building chemical reactions can occur. Thank the microbes that recycle the molecules of our bodies back into the pool of raw materials from whence they came. Those materials will lie fallow there, awaiting the light of fresh creation.

It is this sense of kinship and awe that can illuminate our relation to the other parts of the Creator. In the Christian tradition and many others, each bit of food, each breath of air, each drink of water becomes a sacrament of communion or "co-union" with the Creator. Despoiling the earth becomes a blasphemy, a desecration and denial of the Creator. Every change of direction on our planet, both great and small, becomes an act of co-creation with the Creator.

I have a wall poster that sums it up well: "If we change the world, let it show the mark of our intelligence." When we are about to declare someone our enemy, or beat on a recalcitrant piece of machinery, or manipulate DNA at random, let us reflect on the intelligence of those actions. Let us consider the good and evil that they may do. When we declare something "mine", let us reflect on the meaning and implications of those words.

When our unity with the Creator/creation becomes deeply rooted in our thinking, when the affinity of love guides our course, when our every action is regarded in the Creator's light, it is then that we will begin to live the ethic of the Theology of Ecology.

The Cosmic Deity

Chapter 20 Bibliography

Berry, Thomas, *The Dream of the Earth,* Sierra Club Books, 1988. Thomas Berry defines a restorative, creative relationship with the natural world, drawing on the insights of thinkers from Plato to Teilhard Chardin, Native American elders to Nobel prize winning Scientists, and asks us to tune into the "dream" of the Creator and the creative process going on around us and within us.

Havel, Vaclav. *"A Declaration of Interdependence"* July, 4, 1994. An address given when receiving the Philadelphia Liberty Medal in Philadelphia, acknowledging our interdependence at the most basic level.

Chapter 21

A Vision of Truth

An Ethical Framework

The Emotional Security

"For whatever zeal renders a person capable of sacrifice, veneration, and a pure heart, that is his religion."
— Pierre Van Paassen

When I was a Child ...
I thought like a child.
I reasoned like a child.
When I became an adult,
I put an end to childish ways.
For now we see in a mirror dimly,
but then we will see face to face.
Now I know in part;
then will I know fully . . .
— 1 Corinthians 13:11f
Paul of Tarsus

A vision of truth is all that we can hope for. There will always be a dimming of the truth as filtered through the finite capabilities of the human mind. We can no more grasp the full truth of the nature of creation than we can visualize a photon as both a particle and a wave. Nor can we understand the complete workings of our brain and how each neuron fits into the whole, helping to shape our thoughts and guide our emotions.

What we can do is follow the admonition of the Hopi Spider Grandmother. She told her people to "Try to understand things." If we settle for less, and fall back on the magical notions of childhood thought, we demeans our capabilities and diminishes our unique vantage point in the adventure of creation.

Visions of Truth

The Greek philosopher Eratosthenes showed that the earth was round and measured its size. Copernicus and Galileo pursued the truth of our earth's subordinate position in the solar system in spite of accusations of heresy. Newton offered a clearer view of the universe, how it works and why. He dispelled the notion that magical forces hold up the planets and pull apples and people down to earth. Einstein fundamentally recast the truth as he wove together space and time and revealed the interrelatedness of matter and energy. Hubble found that the universe was expanding, while Penzais and Wilson discovered the lingering whisper of the Big Bang that flung the universe on its outward expansion.

The geologist Lyell illustrated the antiquity of the earth and Darwin discovered the principles of evolution of living species. Mendel showed that the characteristics of living things were tied in a highly regular way to the characteristics of their parents. Watson and Crick revealed the simple four-letter alphabet that spells out the coding in the genes postulated by Mendel, genes which determine the heredity and functioning of all living things.

Rutherford revealed the gossamer nature of atoms and the guiding influence of the organization of their nuclei. Bethe showed how Einstein's famous equation accounted for the production of energy in the sun. Oppenheimer's crew of technicians demonstrated how to unlock some of the tremendous energy locked in the nuclei of atoms. Panofsky and his wonderful atom-smashing machines unambiguously illustrated the creation of matter from energy. William James shed light on the workings of the mind and its relation to the brain. Heisenberg and Bohr disabused us of the scientific certainties that were predicted to be the fruit of a more complete knowledge of the universe. All of them followed the truth wherever it led them.

The world's religious institutions were originally the repository of all knowledge about the natural world and the center of the search for new knowledge of the creation. Their institutions trained scholars and inquiring minds. They maintained the libraries and collected all of the known literature and philosophy. They attempted to put all of this into an understandable order and to interpret its meaning.

Religious institutions gradually relinquished this charter of activity. Their dogmas unfortunately solidified in a way that prevented them from readily incorporating new knowledge as it appeared. When "everything changed", their thinking generally did not. Although the nature of the creation does not change, our perceptions of it do change, sometimes in great leaps, sometimes so slowly that we are not aware of the changes.

There is no greater denial of the Creator than a denial of our knowledge of the creation. A perversion of the knowledge of the creation is a perversion of the reality of the Creator, no matter how fragile that knowledge nor how dimly we perceive it.

We also diminish the Creator when we diminish the creation. The Creator is distorted when the creation is distorted, when we characterize it in a cartoon-like quality. We do this when we try to simplify it so that our finite minds can comprehend it, or when we twist our knowledge to fit preconceived dogmas. We deny the Creator when we reject and deny our knowledge of the creation, deny its elegant simplicity or its complex and varied forms. We venerate the Creator when we try to understand the only manifestation of the Creator that we are privileged to experience. We venerate the Creator when we live in harmony with our resulting vision.

Unbounded Power and Energy

Here then is a vision for our time. The Creator, that unbounded power and energy, in its wisdom has formed itself into the creation, creating space and time, formed itself, its power, into the substance of the creation. It is a creative substance which forms and re-forms itself into the endless variety of the universe. Everything - every particle and every guiding, prodding, organizing force - is an eternal part of the Creator.

This is a vision of the Creator immanent in every event and in every creature, every society of man, every web of organic life, every crystal of rock, every wisp of atmosphere, every linked-up electron, every proton and neutron nestled in the heart of the atom. You and I feel the Creator linking itself through the forces it generates within. Watch the

Creator, off on an adventure, an adventure to create, to experiment, to find what its nature can devise, which manifestation can survive, which novelty will endure. Experience the Creator as a participant rather than an observer, flinging itself through the space-time it creates, displaying its power and majesty in the endless variety of its forms. Contemplate the Creator as the whole of creation, not centered in any one place but immanent everywhere. Discard the anthropomorphic, human-like, and magical view of the Creator, characteristics we cling to from childhood. Recognize that the Creator needs no centralized mind or brain, for it issues no directives.

Marvel in the genius present in every part of the design of the creation. Realize the consonance of what we call love and the affinities which the creation displays in its coming together, its affinities that create and strengthen the harmony we observe, this overwhelming display of love.

Formulating an Ethic

If this view of the Creator as the creation is our measure of truth and a guide for our reflection, wherein lies our ethics? What is our framework for living, and what are the imperatives that guide our actions?

The Hippocratic oath contains the injunction, "First do no harm." What better starting place! We touch the earth and its biosphere in every phase of our daily living. You and I are immersed in the web of living things. We are among the fruits of its past and will be an enduring part of its future. Each of us is united in the web of life with every other living thing. All of us a part of the Creator. Acknowledging this implies a reverence for life, a reverence for the basis of life, and a reverence for each complement of our existence.

The harm we do to one another or to the earth, to the air or the water that sustains us, is an injury to the Creator. Giving part of the Creator as a gift to others is an act of sharing. Giving it back to the Creator is meaningless. As Kahlil Gibran has commented, "*We only truly give when we give of ourselves.*" We are the result of the Creator's craftsmanship. If everything is a part of the Creator, then each part is sacred and should be treated as such. Destroying harmony and interrelatedness is an injury to the Creator, an offense to the Creator.

We can strip-mine the earth in order to hoard its riches or we can carefully use only what is necessary for our lives. We can claim that part of the Creator is mine - my property - or we can share it with others who are equally a part of the Creator. We can impose our will on others or we can seek a harmonious relationship. We can overpopulate the planet or we can plan for future generations. We can hold everyone sacred as brothers and sisters or we can exclude those who differ with us in temperament, belief, or ethnic origin. Only one of each pair of alternatives is compatible with the realization that the Creator is the creation.

This ethic cannot be written out in laws or rules. It cannot be codified into commandments or taboos. It can only flow out of the realization that each part of us and each part of everything is integrally part of that great and wonderful Creation/creator. It will only come with the realization that each act of ours becomes a sacred part of the Creator's action. Each conscious act becomes an enduring monument either to our intelligence or to our folly. The test of any act of volition on our part is whether or not it celebrates the sacred nature of the Creator, whether or not it furthers or hinders the grand adventure.

This is a broad ethic, not just an ethic related to our fellow human beings. It encompasses all of our fellow creatures in a common web of life. The ethic extends to the undergirding, moving, changing earth beneath our feet; to the atmosphere through which we move; and above all, to the entirety of the Creator. We can use or abuse the creation, we can destroy its diversity or nurture it. We can shut out other creatures or we can share our part of the creation with all of them. We now have the power to speed the course of evolution and change its course. Will we acknowledge and be guided by the Creator ethic as we do so?

There are no guarantees. We break the web of life at our own peril. Millions of other living species have disappeared when they either distorted their environment or failed to cope with changes in the adventure. As humans, we have no unique protection other than the intelligence we possess, our faculties to think and plan. These have been built into the blueprint of our minds over untold generations. To fail to perceive the rules of survival or to disobey them puts us all at peril.

Life is not an idyll. Rather, it is a moving, changing, brawling interchange with our fellow creatures and with the moving and changing creation. With tongue in cheek, Mark Twain once described a visit to Heaven, a place of supposed idyllic existence. He observed harps discarded along the path. Apparently the joy of idyllic existence had soon paled, and the harps were discarded in the search for a new adventure.

In the real world, every thing, every creature, every human finds its niche and negotiates a way to survive and flourish. Many without vision lead lives of quiet desperation, while others force changes to the ongoing flow of life. Those changes may have either a fruitful or destructive effect. Only our intelligence and foresight can guide us in making such changes. Our ethic must involve all of our fellow humans, all our fellow creatures, and the whole of the sustaining earth. We can despoil them or we can harmonize with their patterns of existence. Every choice, great or small, is ours. Wars and racial hatred, destruction of the land and air, abuse of our fellow creatures - all are a denial of the creative and loving nature of the Creator, an alienation of ourselves from the Creator.

We act as individuals, but our actions have an effect on everyone and all the rest of creation. Individually we can alienate ourselves, but in doing so, we also stretch the web of life. We cannot divorce ourselves nor can we be divorced from the Creator. If we as individuals put too much stress on the web, it will break, and the individual "sin" will become a collective one.

If we fail the test, if we do not live in the spirit of being a responsible loving part of the Creator, we not only alienate ourselves but risk our extinction as a species. A more enduring, more adaptable species will evolve to replace the errant one, as has been done since the dawn of the Creator's adventure. In the film *O God*, George Burns, as God, is about to depart to visit other creatures when he is implored to stay: "We need you here to help us." His reply was, "I've given you everything you need, all you have to do is use it."

Emotional Underpinnings

Wherein lies that other necessity of human existence, the factor that affords us emotional security? Where are those comforting and assuring symbols? What can effectively take the place of majestic cathedrals invoking the presence of the Creator, mood-changing music and chants, assurances of an everlasting existence, rituals with their promise of personal transformation, hope of rescue from our folly or accidents, a codified framework for behavior, a vision of truth, a channel of communication to the Creator?

I invite you to walk through all of life as through a cathedral, sensing the presence of the Creator in all things and in all creatures. Open yourself to sense the power and majesty of all of the creation as it unfolds before you. Get caught up in the hymn of life with its harmonies, discords, jarring crescendos, and whispering lullabies of love. See if you can discern the grand adventure, the incredible history and unending diversity of these numberless, diverse manifestations of the Creator.

Like a tidal pond on the seacoast, at high tide, you can rejoice in your individual existence. You dance in the sunlight, reflecting the power of the sun with your ever-changing rippling surface. You feel the need to nurture the creatures that dwell in there with you. You are content in the knowledge that you will again merge with the Creator when "your" tide comes in, and continue with the Creator and its adventure.

I invite you to experience the creation flowing through you, through the air you breath, the food and water you consume, the knowledge you accumulate from others or organize from the sights, sounds, touches, and smells that come riding to you on those great communication channels of the creation.

You can rejoice in the transformation of your mind as you sense and comprehend more of the Creator's endless wonders. You gain respect for those who have gone before you. You feel at one with them through the genetic memory that they inherited, modified, and passed on to you. Cherish the code that made a blueprint for you from the flow of bits and pieces of the Creator. You can be secure in your kinship with all humans and all creatures through the shared and common chemistry of life. Know that you cannot escape from those who went before, that you are tied to those about you through your biological and physical kinship. Embracing all this, you may be content, knowing that the fact of your existence endures forever, and that others will bear a part of you imprinted within them as they continue the adventure.

Try thanking the green plants that maintain the oxygen we need. Bless the power of the sun that distills and refines the water we drink. Love and respect the animals and plants that synthesize the proteins and sugars for our bodies, and the acids that free the minerals from rock for our bones.

Remember your journey with the Creator, that every part of you was forged in the act of creation. Remember when you were transformed in the crucible of a white-hot sun, belched out in a supernova explosion, wandered the cold reaches of space until gravity pulled you into a nascent planet. Re-live the molten roiling planet and the slow birth of the continents congealing into mountains and plains. Experience again being belched out in a volcano, buried in the seas, and then joining the long experiment of linking and un-linking forming and un-forming, growing in organic complexity and fragility, changing and evolving.

Try to recall how you were destroyed when a meteor collided with earth, and how you started all over again on the long slow process of forming and re-forming. Relive the adventure of migrating out of the seas onto land, adapting to the harshness of drought and cold and destructive radiation.

When you have realized all this, our lovely heritage, then you will fully experience that underlying love that suffuses all things. It is that web of affinities that ties us together and creates, that nurtures and controls, that compels us to change and then change again, and that affords us our sheltering niche in this web of creation. Experience the overriding nature of this love of the Creator, the Creator that molds and changes us but always keeps us "in its everlasting arms."

Epilogue

I think that the dying
pray at the last,
not please
but thank you
as a guest thanks his host
at the door.

                    Annie Dillard[6]

---

[6] *Tickets For A Prayer Wheel*, Annie Dillard (Harper & Row, 1988) pg 127.

Chapter 22

A Personal Adventure

My life might be called a journey when reflecting upon it, but I can't call it anything but an adventure. True it was guided by the conventions of the society and my family. Nevertheless, no one, knowing me as a child, could have predicted the course of my life, least of all myself.

I had a general acceptance of middle-of-the-road Christian theology. The recorded words of Jesus impressed me by their wisdom and the insights into human behavior. They seemed to me not so much commands given from on high, but common sense based on a deep understanding of human nature. In the mid-1930's there was much discussion about warfare and the relationship of religious tenets to war-making. To me it seemed that the life and words of Jesus were unequivocal in his rejection of war for solving problems, but it wasn't an overriding concern of mine.

The introduction of the draft in 1940 brought the issue home to our family. My older brother would be soon facing it. The necessity for making decisions about this intrusion into our lives thrust it into the foreground. We were descended from and lived in a community of Mennonites and Amish who came from middle Europe. They had completely opted out of the feudal society controlled by the nobility, the church and the military. They had a long standing religious testimony prohibiting military service by their members; and had been persecuted, killed and jailed in Europe for their actions. Society in the United States treated them in much the same way up through the early 20th. century during those times when this part of their testimony and life collided with the war fevers that periodically erupted in the U.S.

Dec.7, 1941, forced some intense thinking and discussion. My brother, most of my Mennonite classmates and I decided that Jesus really meant what he said about loving your enemies instead of destroying them. We took the pacifist position. Life in our high school during the war years took on an abrasive quality between us and most of our classmates. You couldn't just drift along, comfortable in your traditions and cultural expectations. You had to think and justify your actions and beliefs. We were bombarded by signs of "Remember Pearl Harbor" and the like. I remember thinking that Jesus would have told his followers to forget Pearl Harbor and search for solutions other than war.

I entered college before reaching draft age and the war wound down before the draft caught up with me. Attending college where most of your classmates were returning G.I's was uncomfortable. My refusal to take the mandatory Reserve Officers Training Corps classes, didn't help the tense situation.

While in College in Philadelphia, I occasionally attended Friends Meeting for worship. This was my first acquaintance with Quakers, although our Boy Scout troop had its home in an inactive Quaker meeting house. I became an admirer of the Quakers. Their part in operating the Underground Railroad in our neighborhood was part of our folk lore. We heard tales of the secret rooms in several nearby farms where the runaway slaves had been hidden by the Quakers during the day. Stealthy trips at night took them to the next "station" on the Underground Railroad. Canada was their safe haven at the end of the railroad. I was also aware of their steadfast testimony against participating in or preparing for war.

I felt quite at home among them. Particularly, I appreciated their method of worship: meeting in silence broken only by someone speaking from the depth of their convictions. Besides their method of worship, I felt compatible with their belief system. It emphasized individual insight and searching, instead of a codified system of religious thought. I remained, however, with my traditional Christian theological views, some of which might be classified as fundamental, and others as quite liberal.

It was during these college years where I saw at first hand the humiliating discrimination faced by minorities in our society. The weekend work camps of the Quakers, where you worked with a black family helping them to fix up their home, helped me to feel the pain of their situation. The blatant and institutional rejection of Jews in the college fraternity system brought another dimension of society to me that I hadn't experienced before.

My home community had a single racial culture. It was particularly galling to see some religious groups, attempting to justify and enforce discrimination on the basis of Christian theology.

My wife and I were married about a year after I graduated from college. I had begun to work as a development engineer in the new industry of television. We both had exposure to the Quakers in Philadelphia, and their work camps became an important factor in guiding our perceptions of life. We continued working with them by joining their work camp program in our town, after we were married. In spite of this, we felt comfortable in my country Methodist Church. A young liberal-thinking pastor was serving there at the time. He too was a pacifist, influenced greatly by Quaker leaders and their writings.

We both became intimately involved in the activities of the Methodist Church and I still maintained a very conventional theological view. Several times, I remember expressing the view that it surely was good to always have God around to take care of things. I did, however have some ambiguous thoughts about the nature of scriptures or the books on which religious thoughts are based. The writers exhibited a lack of knowledge about the workings of the physical world. They surely did not understand the development of living organisms, or even the scope and breadth of creation. Nevertheless it was tacitly assumed that they represented truth in entirety and were not to be questioned.

The pastor and I attended a Sunday school conference where the major speaker began to open my eyes to some different interpretations of these scriptures. He claimed that at best we could consider them inspired, considering that the word inspired had a root meaning of "breathed into." They were not dictated to a recorder. His insight was that they represented the history of a people's attempt to make sense of the world in which they lived. They were the fruits of the attempt to put it all together into a coherent view of creation. Actually, the Bible represented the entire literature of a group of people. The early traditions had been passed along orally until they developed the ability to record them in writing. They therefore contained history, poetry, tribal rules and speculation of the elders. Interpreting them requires knowledge of the context in which they were written, and appreciation of the culture, language and knowledge of their times.

This was a mildly liberating experience. As the Sunday School superintendent I occasionally discussed these views with the teachers and articulated them to the congregation in general. These expressions became very threatening to some more orthodox members of the congregation. The lay leader was dispatched to quiz me on my orthodoxy and my theology. He apparently confirmed their worst fears. Our children began to tell us that they were getting confused. Their Sunday School teachers were telling them one thing and we were telling them something else at home. Clearly it was time for a change.

The Quakers welcomed us with little or no questioning as to our orthodoxy. They only implied that we continue to seek the truth ourselves. But I had already been asking myself some questions that I couldn't answer with any satisfaction. I wasn't about to subscribe to Mark Twain's statement that *"Faith is believing in something you know is not so."*

The Methodist church had been emphasizing personal prayer. We were assured that marvelous things would happen to a congregation where the members pledged to devote several periods each day to prayer. After many sincere tries, I began to question the process. I also thought that I was being left out of the promise that the Holy Spirit would visit the faithful. That didn't seem to be happening to me nor was it reported by the rest of the congregation.

The Quaker's testimony was that *"there is that of God within every person."* This inner light could be accessed by quiet meditation. I began to use that quiet time to begin to think things through. My thoughts began to concentrate on three areas; communication, action, and goals or purpose. All three involved the nature of God or the Creator, which I assumed were synonymous. I couldn't imagine a universe that was created by one force and then taken over and controlled by another. Nor could I accept a parochial God dealing with just one little planet out of the entire universe.

Since I was an engineer involved with a communication system I tackled that problem first. The communication enigma was of course prayer. What were you doing when you prayed? The assumption was that you were communicating with the Creator. That raised the question of where the Creator was and by what means you were communicating. With every communication that I was aware of, the communication took place between at least two different entities. It also involved some means of transmitting the desired communication. A medium through which the communication can be conveyed is necessary. Then there has to be a receptor at the other end. Lastly, there must be some means of interpreting the information at both ends. The receptor and interpreter are very important. Television waves don't plug directly into your brain. You first have to tune to the communication channel you want to receive. Next you must have the proper machinery to detect the picture and sound information. This machinery then presents it in a way that you can understand. Of course to be useful, it should be a two-way communication channel. I assumed that prayer was a two-way process but I hadn't experienced the return communications in any manner.

Thinking about the communication media further complicated my dilemma. How were thoughts communicated? Was there a multitude of different communication channels between each person and the Creator? What was the language and how was the message received and detected? Was it a party line that everyone used? What was the language used?

Then there was the problem of where was the location of the Creator. If the Creator was located at some central point, this created big problems. It takes time for a message to traverse through the intervening space. The fastest thing we know of is light or some other electromagnetic communication. It takes several years for light to travel just one way to the nearest stars. Indeed, the revelations of Einstein showed that anything traveling any faster was forbidden by the laws of the universe. In any event, communication with a distant Creator required instantaneous transmission. If you assumed the reality of individual prayer, listened to and answered by a distant Creator, you were assuming a lot. You were assuming an instantaneous two-way communication system between each individual and the Creator. You had to cope with the problem of language. The language of each individual channel might have to be tailored to a different language. There are thousands of languages and dialects here on earth. You also had to allow that the Creator was simultaneously communicating individually with billions of people.

That seemed like a hopelessly complicated system. When I voiced this to a "true believer," I was told that "God could do anything he wanted to do." Possibly so, but I had observed that the process of creation had an elegant simplicity, not an intricate complexity. I was comforted by the belief that the Creator was immanent, or everywhere, right there with everyone and with every creature. That view simplified my dilemma with the communication media. The communication time problem was eliminated. However, it complicated my view of the Creator.

This raised all sorts of other theological questions such as: If the Creator was in residence, why did you have to ask the Creator to do something? Was prayer necessary to remind the Creator that it was not being attentive to obvious problems? Maybe prayer was necessary to assure the Creator of my fidelity. But if the Creator was all seeing and forever present, my fidelity or lack of it would be pretty obvious. My own self delusions and professions of loyalty shouldn't make any difference.

I still had no personal experience of answers to prayers. Nothing was recognizable as communications or specific guidance, in spite of a lot of sincere effort. Some people related to me that they experienced warm and comforting feelings that they couldn't properly describe, while others reported that voices told them to do something. Usually these people were dismissed as having recognizable mental problems that produced voices in their head. Others saw things happening that they interpreted as a sign of divine intervention. These events weren't necessarily obvious as divine intervention to other observers. It seemed to me that if prayer were a vital part of the creation and a sure link to the Creator, it wouldn't be so haphazard and unpredictable or unrecognizable.

While prayer remained a puzzle, I accepted the conventional wisdom regarding it, for the time being. Next, I began to think about the Creator's intervention and action in the events of the world. I had been assured that there was evidence of intervention in the course of world events. Individuals were rescued from death or disease by miraculous intervention of the Creator, or so they claimed.

Escape from a very close brush with death in my high school years might be attributed to divine intervention. By all rights or logic, I should have been dead that cold spring morning. I was traveling to school on a heavy high powered motor scooter that I had recently built. It was cold, and since the scooter steered quite well by just leaning one way or the other, I was traveling along with both hands in my pockets to keep warm. A few sharp bumps on the pavement flipped the handle bars to the left against the motor box. I started out over the front, heading directly at the front of an oncoming school bus. Somehow, as I was launched head first out over the front of the scooter, I managed to get my left hand out of my pocket. Reaching back, I grasped the left handle bar. The scooter immediately straightened out. With me hanging over the front of the scooter, I swished by the side of the bus. The white faced driver stared at me as I went by, because he had no time to turn away toward the side of the road. When I related my escape from death to others later, they assured me that God had saved me. I accepted that at the time.

As I began to deal with this matter of Divine intervention, I began to ask on what level this intervention takes place. Does this intervention come about by prompting humans to action? Sometimes this might be a plausible explanation. The creator prods people to take certain actions that will preserve themselves or others.

Since this would not explain mishaps in which another human or creature was not involved, the image of a big hand intervening was explored. The big hand seemed implausible. Certainly no one observed it. An invisible hand might be invoked. It would have to be very powerful to achieve some feats ascribed to it. Besides, I knew that something physical would have to be applied to a physical object to cause it to change course. Maybe a big wind? But what would stir up such a big wind? Would the Creator anticipate the incident and stir up a few molecules of air so that eventually a big wind would provide the proper and timely intervention?

This led me to think about what forces actually act on the materials of this creation. What makes them move? What forces do they react to? Going back to my physics background, I began to realize that the matter of the universe reacts to and is influenced or pushed about by only four forces that are now well known. These are the strong and the weak nuclear forces, electromagnetic forces and gravity. Well, the answer might be in the Creator creating these forces when needed. It could use these to push things around to achieve its objectives. Alternatively the creator could use other mysterious forces to cause the matter of the universe to move in unexpected ways. This "other" force has never been observed or measured. Besides, it became obvious that all of the forces that control, attract or move matter are generated within it. These forces are properties of matter itself. This realization began to shake me up a bit. I had never looked at the universe and its components in this manner before.

This set me off on another train of thought which proved to be unsettling and simultaneously, revealing. I had grown up along with the Atomic Age. We glibly talked about unlocking the power of the atom and threw around terms like Einstein's E = MC². I also grew up in the generation that realized where the power of the sun came from. Next, the expanding universe mystery began to be revealed. The Big Bang as the origin of the universe was being accepted as a reality and the understandings of what took place in this event were being uncovered.

My train of thought was guided by Einstein's description of the Atomic Age. "*It changed everything but our thinking.*" In that instance, I believe he was thinking about weapons and war. He was appalled at the unthinking tendency to accept atomic power as an instrument of war, without realizing the folly of a possible nuclear war. If Einstein's famous equation was universal in its application, it meant that matter could be converted into energy and energy could be converted into matter. This was the underlying assumption of the Big Bang. Initially, there was the "singularity," unimaginably high in temperature. It was a well of tremendous energy in which matter could not exist. As it expanded and cooled, out of it precipitated the stable forms of matter that make up all of the creation.

As I thought through this process, I realized that the entire physical universe was composed of energy. This energy precipitated out as matter, matter that contained within itself the forces that interact with other parts of the universe of matter. These forces couple the parts of the universe together and mold its forms and produce its evolution. There were no outside forces that mold or control the universe. That action comes from within. Energy formed itself into what we call matter and then generated within itself the forces that control it and shape its destiny! A mind shaking revolution began to take form in my perceptions.

This sent me off on another avenue of thought, which took the shape of trying to understand what was going on. I first looked at the concept of what we call matter, physical objects composed of atoms and molecules. Atoms are composed of three basic stable identifiable and measurable building blocks. The protons, the neutrons and the electrons. All atoms are constructed of these same three components. But each atomic element is entirely different in its characteristic from the others.

It was assumed that atoms were immutable until the discovery of radioactivity and radioactive decay of elements. Then it was discovered that the sun is a gigantic atom assembly plant. It is busily making the other elements out of hydrogen and helium by fusing their nuclear parts together in different arrangements. Sure, the alchemists were forever trying to turn the more common elements into gold and silver but they were never successful. The sun's rearrangement of the neutrons and protons did create different materials, different atoms, with entirely new properties. This is accomplished by doing nothing more than changing the organization of those three basic components.

Clearly the properties of these atoms are related to how the components of the nucleus are organized. The number of protons in the nucleus determines its character. The properties of the new or different atom are determined by this particular organization of neutrons and protons. This difference in the number of protons in the nucleus then determines the number of electrons that each nucleus captured in its shell. It became evident much earlier in human history, that the number of electrons in the shell determined just how each element would react with other atoms.

Then I looked at the association of atoms into molecules which could produce materials of entirely different properties from the atoms that made the new material. These new properties are determined by how the different atoms are organized with one another.

I rapidly began to look at other aspects of our life, world, and universe. The reality of all of the things that I examined was determined by their organization, their interrelationship to one another. This applied to the relatively static realm of atoms and molecules. It extended through crystals to the complex dynamic organisms of life. Cultures and civilizations also were defined by their organizational patterns. The nature of everything seemed to be determined by its organization.

Now I had two basic principles. The only substance was energy, and the reality of anything, from materials to thoughts, was its organization.

These were the workings of the Creator. But the other factors were the forces that shape and mold the creation. These forces shape and power the obvious evolution of the creation. These reside within this material that is organized out of energy. Here it was inside, not coming from some far off place or hovering over the local part of creation.

The cosmic concept that began to emerge was my awareness of nearly infinite energy or power. This energy organized itself into the universe and continually reorganized itself in an evolving and expanding universe. It operates by a system that is elegantly simple in its design and is organized and designed so that it continued to create. It is a display of genius!

It seemed that I had come nearly full circle. What I was seeing was really a concept of the Creator, an infinitely powerful genius that created the universe, but created it of itself. The genius of the creation permeated it and was inherent in its basic design. It is a universe that does not require outside force or guidance, but is liberated and empowered to devise the creation out of itself. This was a very unsettling thought in some ways. It made me think of the old gospel song, "*There's no hiding place down here.*"

Originally I was caught up in the "clockwork" universe of Newton. Here, everything should be predictable if you could know what its starting conditions were and could do enough calculations. However my work in developing television camera tubes forced me to begin thinking along the lines of the new physics of quantum mechanics that was developing throughout my lifetime. We were dealing with the solid-state electronic properties of light sensitive materials in these devices. We were also involved in the production of very fine electron beams which were used to interrogate electronic charges. The light sensitive materials develop these charges and utilized the energy of the incoming photons of light to produce them.

We were required, then to come to grips with the disclosures of quantum physics. These were the new understanding of the workings of matter and energy at the atomic and the electron level. Here the idea of **predictability** had to be thrown out and the term **probability** considered. This understanding made me take a closer look at what was going on at the subatomic level, and guided my later observations about destiny and the course of creation's ongoing process.

Originally in my explorations, I thought of the creation as following a predictable or pre-ordained path, journeying to a goal or some objective, as if following a grand plan. I saw it climaxing in the incredible complexity of humans and their brains. Looking backward, you can apparently discern and explain such a course. By looking forward from the Big Bang, there is no discernible path or predictable course. There is certainly no single trend from the simple to the more complex. Not only that, but the universe exhibits a bewildering variety of unique creations. Even in the little speck of the universe we call our planet, the trend is toward diversity. Development does not concentrate only on the development of that sophisticated and complex species, Homo Sapiens. Nature never puts all of its eggs in one basket. We are only one of several hundred million species that have inhabited this planet. The largest mobile creatures so far, are the dinosaurs. They disappeared millions of years ago.

All this seemed to fit together suddenly. It solved the communication problem, and put a face of reality on the concept of the creation. Here were some hard to escape facts:

> The only substance of creation is energy
> The only reality is organization
> All of the forces controlling the substance of the creation and guiding its organization, originated within it.
> The creation is off on an open-ended adventure

I put these facts together to develop the concept of the Creator as creation. I saw unbounded power or energy, organizing itself into the material universe and embarking on an indeterminate open-ended adventure.

Similar trends in religious thinking also became apparent. The Christian tradition accepted Jesus as a part of the Creator. Meister Eckhart and the Quaker founder, George Fox, envisioned a bit of the Creator in each person. In this new view I was extending it to seeing everything as a part of the Creator.

But there remained a nagging fear that I was overlooking something fundamental, or oversimplifying something that was far more complex, something that would invalidate the whole system of thought. On the subject of the conversion of energy to matter my understanding was on shaky ground. True, the power of the atomic bomb and the sun originated from converting some matter into energy. Under closer examination it turns out that those processes merely rearrange the protons and neutrons in the nucleus of atoms. They weigh less in their new configuration. Similarly the fact that the Big-Bang could transform energy into matter was theoretical since no one was there to observe it.

The conversion of matter into energy and the conversion of energy completely into matter was confirmed to my satisfaction after an encounter in the early 70'S. I happened to be on a raft trip down the Grand Canyon and on the trip was "Pief" Panofsky, the director of the Stanford Linear Accelerator. This was one of the world's most powerful atom smashers. He was describing a new use that had been made of this powerful electron accelerator. This machine created a minute "ball" of immense pure energy out of which appeared matter, the building blocks of the universe. Its method of operation was described in earlier chapters.

Later I visited the Stanford Linear Accelerator and its "SPEAR" ring. It seemed that I was being present at the creation, as they described its workings and the results.

There is obviously a lot that I do not know and understand about the creation and the Creator, but I began to feel that I had glimpsed a rather clear picture of the nature of the Creator and the creation.

Some mysteries, however, remain. These have been alluded to in the previous chapters. Stephen Hawking raises some questions when he claims that the universe has positive and negative energy, and the positive energy exactly balances the negative energy. Matter and radiation represent the positive energy. The forces that bind the nucleus and the gravitational ties represent the negative energy. Supposedly, these cancel and the universe has zero energy. Maybe this is right, and as the rest of the universe demonstrates, it has a beautiful symmetry where the positive balances the negative, the Ying balances the Yang.

My exploration didn't stop there. There was the matter of ethics, emotions and the broader field of human-creation interaction. I remember looking at the rules and the commandments handed down by religion. At the time, these seemed to me to be an obstacle course that you had to surmount before you would get some rewards or favored treatment.

When I began to look at the ethics of different cultures, I was impressed by the great number of similarities. Furthermore, the common strands of these different ethics seemed to point to a universal way of living and interacting that would preserve the societies that practiced them. This turned my thinking to the possibility that these characteristics of society had evolved as an important survival feature of those societies. Quite simply, societies that developed these ethics survived.

I have also been convinced, that not only virtually all of the physical characteristics and behavior patterns of each species have evolved as an important factor in the survivability of that species, but also the cultural and ethical systems that they live within, have had an equal value in effecting their survivability. The results of certain types of ethical behavior are not obvious to the participant at the time, but astute observation over a long period can discern those patterns of survival which are desirable. These observations can be passed on to future generations, as laws of conduct that must be enforced by the society to assure its survival.

For instance it is not possible for the person exposed to radioactivity or x-rays to discern any harm at the time of exposure. A careful study of the patterns of exposure of health workers established the cause-effect relationship of cancer and other illnesses of people exposed to radiation. These "wise men" set down rules governing exposure, avoidance, and protection of persons apt to be exposed to radiation. They established an "ethic" of behavior for these situations. The creation has been unforgiving of failures of different species, to adapt to their own unique situation or to a changing environment.

Ethics have therefore been imbedded deeply into society. They are enforced by sanctions. Usually they are blessed as rules given from "on high." This enforces their importance and contributes to the survival of the society. Of course there are differences in the ethics of different societies. Sometimes, these are engendered by the circumstances. In a settled community, bigamy might be destructive. In a nomadic society however, a family left without a forager, protector and hunter would not survive. Hence, there might be a commandment that a brother should take on his dead brother's wife and family.

Early on I was challenged about love and emotions, those great and rich parts of human experience and where they fit into the picture. Then I began to realize the importance of the affinities that characterize the creation. These are the factors that produced the evolution of and the changes in the creation. I soon began to counterpoint these interactions to the various aspects of love. What is love but a drawing together, drawing together to form a more harmonious relationship? It is a creative process in human sexual love, and a sacrificing love when it changes your nature as you submerge yourself into a new union with others. It pulls people together in families and societies, families and societies which are more complex and richer than is life for a solitary individual. All these aspects of love mirror the results of the creativity of the creation. They all operate under the drive of the various affinities that the creation possesses. Not coincidentally, I remembered a part of a creed that I had held in my youth. This was, *"Love is the power of God in human relations."* I also recalled the often quoted words of Jesus that "*God is love.*"

I had originally overlooked one very important fundamental of religions' tradition, that of providing emotional security. This was driven home at a testimonial party for my Uncle who had devoted his retirement years to finding alcoholics who wanted help. He then assisted them in getting into a rehabilitation center, and then he took them into a support group based on a fervent fundamentalist Christian tradition. The success of his group of people in staying free from alcohol was over 60%, while the success rate of the general run of people graduating from that rehabilitation program was less than 20%. Their fervor for the security that this religious tradition gave them, was more than evident in their testimonials for my Uncle and for the Lord. It was obviously the underpinning of their lives. Although their underlying assumptions made no sense to me nor did it provide me with an emotional security, this was a vital factor in their lives. It was only later that I began to study some contemporary psychology of Abram Maslow. He pointed out that unless individuals had some basic security in their lives, they could not develop or progress toward being a more complete person.

This awakened an awareness of the different forms of worship, rituals, creeds and social practices in the diverse cultures of the world. I began to understand how they contributed to the emotional and social stability of their societies. I also began to understand the grave harm that is done to these societies when another culture or religion is forced on them. No better example can be seen than here in the United States. We are still seeing the effects on the emotional stability and the sense of community among Native Americans who underwent this forced cultural change. They were forced to turn over their children to "mission " schools who were torn out of their society, forbidden to use their own language, and indoctrinated in a religion and culture foreign to all of their traditions. Then they were sent back into a culture which had been uprooted from its long held homelands and traditions. Their former ways of life were ridiculed, but they were not accepted as full members of the indoctrinating society.

The things that give a person emotional security are many and varied. They need have no relationship to any reality. The drive to secure emotional security is real and necessary for the individual. For me, the realization that the creation is the Creator, and that I am a part of the Creator and the Creator's endless adventure, provide that emotional security. I am assured of continuing as part of that adventure in the future just as each part of me has participated in the past.

Chapter 21 Bibliography

Twain, Mark (Samuel Clemens), *Following the Equator, Puddnhead Wilson's New Calendar*, New York, Harper and Brothers, 1897.

Chapter 23

Bumps Along The Way

Ruts and Jolts that Shaped My Perceptions

> If an engine has gas, and spark,
> and compression, and it is "in time"
> it MUST run.
> > Grandpa Neuhauser
> > on how things work.

Born at the turn of the century, my parents came from conservative Anabaptist Pennsylvania "Dutch" families. In fact, my grandparents on one side were born into Old Order Amish families. Individually my parents were independent thinkers.

My father, a small town businessman, was a violin player, and an avid supporter of the cultural and musical activity in the nearby small city. He also found time to read a lot of our great literature. Invention of mechanisms for his own use was one of his joys. In his early teens, when automobiles were just coming into use, he was one of a few people in the county who could tune automobile engines.

My mother showed signs of independent thought in her grade school days. Her sisters remember her parading the school grounds during recesses and lunch times with a sign advocating the vote for women. She took business training and was one of the pioneering women in her community to seek work in the business field.

As I look back over my life I realize that I was privileged to be tied into and thrust into many basic inquiries into the nature of the creation. My career had started out with a rigorous engineering education, tempered with practical work in industry. This was a cooperative engineering program where we worked at entry level jobs in industry during alternate academic quarters.

My professional career involved the design and development of television camera tubes, which are the electronic equivalent of photographic film. Here I became involved in a whole new world that my education had not specifically prepared me to understand. I became the Engineering leader for the team of engineers designing these television camera tubes for black and white television and later color television. The most renowned camera tube that we produced was the Image Orthicon. The Encyclopedia Britannica described the Image Orthicon as "the most highly developed camera tube, and it is perhaps the most remarkable electronic device in existence."

I was fortunate enough to have one of my first jobs be the design and fabrication of testing equipment for some of the very early television camera tubes. I essentially had to design and build instrumented television cameras in which the tubes could be evaluated. Later I became involved in the design of the camera tubes.

When you build any electronic vacuum tube, you have to immerse yourself in vacuum technology, where you attempt to evacuate all of the air from inside a tube. A perfect vacuum is impossible to achieve. Even if you could produce a perfect vacuum, you have to cope with the fact that atoms do not remain on the surface of a material forever. They are continually jumping off and filling the vacuum you create. This aspect of matter alerted me in a very practical way to the basic instability of the parts of creation.

Other aspects of this work immersed me in getting a better understanding of atoms and electrons and what forces influence them. We had to devise structures called cathodes that would emit electrons. This is done by heating the proper material to a high temperature so that electrons would detach themselves from the atoms. We utilized these streams of electrons by forming them into electron beams in the vacuum. Then we used electric and magnetic fields to form the electron beam into a very fine stream and move these streams of electrons about with other magnetic and electric fields.

We were also forced to learn a great detail about the materials we used. Glass is strange. It is really a stiff liquid, and not the hard crystalline material you might imagine it to be. You learn that some glasses hold their electrons very tightly and are good insulators, while others allow some of their atoms and electrons to migrate through and conduct electricity. You also find that most materials that you perceive to be completely solid and leak proof are porous. Many have voids through their network of atoms. Small atoms such as helium can continuously travel through these materials.

At times we had to identify the residual gas atoms inhabiting our imperfect vacuum. A mass spectrometer determines their weight or mass. It first ionizes an atom by knocking off an electron or two. It took surprisingly little energy to do this, only a few electron-volts. The mass spectrometer allows you to identify just how many neutrons and protons are in each atom that you are examining. This number identifies just what atom you are dealing with.

Camera tubes detect the amount of light in each part of an image. Then they store the energy that the incoming light waves transfer to the light-sensitive material. In this field of work, you become accustomed to thinking in terms of the energy of each incoming photon of light. You relate the color of detected light with the energy of the photons. The action of electrons in the material that absorbs the light becomes very important. In some materials we utilized this energy to allow electrons to escape from the surface of the light sensitive materials. In others, it allowed the electrons to cast off from their moorings and travel through the material. These electrical charges were accumulated at discrete places and used to produce an electrical television signal. To understand these phenomena, we had to develop an understanding of quantum electronic phenomena. This type of electron physics of "solid state "material was akin to the transistor technology which eventually revolutionized electronics.

Color television immersed us in optic work where light was separated according to its wavelength or color. Here we had to work with materials that bend and reflect light in different ways depending on their "color" or their energy. All of this made us come to grips with the dual nature of light, its wavelike properties and its particle like-properties. We eventually developed camera tubes that were so sensitive that we could "see" individual photons of light as they produced the image. With these tubes you could see how individual photons of light behaved like little particles. You could see them piling onto an image, creating it dot by dot.

Of course we were aware of the transmission of energy through radio waves because our colleagues were developing high power transmitter tubes. These tubes transmit minuscule amounts of energy to each radio or television receiver. The television receiver detects this energy and the information it bears and reassembles it into a full color picture. This compelled us to think about the transmission of energy and the methods of transmitting and detecting this energy.

When you make vacuum tubes, you find that you have to fuse different materials together. Many materials have the propensity to link with other materials to make a strong bond. Then you have to think in terms of how the electrons surrounding one molecule rearrange themselves to link with the electrons surrounding different ones. Then you realize that the strength of the materials and the joints that we formed between different materials was inherent in these electron linkages, and not some mysterious property of the materials.

In the drive to perfect these devices, we had to eliminate small foreign particles that would produce large spots in the pictures. This required us to identify the particles so we knew what materials we had to look for in the way of contamination. We explored interesting by-ways in this quest. Spectrographs heated these small particles and detected the wavelengths of energy that they emitted. The "heated" electrons surrounding an atom jumped up and down in their orbits and emitted light waves that were characteristic of each different atom. By examining the pattern of light, we could identify the culprits producing the spots.

Scanning electron microscopes produce a television picture that show the typical crystalline structure of small particles, illustrating the repetitious and geometrical relationship that the affinities of different molecules produce. This allowed us to deduce what mineral or metal the particle might be. X-ray diffraction studies of materials that we used to detect light, gave us a clue to their structure. This structure was related to the way electrons would be free or impeded in their flow through the material.

I also had the responsibility for helping the designers and users of television cameras make best use of our camera tube's capabilities. This exposed me to worlds of different types of inquiry. Some of our special tubes intensified X-ray images. These allowed the physicians to explore new ways of looking at a functioning human body with minimum X-ray exposure. Sunspots were viewed using other camera tubes, to explore the processes taking place in the sun. Hooking these cameras up as the eyes of a telescope disabused the credulous of the notion of canals on Mars. These devices, eventually became much more sensitive than photographic film. They produced images of the furthermost reaches of the universe. Galaxies and quasars, billions of light years away, are seen through their eyes.

It is difficult to determine just what is going on in living cells. They are transparent to light. Previously, the only practical way to see what is inside a cell was to stain it with a material that absorbs light. Then you can see into it with a microscope. Unfortunately, the stain kills the cell. You can only speculate what is going on inside while it is living. I had the privilege of helping a top medical researcher develop an ultraviolet-sensitive television camera system. This system used short pulses of ultraviolet light (which is absorbed in many cell materials). This camera produced an image of the internal working of living cells. By using different wavelengths of ultraviolet light, it became possible to identify different chemicals in the cell. Then it became possible to determine where different nutrients were utilized in the cell and what new products the cell developed from these nutrients. We used the ultra-violet light in short measured pulses since it is lethal to cells. The energy of the ultraviolet light easily breaks the chemical bonds of living material and creates new chemicals.

This led me to appreciate the ephemeral nature of living things, and the chemical basis of life as controlled by the chromosomes and genes. It also led me to more clearly understand the role of energy transfer in the chemical processes taking place in living organisms and the factors that could produce genetic change or damage.

My colleagues in related electron tube development work, opened new avenues of thinking and knowledge. The engineers making the extremely sensitive light detectors, were plagued by spurious light flashes. They detected these in complete darkness. This led them to realize that even the purest materials of which the tubes were made contained radioactive isotopes. These decay on a regular basis, and give off the radiation energy that was being detected as flashes of light. This led me to realize that radioactive decay and change of one atom into another were an every day and pervasive reality. It is almost impossible to find any material that does not contain some radioactive isotopes.

The energy they put out is a powerful agent for change in a world of apparent stability. These fellows also provided the radiation detectors necessary to understand and control nuclear reactions. Through these, our little professional community became enlightened by the discoveries that the atomic scientists and the atom smashers were revealing.

Other engineers were crafting very powerful radio wave producing tubes that could pump large bursts of energy into a vacuum chamber. The intent was to produce the conditions that exist in the center of the sun. In the heart of these giant complex machines, its inventors were beginning to fuse the nuclei of certain isotopes of hydrogen causing them to release tremendous amounts of energy, in effect, to produce the conditions inside the sun that produce the sun's awesome energy.

My favorite philosopher, Walt Kelly, creator of the comic strip Pogo, illustrated the process of the metamorphosis of my thoughts. In a sequences involving his swamp critters, one character suggested that they discuss weighty matters; "*things like life and death, and not 10 tons of coal.*" The critter replied, "*Here I was expecting a nice fun afternoon discussing things, shouting and screaming at one another. Now you've gone and spoiled it all - you got me to thinking.*"

My direct exposure to all these different aspects of the creation, from the nuclear center of atoms to the far reaches of space, from the chemistry of life to the indeterminable nature of matter, ranging from the interchange of energy to matter, to the curving of space by gravity, "spoiled it all" for me. It disturbed my comfortable conventional world, and it got me to thinking.

Chapter 22 Bibliography

Kelly, Walt, *Potluck Pogo*, New York, Simon and Schuster, 1954.

Appendix A

Additional Description
Of the Four Forces of Creation.

The Electromagnetic Force[7]

Electrons have what is called a negative electrical charge. This electric charge produces an electric field surrounding the electron. Protons have an equally strong positive charge and electric field. The electron's negative field is strongly attracted to the positive field of the proton. This field is the force that pulls the electrons and protons toward one another. These all important fields of force create the structure of our world in its various and multitudinous forms. How this force creates the tangible parts of our universe is really a thrilling story.

We'll start with the atom, where this force actually builds atoms by tethering electrons to protons. Electrons envelop the nucleus of an atom, which is an assembly of protons, in a cloud-like shell. Electrons are attracted toward this nucleus by an electric field generated between the positively charged protons and the negatively charged electrons. The attractive force between a negatively charged particle and a positively charged particle increases greatly as the charged particles approach one another.

The electric field between two particles is very intense when they are close together, but it drops off rapidly (inversely as the square of the distance) when they are moved apart. This means, for example, that when the separation increases by a factor of ten, the force between the particles is only one hundredth as strong as it was at its original distance.

Atoms by themselves are very small, less than one hundred-millionth of an inch in diameter. The nucleus is even more minuscule. It is less than one ten-thousandth of the diameter of the atom itself. Since each proton is nearly two thousand times as massive as an electron, most of the weight of the atom is concentrated in the nucleus. If the nucleus

---

[7] I have introduced the term electromagnetic force since the electrostatic force of the electron's charge is both manipulated by a magnetic field and the motion of an electron produces a magnetic field. Both electric fields and magnetic fields are inexorably intertwined and are commonly described as a single electromagnetic force.

were scaled up to the size of an orange, the first shell of electrons would be about half a mile away. To humans living at human scale, these dimensions are truly astounding!

The small nucleus determines the nature of the atom. It simply decrees how many electrons are to be held in the electron shells; one electron in the shell for every proton in the nucleus. The number of electrons in the shell determines how a particular atom interacts with or attaches itself to other atoms. It is the electrons of one atom interacting with the electrons of other atoms that forms all molecules, chemicals, and physical structures.

Although we are used to thinking of most materials as strong, dense, and solid, actually the atom is a structure that is mostly empty. In spite of its fragile-appearing, mostly hollow nature, the atom and its electron shells are very strong. The "firmness" of an atom really means the firmness of its electron shells. And here we find that the strength of the force tethering electrons to their nucleus is a fine strength indeed

It is difficult to strip the electrons from the shells, and it is difficult to crush the shell. If the atom is subjected to enough pressure, the pressure can collapse the shells and force the electrons into the nucleus. This amount of pressure can only be generated at the center of objects that have a mass several times greater than that of our sun.

Repulsive Electric Fields

We started out by talking about the electromagnetic force but so far have used only the term "electric field." This is the force of attraction between negatively charged electrons and positively charged protons.

However, electric fields may also be *repulsive* fields, since like-charged particles repel one another. For instance, the positive charges of the protons of a nucleus exert an enormous repulsion on one another. The nucleus would fly apart if another, stronger force did not hold it together. Later we will examine this other essential force, the strong nuclear force.

Meanwhile we must recognize that electrons also exert a strong repulsive force towards one another, if and when they are close together. But because the distance between electrons in their shells is relatively great -- compared to say the distances between protons in the nucleus -- the only force necessary to hold them in their shells is their electric attraction to the protons in the nucleus.

Electromagnetic Fields

A magnet produces a magnetic field. We are all familiar with magnets and know that they can either push or pull. We cannot see or feel the magnetic field between magnets or between magnets and "magnetic" material, but the effects are striking.

Magnetic fields are produced by electrons in motion. A minute bit of magnetism is generated around every electron, sort of like having a shadow. These minute bits can add up. Every atom, for example, has a small magnetic field produced by the movement of the electrons circulating in its shells. In some materials the atoms are arranged in a rather rigid structure, allowing the magnetic fields of many atoms to line up in the same direction. Each atom then adds its small magnetic field to the others, together producing a stable magnet with a strong field.

Some of us are also familiar with the magnetic fields produced by magnetic coils. These are coils of wire that produce a strong magnetic field when electric current is forced through them. (An electric current is a flow of electrons through an electrically conducting material like a copper wire). The stream of moving electrons in a wire produces a magnetic field just like the electrons that circle around in the shells of atoms. Winding the wire in a tight coil allows the field to repeat and strengthen itself again and again, resulting in an electromagnet that might be found in a motor, a television receiver or the pulsating speaker of a ghetto-blaster. A reverse action takes place when a magnetic field moves in relation to a wire. In this case the magnetism compels any loosely attached electrons to move in one direction in the wire. A practical example is an electric generator. Here vast numbers of electrons are forced to travel through tightly coiled wires by a powerful moving magnetic field. The resulting flow of electrons is the electric current put out by the generator.

In a more general sense, then, we may perceive an elegant reciprocal relationship. A moving electric charge generates a magnetic field, and a moving magnetic field produces an electric field that moves an electric charge. This inter-relationship was puzzling until James Clerk Maxwell in 1860 developed a convincing and elegant mathematical analysis relating electric and magnetic fields. He showed that both electric and magnetic fields were aspects of a common phenomenon that he called the *electromagnetic field*. The creation may sometimes look chaotic, but closer inspection typically reveals a good housekeeper's tidiness!

Electromagnetic Radiation

Shortly thereafter another fundamental property of electromagnetic fields was discovered. They are the means by which energy is transferred from one electron to another, whether these electrons be in the same molecule or a universe apart. This kind of energy is called *electromagnetic radiation,* and we know it as light, heat, radio waves, x-rays, and other radiant energy. This energy -- electromagnetic energy -- is often referred to as "waves" because each bit of it vibrates from side to side with perfect regularity as it simultaneously shoots forward through space in a straight line and at constant speed. Tidy indeed!

Electromagnetic fields give rise to electromagnetic energy. This travels through space at "the speed of light", the greatest speed anything can attain. And light itself is of course, electromagnetic energy.

This explanation of the relationship between electric and magnetic fields and their propagation by electromagnetic waves opened a broad understanding of the nature of our universe. Heat, radio waves, x-rays, light, and gamma rays were all found to be electromagnetic waves. They all have the same wave nature, that is they vibrate as they travel forward. And something more fascinating: the energy that they transmit is conveyed in precise bits, discrete quantities akin to particles. These individual units or quanta of electromagnetic energy are called *photons,* since they were first used to describe the transmission of light. But photons of visible light are not identical to say radio photons. The difference between a light ray/photon and a radio wave/photon lies in the frequency of the oscillations of the wave. Just as sound waves can have different pitches, so electromagnetic waves can have different frequencies. For example, a ray of green light vibrates about a billion million times per second, whereas an AM radio wave vibrates only about one million times per second, making them feel very different to us! (One vibration per second is often called one hertz (Hz), so the AM radio frequency mentioned above can also be described as one million hertz, one megahertz, 1 MHz, or 10^6 Hz. The light wave has a much higher frequency, about 10^{15} Hz).

Another measure of this difference is the distance between the peaks of the waves, called the wavelength. The more frequent the oscillations, the shorter is the length of each wave. (Waves with higher frequencies and shorter wavelengths also contain more energy in each packet or photon, as we'll see later). The green light has a wavelength of about 5 ten-millionths of a meter, 0.0000005 m, whereas the radio wave is several hundred meters between peaks, i.e. almost a quarter of a mile! Fortunately a household microwave oven uses a wavelength that is easy to comprehend -- about an inch between peaks. The energy in each of its packets or photons is just the right amount to be absorbed by the electrons orbiting between the hydrogen and oxygen atoms of a water molecule. Thus microwave ovens heat water-filled foods very efficiently - and are mostly ignored by solid substances such as glass and plastic food containers.

There is no distinction between the photon of a radio wave, light wave, x-ray, or any other electromagnetic wave except their frequency or wavelength and their corresponding *energy*. The differences in energy between different radiations are crucial to understanding how our universe works. A single photon of visible light has an energy of between one and two electron-volts. A gamma ray photon possesses hundreds of thousands of electron-volts of energy, whereas a radio photon possesses only a tiny fraction of one electron-volt.

Electromagnetic waves are the means of transferring energy between electrons when they are far enough apart that they no longer interact by simple repulsion. Electrons initiate these waves by suddenly losing energy and emitting a photon equal to the energy that the electron has lost. This photon of electromagnetic energy travels at the speed of light until it encounters another electron that can absorb the energy. The recipient electron gains exactly the energy of the photon, causing it to vibrate faster or go into a higher-energy orbit around its nucleus. At the level of a substance that we can see and feel, we say that it has gotten warmer, is moving faster, or both.

Electrons are implicated in most motion, action and power. The typical earthbound forces that we encounter, including wind and waves on water, originate from the motion of molecules and atoms as they vibrate and push one another. These forces are transferred from one electron shell to the next. If the energy of the electrons dissipates, atomic and molecular motions decrease and the molecules cool. If electrons give up enough photons of energy, the material they belong to eventually freezes into an unmoving and rigid structure.

The photons themselves are very efficient. They are not deflected or diminished in energy until they collide with a recipient electron and are absorbed. This distance may be very short or very long. For example, photons of visible light seen by astronomers from the most distant reaches of the universe have been traveling for billions of years. These are the ones that escape into space. We may suppose that most do not get this far -- the others are absorbed within the emitting star by electrons which are only the minutest distance away. How lucky the intergalactic travelers!

Even better, these travelers arrive unmarked by age. Despite their immense lifetime, they are exactly the same as the newly minted photons reaching your eyes from this page. The ancient light from distant stars tells us about its emitting atoms just as the light from the printed page tells us about the reflective properties of today's paper and ink.

Atom-Atom Interactions

So far we have talked about individual atoms, their seeming fragility, and the relatively empty spaces within the shells of electrons. For the most part, the atoms of the world we live in are linked up with one another to form either substantial structures or fluids. In the long history of the universe this was not always the case.

In the early stages of the creation, virtually the only atoms present were hydrogen and helium. There was nothing solid or substantial about this dense sea of super-hot atoms. When things cooled a little, however, hydrogen atoms were the first to organize themselves into more complex structures.

A hydrogen atom, when cool enough, can make contact and pair up with another hydrogen atom. This is because the shell formed by its lone electron can accommodate a second electron. In fact, hydrogen seems to *want* to have another electron to make its shell complete. When two hydrogen atoms approach each other, they are able to complete each other's shell by sharing their two electrons equally. In the process the electrons lose some energy and give off some electromagnetic radiation. Once this has happened, the two atoms are bound tightly together. They can be separated only if the electrons are given additional energy equal to or greater than the energy that they gave up when they paired.

This pairing of hydrogen atoms was the earliest assembly of atoms into molecules. It was another landmark step in the long journey from the Big Bang to today's conscious beings.

Now if hydrogen atoms like to form couples, helium atoms remain stubbornly solo. They already have two electrons in their shell. The electromagnetic force does not impel them to seek another one, and so they remain free of any electron ties to other atoms. After their appearance in the early moments of creation, they have remained the Lone Rangers of the universe ever since.

Later, different and heavier atoms were formed in the stars. These heavier atoms have more electrons and these electrons assemble themselves into various layers or shells around the atom. For most of them, their outermost shell can accommodate more electrons than they possess. Remember that single atoms are only assembled with the same number of electrons as there are protons in the nucleus. Thus atoms with unfilled shells seek combinations with other atoms that allow their thirst for filled-up shells to be satisfied.

The union of two different types of atoms creates what is called a *compound,* a material whose molecules have quite different properties from either of the two different atoms from which it was put together. More complex compounds are formed when more than two different atoms share their electrons. Although there are only about 100 types of stable elements found in nature, an almost unlimited number of different compounds and complex molecules can be created from them. The formation of molecules and compounds is a dynamic, creative process. Complex groups of atoms frequently assemble themselves into chains, rings, or branches, sometimes thousands of units long. (Polymers such as plastics are long chains in which an identical sequence of atoms is repeated over and over again). Most of the organic molecules that make up our bodies consist of such complex atomic chains twisted into different useful shapes. By the time these complex molecules began to form, the creation had come a long way from that early universe of the hot unattached hydrogen atom.

Although the bonds between different atoms differ in strength, they are everywhere responsible for the rigidity, flexibility, fluidity and other characteristics of the materials of our world. The force that holds ordinary matter together resides in the ties between the electron shells of the different atoms.

The electromagnetic force associated with these charged particles does the work. It binds structures as strong as iron, as hard as diamonds, and as fluid as water, but it is always the same force interacting in different arrangements or patterns. The physical and chemical nature of all materials may be explained by the way this one natural force organizes matter; it is not necessary to postulate any other forces.

If an electron has or receives too much energy to remain in its shell, it can break loose from the atom or it can even break the bonds holding a compound or molecule together. This rupture allows the component atoms to reorganize themselves into new structures. In general it is easier for atoms and molecules to make rearrangements that allow their electrons to lose energy and become more stable. For instance, when a substance crystallizes, its electrons lose some energy and we say the atoms are in a lower energy state. To unmake the crystals requires the replacement of this energy. If the amount of energy is large, then any further rearrangement will be correspondingly difficult. Diamonds, for example, are famous both for the amount of heat and pressure needed to make them and for the amount of energy needed to unmake them. Although they may not be "forever" in the history of the universe, they certainly are permanent in the time scale of any happy bride and bridegroom.

If large numbers of atoms or molecules rearrange themselves suddenly and simultaneously, releasing energy very rapidly, we call this an explosion. Controlled explosions can power automobiles or move mountains. Uncontrolled explosions can be as fun as a firecracker or as devastating as a bomb.

How do we experience the energy of an explosion? First, if the material of the explosion is hot enough, some of the energy is flashed off as photons of visible light and we see a pulse of illumination. This reaches our eyes in microseconds if the explosion is here on earth. At the same time air molecules are set into motion like ripples on a pond. The violent disruption of surrounding air molecules by an explosion transmits itself to our ears as the atoms and molecules in the air bounce against one another, spreading outward, until the pulse reaches our eardrums and we hear the disruption as a sharp sound. The ripple of a sound through air is a mechanical process, not an electromagnetic one, so it proceeds much more slowly. That is why we always see the flash of lightning before we hear the thunder, even though the events begin at exactly the same instant.

Though stars may explode with the power of trillions of atomic bombs and the sun rumbles and roars within, we cannot hear the titanic explosions nor the whispered symphony of the stars or the crashing trumpet of our nearby sun as it peeps over the horizon, because there are no atoms close enough together in the intervening space to convey this sound to our ears.

Summary

The electromagnetic force acts between charged particles - electrons and protons - to build atoms, the familiar basic building blocks of our universe. It does not act on neutrons or neutrinos. From the interaction of the atom's electron shells comes all of the molecules and compounds that comprise the diversity of the universe, responsible for a bewildering number of new materials with unique properties. This force is transmitted from electron to electron by photons of electromagnetic energy, and when they act in concert, they give rise to most of the other familiar forces and energies in nature. In particular the electromagnetic force allows the communication of sight, sound, and other sensations. Of the four forces, this is the one that speaks to us with intimacy and fills our lives with the sense of excitement, connectedness, and change.

Appendix B

More on Long Term Stability of Atoms and Their Parts

One prediction is that protons revert back into energy at an average age of 10^{35} years. That is roughly one trillion-trillion times as long as the life of the universe so far! Even if it is true that the universe is slowly dissolving away as its protons spontaneously burst into energy, 10^{35} years is a good approximation of forever when compared to the expected life of the earth or its inhabitants.

Still, the possibility of proton decay is taken seriously enough. Enormous efforts are being made to observe large numbers of protons for a long time to see if any of them decay. To detect this phenomenon we could either watch several protons for 10^{35} years, hoping to detect one of them decaying, or we could watch many more than 10^{35} protons for a few years to see if any one of them decays. The latter course is now being fervently pursued. Any evidence for the decay of protons could help to explain some of the remaining problems of the Big Bang theory, such as why there is so much more matter than antimatter in the universe.

We'll explore this in greater detail in the chapter called the Long-Long Adventure.

DNA Stability.

DNA is a seemingly fragile structure. There are many things about its structure that enable it to endure and be the agent of stability in living things as well as the agent and carrier of change.

Because of the clever packing of the DNA chains, one of the more delicate structures of life, is also one of the most durable. When fossils are found containing traces of the original organism, DNA molecules are usually among the remains. This ancient DNA - perhaps billions of years old - cannot be chemically distinguished from modern DNA, although we know it spelled out blueprints for living creatures radically different from the ones we know. (Readers may recognize this is as an essential premise of *Jurassic Park*).

For billions of years, the words of the DNA code have persisted in nearly identical form - a style of writing that has been accurately passed on to every succeeding generation at least 100,000,000,000 times. In the biological world this is very long-term stability indeed. If you wanted to write a recipe that could still be read a billion years from now, writing it in DNA molecules would be a very good choice, probably about 10,000,000 times better than writing it on one of today's computer disks!

When we consider the durability of DNA, clever packing alone does not seem to account for its stability. Obviously DNA does get damaged from time to time, and in the course of a billion years a great deal of damage would accumulate. How do the very precise DNA chains that specify the functioning of a specific living organism continue to function undiminished over many generations? Why don't we see many more mutant offspring showing the results of genetic damage? What produces the unexpected stability in the face of the disruptive forces that sooner or later assault the strands of DNA? Apparently the design genius of DNA lies in two features that allow damaged DNA to be either repaired or discarded. The repair function is enabled by the double helix design of the DNA chains. The discard function is enabled by what H.G. Wells has called the greatest invention of nature: sexual reproduction, and its corollary, death.

Sex Provides Both Stability and Change

When human egg and sperm cells unite, each brings 23 chromosomes to the new cell. This is a fertilized egg with 46 chromosomes that becomes the embryo. Each parent supplies his or her copy of the complete genetic code to join the copy supplied by the other parent. It also means that each parent *discards* a copy of the code at the moment the germ cell is made. During cell division the double helix DNA structures not only unwind, they also (briefly) unzip their ladder of base pairs and allow sections of single-stranded DNA to look for their counterparts in the other parent's DNA. Frequently, portions of one strand are exchanged for the corresponding portions in the counterpart strand - in effect, exchanging words of their genetic text. In the process, one book of instructions is compared to the other, and if there are major discrepancies, these discrepancies become resolved. From these different mechanisms a strong pattern emerges, that of preserving the integrity of the DNA blueprint.

So far we have talked about how the DNA mechanism works to ensure stability. But in species with two sexes, such as ours, it also brings about a guarantee of carefully controlled change. Wells' comment about sexual reproduction refers to the fact that it brings together two different people and two slightly different copies of the human genetic code. Such genetic fusion not only allows a certain degree of change to happen, it *forces* it to happen. The genetic characteristics that each parent brings to the union have survived the test of life and have a demonstrated stability. Forcing them together provides some mild instability and offers an opportunity for innovative change. The creation reaps the benefit.

Thus a single process, sexual reproduction, leads to both stability and instability. The fellow traveler of sexual reproduction, inevitable death, also acts to promote both stability and change. On the one hand it removes harmful mutations which weaken the species. On the other hand it ensures that there will always be turnover and that new genetic characteristics will be able to come to the fore.

To all who helped make this book possible: The Lancaster Chapter of the International Torch Clubs who heard me articulate some of the themes as I presented them in papers at their monthly sessions and who collectively critiqued my logic and ideas; The Lancaster Friends Meeting members who listened to some of the insights that I gleaned from the periods of silent meditations in Meeting for Worship; my friend and co-worker, Nick Nixon, who listened to my discoursing concepts of science and religion while watching the twilight after dining in at a restaurant atop the highest tower in Atlanta GA and encouraged me for lo these many years to put them into a book; and my late wife, Virginia, who listened patiently and skeptically to my plans to incorporate an up welling of ideas and conclusions into a book.

Reviewers were many! Among them were Mary Jean Irion who read my first tentative presentation of these ideas and encouraged me to more fully develop them; Professor Charles Holzinger for a critical review of an early draft; Professor Richard Veith, who invited me to share my ideas with one of his seminary theology classes; Professor Dan Schlitt of Lincoln, NB who helped refine the scientific concepts; and Dr. Wolfgang Panofsky, former director of the Stanford Linear Accelerator, who helped me to clarify the basic scientific concepts presented in the book.

Major thanks also goes to Tom Holzinger who spent may days doing a professional editing job. He critically challenged many of the concepts while helping to refine the arguments and the language. My sister, Susan Atlee helped me realize the importance of incorporating elements of style into my writing, and showed me how to infuse them into the manuscript. My wife, Dorothy, deserves much praise for doing final editing and formatting of the book and also helped with all of the myriad details necessary to get a book published.

INDEX

INDEX

INDEX

ORDER BLANK

Please send me ____ copies of *The Cosmic Deity: Where Scientists and Theologians Fear to Tread.* Each copy is $23.95 plus $3.05 postage and handling for a total of $27.00. Order 6 or more copies for $17.00 each including postage and handling.

Name

Address

e-mail address ____
(Optional)

Payment method - Check One:

☐ Master Car
☐ Visa   ____ ____ ____ ____   ____
             Credit card number   expiration date
☐ Check enclosed
Send order to:
Mill Creek Publishers
PO Box 10892, Lancaster PA 17602

or order via email or web address:
mcp@paonline.com
www.millcreekpublishers.com

or check your local bookstore

Biography

Robert G. Neuhauser was born in 1927 in Lancaster County Pennsylvania. He grew up and was nurtured in a family that was immersed in the Anabaptist tradition of the Amish and Mennonite faith as well as Methodism. In mid life he migrated to the Quakers, The Religious Society of Friends.

He was educated in Electrical Engineering at Drexel (University) and worked all of his career in Television engineering at RCA. He managed the development of camera tubes for television cameras, one of which, the Image Orthicon, was described by the Encyclopedia Britannica as " . . . the most highly developed of the camera tubes and is perhaps the most remarkable electronic device in existence." He is a Life Fellow of the Society Of Motion Picture And Television Engineers and was awarded their David Sarnoff Gold Medal for his leadership in developing television camera tubes for color television.

An award winning author, he has garnered awards for his writing in both the technical and philosophical realms. In 2000 he received the International Association of Torch Clubs' Paxton Award for the best paper/talk of the year. He has published many magazine articles and one book on television camera tubes. An accomplished public speaker he has presented talks in many countries throughout the world.

His writing attempts to bridge the gap between scientific knowledge and religious thought. He brings a thoughtful and provocative insight into the nature of the Creator that can resonate with the theological reevaluations taking place in the religious community and with skeptical scientists who contemplate the rules by which this universe operates but wonder who made the rules.

He has provided leadership in his community for breaking housing segregation barriers, finding refuge for foreign refugees fleeing for their lives and helping to solve the problem of homeless women with children. With the Quakers he has served on the corporations of both The American Friends Service Committee and The Friends Committee on National Legislation.

He is the father of four professional children, a traveler, skier, pilot, hunter, gardener and boater. For the better part of his life he has been pondering the nature of the creation and its origin.